The Mulatta Concubine

The Mulatta Concubine

TERROR, INTIMACY, FREEDOM, AND DESIRE IN THE BLACK TRANSATLANTIC

Lisa Ze Winters

The University of Georgia Press
ATHENS

Parts of chapter 4 first appeared in different form as "'More desultory and unconnected than any other': Geography, Desire, and Freedom in Eliza Potter's *A Hairdresser's Experience in High Life*," *American Quarterly* 61, no. 3 (2009): 455–75, Johns Hopkins University Press, publisher. Copyright © 2009, the American Studies Association.

Paperback edition, 2018
© 2016 by the University of Georgia Press
Athens, Georgia 30602
www.ugapress.org
All rights reserved
Set in 10/13 Adobe Caslon Pro by Kaelin Chappell Broaddus

Most University of Georgia Press titles are
available from popular e-book vendors.

Printed digitally

The Library of Congress has cataloged the
hardcover edition of this book as follows:

Winters, Lisa Ze.
The mulatta concubine : terror, intimacy, freedom, and desire in the
Black transatlantic / Lisa Ze Winters.
xiii, 222 pages : illustrations ; 24 cm. —
(Race in the Atlantic world, 1700–1900)
Includes bibliographical references and index.
ISBN 978-0-8203-4896-4 (hardcover : alk. paper) —
ISBN 978-0-8203-4897-1 (e-book)
1. Racially mixed women—United States—History.
2. Racially mixed women—Atlantic Ocean Region—History.
3. Free African Americans—Social conditions. 4. African American
women—Social conditions. 5. Blacks—Race identity—Atlantic Ocean
Region. 6. Atlantic Ocean Region—Race relations—History.
7. African diaspora. I. Title.
HQ1410.56 2015
305.48'8960730163—dc23

2015013510

Paperback ISBN 978-0-8203-5384-5

VèVè Amasasa Clark

Lynnéa Yuvella Stephen

Doris Marie Crandall Dawson

Earle Roberts Dawson

IN LOVING MEMORY

CONTENTS

ACKNOWLEDGMENTS

The wonderful paradox of writing is that it allows me at once to live in the refuge of a most peaceful solitude and, when that solitude runs headlong into anxiety and fear, to be held tightly by a community of friends and family who step in to help me move my writing in ways impossible to do on my own. Over the many years of writing this book, there were days, even months, when what kept me going was the anticipation and responsibility of sitting down to write these acknowledgments. It is my sincere hope that the people listed herein will see their labor and generosity reflected in what is strongest about this book. Any omissions in that list are unintentional, and I hope that anyone inadvertently slighted here will allow me the opportunity to rectify the error in person. Any missteps or errors in the pages that follow are mine alone.

I have enormous gratitude for the numerous librarians and archivists upon whose expertise my project depends. Thanks are due to the staff of the Bancroft Library, the Historic New Orleans Collection, Tulane University's Amistad Research Center, the University of New Orleans's Special Collections, and the Archives nationales d'outre mer in Aix-en-Provence, France. I am especially grateful to Phyllis Bischof, Librarian Emerita for African and African American Collections at the University of California, Berkeley; Gregory Osborn at the New Orleans Public Library; and Mary Linn Wernet at the Cammie G. Henry Research Center at Northwestern State University in Natchitoches, Louisiana. At Wayne State University, Judith Arnold and Joshua Neds-Fox have kindly provided ready research support and advice.

My research has received essential financial support from a number of sources. Funding from UC Berkeley's Graduate Opportunity Program, UC Berkeley's African American Studies Department, and the Ford Foundation Predoctoral Fellowship Program provided me essential financial support toward the PhD. The University of California President's Postdoctoral Fellowship Program afforded me time to figure out the terms and stakes of this project. At Wayne State University I have received sustained financial support from a variety of sources, including a University Minority/Women Summer Research Grant, subventions for illustrations and indexing from the English Department and the College of

Letters and Sciences Faculty Fund, the English Department's Josephine Nevins Keal Fellowship, and a sabbatical leave. An earlier version of chapter 4 appeared as "'More desultory and unconnected than any other': Geography, Desire, and Freedom in Eliza Potter's *A Hairdresser's Experience in High Life*" in a special issue of *American Quarterly* ("In the Wake of Katrina: New Paradigms and Social Visions") 61, no. 3 (2009). I am grateful to the editors for permission to reprint the material here.

My debt to my teachers is immeasurable. I was lucky enough to be one of a number of UC Berkeley undergraduate students whose lives were touched by Roy T. Thomas, a senior lecturer in the African American Studies Department. When I entered his course as a sophomore, I was nearly ready to drop out of college. He opened a world to me. Candice Francis taught me how to write. Opal Palmer Adisa and Paula Gunn Allen gave me confidence in my voice. Barbara Christian created a joyful and reverent space in her classroom; I am grateful to have experienced this space and her teaching as both an undergraduate and a graduate student. Patricia Penn Hilden extended a sure and steady hand when I found myself disoriented my first year of graduate school; she acted as a gracious interlocutor and fierce champion of my possibilities throughout my graduate career and beyond. Stephen Small provided tough yet generous guidance on questions of interdisciplinary methods and methodologies. Donald Moore was equally generous in taking time to consider my work seriously and extraordinarily gentle in encouraging me to develop a more rigorous theoretical framework. I have looked up to Pier Gabrielle Foreman since I was an undergraduate; her support of my project has meant the world to me. Ruth Wilson Gilmore's gentle patience and generosity in offering me an impromptu tutorial on the discipline of geography has stayed with me to this day. Lindon Barrett, without knowing me or my work, responded immediately and enthusiastically to my initial, tentative email to him inquiring whether he might consider serving as my mentor for the UC President's Postdoctoral Fellowship Program. His generosity was unconditional and humbling, and his insight, encouragement, and support left an indelible mark on me. I am forever grateful for our short time together.

VèVè Clark, Saidiya Hartman, and Ula Taylor deserve so much more praise and gratitude than I can ever express in these pages. I met all three of them during my last three semesters as an undergraduate student; Dr. Clark and Dr. Hartman were advisors for my senior honors thesis. Dr. Clark called her students her intellectual children; she was absolutely my intellectual mother. It still stops me short when I realize I have written this book without being able to call her and sort out my thoughts, ideas, theories, and speculations. In no way, however, did I write this book without her. VèVè, I've done my best not to bring you any retreads. I miss you terribly. Well beyond the call of duty or obligation, Dr.

Hartman and Dr. Taylor have given me courage when my own failed and shown me grace and compassion most generously and most kindly. I thank you for your continued guidance, support, and example. Twenty years after I first entered your classrooms, I still want to be like both of you when I grow up.

My colleagues and friends have been instrumental to this project's completion. At Wayne State University, Lisa Alexander, Melba Boyd, Sarika Chandra, Lara Langer Cohen, Ollie Johnson, and Kidada Williams read various chapters in various stages and offered me feedback and support at critical times. Kidada Williams probably read every page of this manuscript at every stage, Lara Langer Cohen's gentle yet persistent check-ins held me accountable for writing when I least wanted to, and Sarika Chandra made it her mission to motivate me when I wanted to give up; I couldn't ask for better allies or friends. Current and former colleagues in English and African American studies (until recently Africana studies) have offered me camaraderie and moral support throughout. Special thanks are due to Beth Bates, Simone Chess, Robert Diaz, Todd Duncan, Jonathan Flatley, David Goldberg, Jaime Goodrich, Eboe Hutchful, Margaret Jordan, Chera Kee, John Pat Leary, Xavier Livermon, Perry Mars, Daphne Ntiri, Ross Pudaloff, and Donnie Sackey. Staff in African American studies and English work hard to make things easy for faculty. For their kind responsiveness to my many and various requests for help in figuring out one logistical problem or another, I am especially grateful to current and former staff, including Tia Finney, Annette Hawkins, Diara Prather, Sue Rumps, Alisia Taylor, and Kathy Zamora. In their capacity as department chairs, Richard Grusin, Ellen Barton, and Melba Boyd provided essential encouragement and support for the project. Outside Wayne State, Marisa Fuentes and Jessica Marie Johnson have been generous in their feedback at key stages of the project. Eric Avila, Scot Brown, Dennis Childs, Carter Mathes, and Danny Widener have each helped me maintain perspective and stay grounded within the academy. Sarita Cannon, Ralina Joseph, and Cherise Smith were the first to show me how important an honest and compassionate community of writing was for one's work and well-being; I thank them for inviting me in. My friendships with Amy Ifátólú Gardner, Sara Johnson, Myisha Priest, and Erin Winkler sustain me. I could not have completed the project without their loving, generous, and unconditional intellectual and emotional support. Lynnéa Stephen never let me not believe in myself. My memories of her candor and critique and of our highly exclusive mutual admiration club take me back, hold me still, and move me forward.

Thanks are due to all at the University of Georgia Press for making it possible for this project to become a book. I am grateful to Mick Gusinde-Duffy for seeing potential in my prospectus and inviting me to submit the full manuscript for review. The press's anonymous readers' comments were at once affirming and instructive in helping me clarify and sharpen my arguments. Walter Biggins's compassion and patience helped to keep me calm and focused as I completed revisions. John Joerschke was a pleasure to work with as he steered me through the publication process. Mary M. Hill's copyedits were attentive and graceful; her ability to know and make clear what I was trying to say has been a revelation.

Much of this book invokes and explores the significance of the Haitian vodou lwa Ezili and to a lesser extent the African diasporic goddess Mami Wata. I am not a practitioner, yet I hold both in reverence and their devotees in respect. I have done my best to honor each figure's presence in diaspora as one that is both sacred and consequential. I am most grateful to the scholar-practitioners who know them intimately and have made them visible to outsiders.

Throughout it all, my family's support and love have been unconditional. Veronica Conway and Zoë Howell are more my sisters than friends. Though they live lives completely outside academia, they understand better than anyone how I inhabit this place. Thank you for loving me as I am. Teena Priest has shown me kindnesses as if I were her daughter's sister; her warmth and generosity are an incredible gift. Carla Vecchiola, Orlando Ford, and their son, Renato, have offered incredible support in their care for my daughter and with their patience with the constant cancellations and rescheduling of play dates my writing demanded. Frédéric and Susan Ze are my parents, and they are extraordinary. They have helped me with tricky translations and watched my daughter so I could write. My mom has been my stalwart and trusted comrade-in-arms, traveling with me to archives in New Orleans and Aix-en-Provence, helping me navigate French etiquette and protocol, and shipping my books back to me after I spent visits home immersed in my writing. Thank you both for always being my advocates and protectors, for always believing in me and unconditionally supporting me emotionally and financially, for catching me when I stumble, for forgiving me my teenage years and my twenties, and for not changing the locks without giving me a key first. My grandparents Doris Marie Crandall Dawson and Earle Roberts Dawson modeled and offered compassion and integrity and were extraordinarily generous in spirit and in action. I miss you both. Monique Ze, Martina Damko, and Rémie Loudy do what sisters do, and I am grateful for all of it. My nieces and nephews have given me immeasurable joy and always remind me what matters. My mother's brothers and their partners, Jim Dawson and Wayne Flottman, and Richard Dawson and Adele Wallace, have regularly provided necessary laughter and respite from the stresses of writing and the tenure-track when we converge for holidays at my parents' house. Ken Winters has shown me an expansive love and unfaltering patience beyond what anyone could reasonably request. He is my partner and my best friend, and he has kept me here, in this place, in this fight. My stepdaughter, Amenta, has taught me everything about courage, forgiveness, love, and perseverance, for which I owe her my deepest gratitude and respect. And finally, there is Amara, who has shown me what is possible, what it is to be free, what it is to imagine. You are everything.

The Mulatta Concubine

INTRODUCTION

In 1728 a free African woman boarded the slave ship *La Galathée* at Gorée Island, an Atlantic entrepôt off the coast of Senegal (Hall, *Africans*, 128; Spear, *Race*, 80).[1] According to the historical record, the woman was a *mulâtresse*, a woman of mixed European and African descent, and she brought with her three slaves. She made the transatlantic voyage from Gorée to New Orleans in order to join a French gunsmith previously stationed at Gorée and deported to the American colony as sentence for an unspecified crime.

We do not know whether her passage was free of the sexualized and racialized violence and terror endemic to the transatlantic slave trade. We do know she and her slaves arrived alive in New Orleans (Hall, *Africans*, 128). Once in New Orleans, the woman disappeared from the historical record as abruptly as she entered it.[2]

The woman's presence on the ship and its trace in the archive are as startling as they are fleeting. The questions they demand of those of us who are interested in the intersections of race, gender, and mobility in the Atlantic speak to how we read, imagine, and understand narratives of origins, memory, and freedom in the production of African diasporic subjectivities. How freely did she make her choice to follow the deported French gunsmith? What family, if any, did she leave behind? How did she imagine her relationship to the slaves she held or to those slaves on the ship who were bound for the American slave market? Was her passage indeed free of sexualized violence and terror?

Of course, the official record does not, or cannot, yield these answers, at least not willingly. Given the intellectual and academic rigor of the scholars who offer this woman's presence in passing as anecdotal evidence for their examinations of interracial sex in colonial New Orleans, one can say with near absolute confidence that no one will happen upon this unnamed woman's diary or letters home describing her passage across the Atlantic, her memories of home, her encounter with the marvelous social and physical landscape that was colonial New Orleans. The apparent singularity of her journey appears as a fragment in an archive of official documents already primed not to tell her story. And yet this same archive tells us she is not singular. In the official archive that produces the

barely sketched details of her existence is a preponderance of visual and written representations of free(d) mulatta women across Atlantic slave societies attached—discursively, economically, culturally—to European men.

Thus, while this unnamed woman's free status sets her apart from the captives
aboard *La Galathée*, her legal, sexual, gendered, and racialized status marks her
as a subject whose presence pervades African diasporic history: the free(d) mulatta concubine. These women's underexamined presences across the eighteenth-
century Atlantic and their traces in nineteenth- and twentieth-century historical
and popular archives compel this book. For against the individual transatlantic voyage of this African mulâtresse, apparently sexually and affectionately attached to a white man (for she followed him), are the elaborate, fantastic, and
repetitious depictions of the free(d) mulatta concubines—the infamous *signares*
of eighteenth-century Senegal, the notoriously beautiful quadroons of antebellum New Orleans, the seductive mulâtresses of colonial Saint-Domingue, or the
Haitian vodou deity Ezili Freda—that pervade African diasporic history and
memory and propel my project.[3] The details of this woman's individual experience aboard the slave ship appear irretrievable. I suggest, however, that her
movement across the Atlantic aboard a slave ship from one iconic diasporic
place to another produces a fissure, a space in how we who are interested in such
questions might read and understand the intersections of race, sexuality, intimacies, geography, and freedom in the context of an African diaspora. Read against
the ubiquity of visual and written depictions of the free(d) mulatta concubine
across diasporic time and space, her presence demands a consideration of how
these women, whom the official archive consistently depicts as free and authoritative over their bodies and sexuality, fit into an African diasporic community
produced by and through its subjection to the transatlantic slave trade.

*The Mulatta Concubine: Terror, Intimacy, Freedom, and Desire in the Black
Transatlantic* produces and draws from an archive that includes eighteenth-
century contemporaneous accounts of these women and nineteenth- and
twentieth-century historical and popular representations of them in order to
make three distinct but interrelated arguments. First, I argue that reading diaspora through the lens of the free(d) mulatta concubine demands a rethinking of
the interrelated questions of origins, memory, terror, freedom, and evidence in
the production of African diasporic subjectivity. I contend that understanding
how the figure of the free(d) mulatta concubine inhabits the black transatlantic
is an essential component for understanding both the multiple dimensions of
the unfreedom of African diasporic subjects and the possibilities for the imagination and practices of their freedom across time and space. Second, I insist that
central to the free(d) mulatta concubine's significance in the black Atlantic is her
dual manifestation as both a historical actor and an African diasporic goddess.

Such duality demands that we consider diasporic subjectivity as a geographically and temporally synchronic process. That is, reading diaspora through the lens of the free(d) mulatta concubine illuminates how, for African diasporic subjects, to imagine and experience freedom is to inhabit simultaneously multiple temporal and spatial geographies. Finally, by (re)constructing a genealogy of the transatlantic circulation of visual and written representations of the free(d) mulatta concubine, my project challenges how we scholars produce and recognize archival evidence. Braided together, these arguments suggest that scholars of the African diaspora must examine more critically what freedom may have looked like and meant to enslaved black subjects. Ultimately, my book argues that transatlantic circulation of the free(d) mulatta concubine illuminates African diasporic negotiation of and resistance to the terror that defined black experiences of slavery *and* freedom.

Possibility, Presence, and the Free(d) Mulatta Concubine

The mulatta concubine in diaspora is everywhere. She is in representations of Thomas Jefferson's long-term "relationship" with the enslaved Sally Hemings, begun when she was fourteen and he forty-four (see Gordon-Reed, *American Controversy*). She is the protagonist who emblemizes Cuban national identity in Cirilo Villaverde's 1882 novel, *Cecilia Valdés: Novela de costumbres cubanas*. She is allusively present in the fantastical and garish transformation of an enslaved black woman to sexually powerful white (by virtue of makeup) mistress in the Brazilian film *Xica!* She is remembered as the owner of the infamous *maison des esclaves* (house of slaves) on Gorée Island, the former Senegalese slave entrepôt and now major slavery tour destination. She is the enslaved Joanna, "immortalized in John Gabriel Stedman's *Narrative of Five Years' Expedition against the Revolted Negroes of Surinam* (1806 [1796])" (Sharpe, *Ghosts*, 46). She is the commodity that drove the fancy slave trade in the antebellum United States.[4] She is present in travelers' descriptions of antebellum New Orleans's free women of color. She is "that seductive mulatto woman" in colonial Saint-Domingue (Moreau de Saint-Méry, *Civilization*, 81–89).[5]

Indeed, she is so pervasive that to name her "mulatta concubine" becomes redundant. Thus, in her analysis of eighteenth-century Anglophone representations of enslaved concubines, Jenny Sharpe notes "the practice of using 'mulatto' as a generic term for concubines, whether they were black or racially mixed, slave or free" (*Ghosts*, 45). And in her excavation of "the system of desire, violence, and exclusion that characterized slave societies in the French Caribbean," Doris Garraway explains that "the evolving discourse on miscegenation invested both black women and mulatto offspring with the stigma of illicit, adulterous desire, which was capable of disrupting colonial reproductive dynamics and posing a threat to white men" (*Libertine Colony*, 197, 205). In the United States, as Emily Clark argues, the stereotype of the quadroon concubine in New Orleans had consequences for the city's "living women of color, free and enslaved," as "visitors came to New Orleans expecting to find beautiful quadroons to dance with and bed" (*Strange History*, 161). Across the Americas, the inextricability of the mulatta's presumed sensuality, seductiveness, and availability from her ambiguous racial appearance, whether she was free(d) or enslaved, is inescapable.

While such inextricability is one overwhelmingly produced by white (European, Creole, and Anglo-American) writers and has thus engendered necessary critique and dispute, what interests me here is how the production of the stereotype invites us to consider the sexual and racial economies central to the maintenance and reproduction of chattel slavery in the Americas. That is, what the stereotype of the mulatta concubine does here is to highlight interracial sex between white men and women of African descent (and consequently render invisible that between white women and black men) and place it firmly in a nexus of "desire, violence, and exclusion" (Garraway, *Libertine Colony*, 205). For example, while the specific details, mechanics, and logistics of slavery's operations varied across colonial and geographic spaces, authorities persistently issued legal codes in efforts to define and enforce distinct racial categories and discrete relationships to slavery and freedom. Thus, across slave societies, officials codified interracial sex in order to produce and preserve racial distinctions and power relationships. The oft-cited 1662 Act XII in Virginia mandated: "WHEREAS some doubts have arrisen whether children got by any Englishman upon a Negro woman should be slave or free, *Be it therefore enacted and declared by this present grand assembly,* that all children borne in this country shalbe held bond or free only according to the condition of the mother, *And* that if any christian shall commit ffornication with a Negro man or woman, hee or shee soe offending shall pay double the ffines imposed by the former act" ("Slavery and Indentured Servants"). The act's acknowledgment of "doubts" regarding the "condition" of the child of an "Englishman" and a "Negro woman" offers a glimpse of what life looked like for enslaved women in colonial Virginia. First, that the act settles the question by deciding that the child should follow the condition of the mother suggests a confidence on the part of the authorities that the intersecting racial and sexual economies of slavery were inevitable—that the mother of a mixed-race child would in fact be enslaved and that such a law would ensure the stability of such an institution. Second, the act suggests that enslaved women who bore children had in fact agitated for their children's freedom. Likewise, looking at the French Caribbean, Garraway examines "how the escalation of racially segregationist measures" in colonial policy "sought to block the social or material enfranchisement of the slave concubines and mixed-race children of white men" (*Libertine Colony*, 209). Finally, and perhaps most urgently, as Garraway and others have observed, laws proscribing and otherwise policing interracial sex and the concomitant cultural stereotypes of the mulatta concubine across slave societies displaced the locus of authority and self-determination—what might be called agency—from the will of the white male slaveholder onto the body of the enslaved black woman. As Saidiya Hartman insists, dominant discourses of the "phantasmal ensnaring agency of the lascivious black" insured that "rape disappeared through the intervention of seduction" ("Seduction," 544–45).[6]

That such mythical agency is indeed "phantasmal" is most obvious when the mulatta concubine is enslaved. There, the labor of black feminist scholars and black women writers has in substantive ways dismantled white and male fantasies of the lascivious, predatory jezebel in order to make plain the centrality of sexual violence to the day-to-day lives of enslaved women.[7] And yet, there endures in a U.S. landscape of social media and popular culture fantasies of the "phantasmal ensnaring agency" of women of African descent, enslaved and free. For example, in 2010 a controversy erupted across a black social media landscape when "writer and social commentator Touré let out a stream of bizarre tweets that praised raped slaves for seducing their white masters" (Hopkinson, "Truth").[8] More recently, the ABC television show *Scandal*, which depicts President Fitzgerald "Fitz" Grant, a white Republican president married to a white woman, and Olivia Pope, an African American woman and powerful D.C. "fixer," as star-crossed lovers, has engendered controversy over how the show depicts the interracial relationship. In one episode, "Olivia remarked to Fitz that she was feeling 'a little Sally Hemings–Thomas Jefferson' about their relationship" (Paskin, "Network"). The president's response to Olivia included him insisting, "You own *me*, you control *me*, I belong to *you*" (Washington, "Emmys 2013"). As writer Stacia Brown puts it, while "Olivia is no slave," the fact that the "leader of the free world" claims that it is Olivia, a black woman, who owns him (sexually and emotionally) is "giving too many shades of Sally Hemings" ("Is Olivia Pope"). Olivia Pope's character is neither light skinned nor mixed race or biracial. However, the exchange between her and the president suggests that the cultural grammar of the seductive enslaved mulatta—here Sally Hemings—not only persists in the face of black feminists' and black women's labor to undo it but frames readings of and possibilities for all black women's sexual lives, regardless of skin color or apparent relationship to freedom.

This project presses against the persistence of these interdependent lexicons—that of the fantastically agential enslaved black and mulatta women and girls and that of the contemporary free black woman firmly bound by the racial and sexual economies of the "afterlife of slavery"—in order to consider what may be an unstable, undependable, and capricious but ultimately discernible and consequential difference when our focus shifts from the captive black and/ or mixed-race female subject to the ostensibly free(d) mulatta concubine. The stakes of shifting the questions of the mulatta's authority over her own body, her sexuality, and her will from enslaved subject to free(d) are these: surely, there has to be something different about freedom; surely, the free(d) woman of color experienced her day-to-day life in ways qualitatively and substantively different from that of enslaved women; surely, these differences matter. How, then, to measure and theorize these differences? How, then, to speculate about or otherwise imagine the possibilities for agency for free(d) black women? How, then, to contend with the spectacle *and* specter of free(d) women of color who appear to profit from their sexual relationships with wealthy white male slaveholders?

To write these women as "free(d)" is to underscore the precariousness of their freedom: whether free by birth or by manumission, these women experienced a tenuous freedom inextricable from the circum-Atlantic/transatlantic economies of race, sex, gender, and slavery intertwined in African diasporic history. Likewise, to write these women as a singular concubine underscores their inescapable connection to slavery. It also emphasizes the complexity of their visibility in historical and popular narratives. To name them "concubine" directs us to consider the multiple, intersecting legal and cultural codes that shaped the dimensions of their sexual relationships with white men. That is, whereas the acceptance, success, and benefits of such relationships varied across Atlantic slave societies, the extralegality of these unions vis-à-vis colonial and state authorities was consistent. In addition, whereas the social and economic statuses of the women were also diverse, the stereotypes of excessive sexuality, seductiveness, and ethereal beauty attached to them make the historical subjects almost impossible to see clearly. Or, in the words of a friend, the free(d) mulatta concubine in history and memory is never "broke down." To always cast and emphasize her extraordinary, ephemeral beauty is to obfuscate the quotidian monstrosity of the desire to which she was subjected. Likewise, to name the women "concubine," a term that at once foregrounds and obscures the subjugation of the named subject's will and desire, emphasizes the repetitious nature of archival descriptions of these women across time and space: these are visual and written depictions that invoke both fantasy and notions of the fantastic in defining how we remember the historical subjects who navigated the treacherous racial and sexual economies of Atlantic slavery.

Finally, to call the women "mulatta" underscores the term's vexed etymology and common usage. Typically used to describe women of mixed European and African descent, the term is at once precise and capacious. Hortense Spillers's explanation of the term is instructive, calling it "a special category of thingness that isolates and overdetermines the human character to which it points. A semantic marker, already fully inhabited by a content and an expectation, America's 'tragic mulatto' exists for others—and a particular male other—in an attribution of the illicit that designates the violent mingling and commingling of bloodlines that a simplified cultural patrimony wishes to deny" ("Notes," 303).[9] In order to emphasize "the figure's status as an unreal, impossible ideal" and the absolute objectification of her body, Jennifer DeVere Brody coined the term "mulattaroon" (*Impossible Purities*, 16). While I find Brody's term both provocative and useful, I employ the more familiar "mulatta" in an effort to invoke and critique the vexed nomenclature of a specifically raced and gendered historical subject. Indeed, I want to stress the visual markers of my subject, to emphasize her visible difference from more readily recognizable black female subjects, as well as her discernible proximity to blackness. I do so neither to privilege her nor to rescue her from imaginative or historical margins. Rather, I do so in order to attend to the specificity of her appearance in the archive, to consider how and when black women are marked mulatta, how and when the skin color of women of African descent appears to matter, how and when the details of her appearance obscure the racialized and sexualized power relationships of slavery, and how and when these same details lay bare the economies of these relationships.

Under these terms, the complexity of the free(d) mulatta concubine's agency is perhaps most apparent in the case of that African mulâtresse who boarded and sailed on the slave ship *La Galathée*. That is, in the context of the Americas, that the free(d) mulatta concubine's liberty was tenuous and inextricable from the sexual and racial economies of slavery is a fact made unambiguous in the official archive despite white patriarchal discursive attempts to obfuscate such inextricability. For example, the free women of color in colonial Saint-Domingue enjoyed the reputation of being "economically prudent, thrifty, and even entrepreneurial" and were "on average ... more independent and financially much better off than white women" (Garraway, *Libertine Colony*, 235). And yet, as Colin Dayan observes, while they were "served, fed, honored, and adored," free women of color were "at the same time excluded from marriage, threatened by poverty, and often abandoned" (*Haiti*, 57). The threat of poverty and abandonment frame Médéric-Louis-Elie Moreau de Saint-Méry's description of the mulatta woman's relationships with enslaved black women. According to Moreau, while free women of color were "very imperious and much dreaded mistresses," it was nonetheless "quite common to see these free mulâtresses living in the greatest familiarity with female slaves—but not those that belonged to them."[10] Most significantly, according to Moreau, "I observe that in this regard, this familiarity, sometimes based on kinship, has very often for its cause, the presents that the freed women received from the slaves who had lovers in their masters or other whites, who gave them the means to be generous. In general, the mulattoes even received much aid from the slaves with whom they had various relationships, without being embarrassed."[11] Moreau's description stresses the intricacies and bonds of the sexual and racial economies of slavery. He draws attention to the kinship relationships between free(d) and enslaved women at the same time he suggests the intimate relationships between the legal statuses of both groups of women. His note that "these are slaves who have lovers in their masters" underscores white masters' perversions of love and desire in colonial slave societies, so hauntingly explored by Dayan, who insists, "But no matter how degrading, how despotic the effects of slavery there remained a place for love" (*Haiti*, 56). And finally, the insecurity of the free woman of color, highlighted in her dependence on her enslaved sisters for gifts and aid, underscores the precariousness of freedom for the ostensibly free(d) mulatta concubine in the Americas.

In contrast to New Orleans, where the African mulâtresse arrived, the Senegalese island entrepôt of Gorée, where she embarked upon the slave ship, along with its historical sibling Saint-Louis Island, appears at first in both the archive and the present moment to be a place where the security and prosperity of the free(d) mulatta concubine was both more assured and more stable. At Gorée, the mulâtresse embarked at a place that would produce two icons of the transatlantic slave trade: the celebrated signares and the notorious *maison des esclaves*. The signares, whose name "derived from the Portuguese *senhora*, denoting a free woman of property and social consequence," may succinctly be described as a class of African and mixed-race women known for their profitable, serial marriages with French men stationed at the islands of Gorée and Saint-Louis during the course of the eighteenth century (Brooks, *Eurafricans*, 206). Almost uniformly represented as mulattas in contemporaneous and scholarly accounts, the signares' significance lies, in part, in their establishment of a class of mulatto intermediaries, *habitants*, who would eventually come to play substantial roles in colonial and independent Senegal.[12] While sources across time routinely linger on the women's beauty, seductiveness, and vanity—commensurate with eighteenth- and nineteenth-century descriptions of the free(d) mulatta concubine in the Americas, eighteenth-century French travelers also often described "mariages à la mode du pays" as the central sexual economy of the women's lives. As George Brooks explains, "Frenchmen living at Saint Louis and Gorée married African and Eurafrican women—a few before a priest but most à la mode du pays (country-style in English usage)—accommodating Wolof and Lébou marriage and inheritance practices" (*Eurafricans*, 210). As in the Americas, Europeans cohabiting with and marrying women of African descent did so in contravention of official policies and dictates.[13] However, on Gorée and Saint-Louis, where the demographics, geography, and landscape together helped to produce a type of slave society very different from that in the Americas, the signares were able to exploit unions that "corresponded to an expectation of marriage among African people of the interior yet was transformed to meet the realities of life in the coastal town" (Jones, *Métis*, 35). With the islands' populations, including the resident Europeans, viewing "mariage à la mode du pays as legitimate marital unions," the signares enjoyed high social status on the islands, "played central roles in shaping the cultural traditions," and achieved wealth through the acquisition of gold and the building of properties on the island (37). Thus, "by 1749, ten of the thirteen private properties on Gorée belonged to Eurafricans, nine of whom were women" (Brooks, *Eurafricans*, 211). Indeed, the term *signare* emerged first as an honorific title; as Marie-Hélène Knight-Baylac explains, the name was "first only given to those who owned a residence, as [doing so] required a degree of dignity" (citing Pierre Cariou, "La vie à Gorée," 401).[14] According to prevailing accounts then, free African and mixed-race women living on Gorée and Saint-Louis during the eighteenth century and involved in domestic unions with European men enjoyed a stability, a security, a possibility for prosperity, and above all else a type of freedom not available to free women of color in the Americas.

And yet. An unnamed free African mulâtresse boarded a slave ship, accompanied by her three slaves, to make a transatlantic journey from a place that was her home, a place where the historiography tells us she was safe, to a place across the ocean, a place to which ships from her island carried captives and deported criminals, in order to join her French gunsmith husband. Unclear from the record is whether she was deported as well or otherwise enjoined to follow him to the only recently established and thus socially tumultuous French colony New Orleans. Given that in the case of *mariage à la mode*, "both parties understood that the marriage ended upon the death or permanent departure of the man from Senegal," the African mulâtresse's own departure, to follow this man, is all the more startling, at least from the story the archive tells and allows us to imagine (Jones, *Métis*, 19). That is, as Hilary Jones insists her audience recognize, the "gendered aspects of imperialism remain underappreciated," as the histories of colonial and colonized spaces "are too often told through the lens of male power and privilege"; this framing conditions what we might imagine (*Métis*, 21). At the very least, surely, this African mulâtresse would have understood the fate of the other Africans bound in the ship's hold. Indeed, William Pietz recounts Willem Bosman's account of how an African man at the slave port Ouidah subdued his wife by threatening to sell her and put her on a slave ship bound for the Americas. The husband "led her down to the shore in sight of a European ship, whereupon her terror that he was about to sell her into slavery cured her permanently of her deceitful hysterics and turned her into a dutiful wife" (Pietz, "Problem," 120). The specter of terror informs the questions the woman's departure from Gorée raises and underscores what we do not know, or at least what the historiography does not explain, about a figure who would otherwise be celebrated as a signare, iconic and central to the production of a quintessential African diasporic place.

The unnamed African mulâtresse's movement from one place to another disturbs such discrete representations of the free(d) mulatta concubine as an object of analysis and invites us to consider how the free(d) mulatta concubine as a subject travels and moves across black Atlantic geographies. And here I tread carefully, for the terrain is perilous. To say she travels with and through the Middle Passage violates the unimaginable horror experienced by those captive Africans who could only endure the voyage. And yet, somehow, this is what she does. Within this context, this woman's movement across the Atlantic, as *a black female passenger aboard a slave ship*, disturbs because it demands attention to the terror of her journey against the possibility of her individual safety and liberty *and* the impossibility of the safety and liberty of the captive Africans transported on *La Galathée*. Her movement raises questions not about white colonial and national power and domination but rather about *her* identity, about how she imagined herself, about how the captives she held as property experienced and imagined her, and about whether and how the other captives held as cargo on the ship recognized and made meaning of her presence.

The mulâtresse's presence, in isolation, is at once startling and utterly mundane. On the one hand, her departure complicates narratives of the signares that cast them as powerful free women of African descent who steered life on an Atlantic slave entrepôt. On the other hand, her apparent choices make literal some of the most salient stereotypes of the mulatta concubine: she distances herself from an identifiable black kinship community; she holds captive subjects in bondage and subjects them to the most brutal of journeys; she sleeps with and remains loyal to a historical subject who by virtue of his occupation personifies the methods of white European domination of black people in Africa and the Americas. In its isolation, in its breathtaking brevity, in its reduction to a note in the records of a French slave-trading company, the appearance of this unnamed woman's journey in the archive can upend neither dominant narratives of the signares in eighteenth-century Senegal nor prevailing stereotypes of the free(d) mulatta concubine in the Americas.

Read against the grain, however, her presence does something both to how we imagine the free(d) mulatta concubine and, as a consequence, to how we think about diaspora. She moves from one place where subjects like her played central roles in that location's prevailing racial and sexual economies of slavery and freedom to another, distinct place where subjects like her, too, were central to these economies in their geographically specific manifestations. Against this movement are the repetitious depictions of the free(d) mulatta concubine, depictions that regularly frame her in terms of what she means to the discrete colonial, linguistic, or geographic spaces in which we find her. That is, stereotyping the free(d) mulatta concubine, especially in the Americas, was a tactic central to defining and maintaining the boundaries and privileges of whiteness, patriarchy, and nation in colonial places and newly independent states. Against the spectacle of her supposed sexual and racial transgression and the phantasm of her extraordinary agency, the free(d) mulatta concubine ultimately emerges in the archive as an object produced through slavery's economies and most useful for how she helps explain the paradoxical aspects of white patriarchal and imperial power. To read the free(d) mulatta concubine solely as evidence of the contradictions, hypocrisies, and logistics of white heteropatriarchal nationhood, however, is to capitulate to the dominant discourse's authority to define not only the content of the story but also the heart of the story's meaning.[15] This project opens with a *traveling* African mulâtresse in order to widen the concern from the mechanics and material consequences of white heteropatriarchal desire and also consider how black Atlantic subjects encountered, processed, and theorized the event of the free(d) mulatta concubine *in diaspora*.

In Diaspora: "What Happened Then"

My project joins a rapidly growing body of scholarship that attends to the multiple ways free(d) women of color inhabited colonial and slave societies, their negotiation of these spaces "characterized by complicity and contradiction, by contrariness and collaboration, by inconsistency and complexity" (MacDonald-Smythe, "Trading Places," 90).[16] The preponderance of this scholarship excavates individual lives within discrete national, colonial, and physical contexts and localities. This work is producing richer and more nuanced understandings of how free(d) women of color navigated the particular dimensions of the local societies they inhabited. As Amrita Chackrabarti Myers explains in her study of black women in antebellum Charleston, "A person's understanding of notions such as liberty, freedom, and citizenship are dependent on their chronological context . . . residential position . . . and factors of social space" (*Forging Freedom*, 2). Furthermore, as Myers insists, "Discussions of the black definition of freedom have a rich literature, the majority of which is grounded in the Reconstruction Era. There is less scholarship, however, addressing how free blacks in the early national and antebellum periods, particularly black women, envisioned freedom" (2–3). Thus, centering the imaginations and desires of free(d) women of color, *some* of whom occupied or otherwise had to navigate the economy of the free(d) mulatta concubine, this scholarship resituates the stakes of reading the figure, shifting from understanding white nationhood to exploring the multiplicity of experiences of blackness, gender, and freedom within discrete and specific locations.

While this scholarship often places its nation- or place-bounded inquiries within a broader Atlantic and/or African diasporic context, its emphasis on most fully developing detailed portraits of how free(d) women of color inhabited their particular locations demands a primary attentiveness to and sometimes inadvertent reification of discrete national, colonial, or linguistic boundaries. As Linda Sturtz contends in her examination of a mixed-race eighteenth-century Jamaican woman (and citing Herman Bennet's work in colonial Mexico), "Only by historicizing individuals like Mary Rose and the 'multiplicity of cultural formations' in which they lived in various times can we understand the variety of lived experiences of people who lived in the diaspora, and in an ongoing process, performed their identities and created communities" ("Mary Rose," 78–79). Such work thus illuminates how black subjects were aware of and understood their place beyond the localities in which they found themselves. Left undertheorized, however, are how histories of free(d) women of color intersect with and shift theories of diaspora and, inversely, how reading these subjects through diaspora helps us understand something more about the women themselves.

And to be sure, the fact of the free(d) mulatta concubine's ubiquity across diaspora does not inherently demand or justify a reading of her as a diasporic subject. As Tiffany Patterson and Robin D. G. Kelley point out, "Neither the fact of blackness nor shared experiences under racism nor the historical process of their dispersal makes for a community or common identity" ("Unfinished Migrations," 19). Citing Stuart Hall, Patterson and Kelley further remind us, "The linkages, therefore, that tie the diaspora together must be articulated and are not inevitable. These linkages are always historically constituted" (20). Thus, while the free(d) mulatta concubine appears everywhere in diaspora, the event of her appearance is always tied to the specific and often particular circumstances produced by the sexual and material desires of the European white men who laid claim to her body (and that of her black African and indigenous American mothers) across spatial geographies and racialized economies. Rather than a diasporic subject, she appears more readily as a colonial object and trope produced not by African or black agency but rather by European desire and domination.

Furthermore, as Hall insists we recognize, while "the past continues to speak to us . . . it no longer addresses us as a single, factual 'past' since our relation to it, like the child's relation to the mother, is always-already 'after the break.' It is always constructed through memory, fantasy, narrative and myth. . . . Hence, there is always a politics of identity, a politics of position, which has no absolute guarantee in an unproblematic, transcendental 'law of origin'" (Hall, "Cultural Identity," 226). Against Hall's injunction, to insist that the evidence demands that we read the free(d) mulatta concubine as a diasporic subject rather than as a mere colonial trope or object risks eliding the "politics of position" that guide such an inquiry in the first place. The danger here is not merely discursive. It is not incidental that Hall opens and closes his probing examination of cultural identity and diaspora with extended quotes from Frantz Fanon's *Wretched of the Earth* (and in fact leaves the last word to Fanon). Against this backdrop, one that at once recognizes how diasporic "identity is constituted, not outside but within representation," that asserts that the cultural forms that produce such representation in fact "constitute us as new kinds of subjects, and thereby enable us to discover places from which to speak," and that invokes the interdependent links between revolution and consciousness, to assert the centrality of the free(d) mulatta concubine to black diasporic identity is vexing indeed (Hall, "Cultural Identity," 222, 237).

Thus, particularly in the early stages of this project, when I most struggled to articulate concisely not only the scope but also the stakes of my project, I have often and reasonably been met with a persistent and skeptical question: Do I mean to rescue or redeem the figure of the free(d) mulatta concubine? A politics of position and identity propels both the question and my own response, which has always been a "no," once vehement and now, perhaps, more equivocal. The question's reasonable skepticism is grounded both historically and presently, given the social and material privileges accorded lighter-skinned women of African descent through the contemporary moment. And again, position matters: my centering of the free(d) mulatta concubine is most fraught within a U.S. literary historical context: as Teresa Zackodnik explains in her overview of the uses of and scholarship on the tragic mulatta trope, "We have understood the early history of this figure to be that of a doomed 'whitened ideal' who communicates white notions of racial difference to a largely white audience or who expresses white women's concerns about their material condition" (*Mulatta*, xiv).[17] Thus, I began my project understanding that to insist on *centering* the persistently marginal and pathological free(d) mulatta concubine in a theory of African diaspora and thus, by extension, a theory of blackness most understandably raises suspicion, as it risks privileging a figure so many view as standing not only outside but antithetical to the protracted work of excavating, seeing, and listening for the elusive experiences, voices, and testimonies of definitively unprivileged and captive black subjects who endured the Middle Passage and constituted the majority experience of the African diaspora on this side of the Atlantic, in the Americas.

And yet, the free(d) mulatta concubine *is* at the center. Across Atlantic land-scapes, her body bears the markings constitutive of an African diaspora espe-cially, as Hershini Bhana Young posits, "if one of the crucial constitutive factors of blackness and the African diaspora is, in fact, this racial injury" (*Haunting Capital*, 2). Light-skinned, female, and always beautiful, nearly always under-stood to be a New World subject, her body is evidence of the racialized and sex-ualized trauma, the violence of white male desire, the geographic displacement, and, perhaps most importantly, the fractured and interdependent reproductions of kinship and capital so central to economies of American slavery. And across both sides of the Atlantic, so too does her presence press upon that persistent, nagging question in diaspora, that of the participation of African and African diasporic subjects as kidnappers, negotiators, sellers, buyers, and enslavers of cap-tive black people. Her presence at once epitomizes what it is to be in diaspora and lays bare the fragility of any notion of kinship shaped and haunted by slav-ery and its "afterlife."[18]

Furthermore, while it is the enslaved mulatta who may most urgently em-body the injuries central to African diaspora history and memory, especially in that subject's unequivocal experience of sexual violence, it is the specter of the free(d) mulatta concubine that speaks to a fraught anticipation of the costs of freedom. And because we inhabit the "afterlife of slavery" where black subjects, while certainly no longer subjugated by racialized chattel slavery, also certainly have not yet fully experienced freedom, this *anticipation* of freedom, the desire to imagine and enact freedom's possibilities, persists (Hartman, *Lose*, 6). Indeed, as the work of Hartman, Young, Dayan, Ian Baucoum, and others makes clear abundantly and variously, our present, one made possible and indeed a "future created by" (Hartman, *Lose*, 133) the racial sexual, mercantile, and legal econo-mies of slavery, is "a moment of repetition, a moment in which the past returns to the present in expanded form, a moment in which present time finds stored and accumulated within itself a nonsynchronous array of past times" (Baucoum, *Specters*, 29). It is precisely the past's intrusion on the present that demands we attend to the myriad representations of a figure at once marginal and central to the very notion of an African diaspora. As Hartman insists, "The stories we tell about *what happened then*, the correspondences we discern between today and times past, and the ethical and political stakes of these stories redound in the present" (*Lose*, 133). That the free(d) mulatta inspires stories both fantastical and burdened matters too. That is, if, as Angeletta Gourdine contends, "the syncre-tism that frames any notion of diaspora manifests itself in a slight elision of the boundary between fiction and reality," then the figure of the free(d) mulatta con-cubine, as much myth as historical fact, perhaps inhabits that elision most visibly (*Difference*, 104). To place her in diaspora, then, is neither to rescue nor to redeem her but rather to explore more fully the story that this figure, most assuredly dia-sporic, can tell us about "what happened then" and perhaps, too, about what can happen now.

"The Question Must Be Asked": Archive, Linearity, and the Story Told

The African mulâtresse's presence aboard a slave ship as a free(d) mulatta concubine and the consequent reminder that subjects like her very well thrived in a slave port thus invite us to imagine how black subjects, enslaved and free(d), imagined freedom as a possibility. And here again, to begin to speculate what enslaved and free(d) black subjects may have known and imagined when they saw the free(d) mulatta concubine aboard a slave ship, in an urban slave society landscape, or in their homes as blood kin is to tread upon treacherous ground. Hartman's cautions haunt any attempt to read against the archive. Ruminating on the archival trace of two enslaved girls who "died on board the [slave ship] *Recovery*," Hartman presses the tension produced and reflected by the desire "to fill in the gaps and to provide closure when there is none" ("Venus," 7, 8). She insists: "Narrative restraint, the refusal to fill in the gaps and provide closure, is a requirement of this method, as is the imperative to respect black noise—the shrieks, the moans, the nonsense, and the opacity, which are always in excess of legibility and of the law and which hint at and embody aspirations that are wildly utopian, derelict to capitalism, and antithetical to its attendant discourse of Man" (12). In the same vein, Dayan describes her own methodology in a tren-chant critique of Paul Gilroy's *The Black Atlantic*, insisting, "I try to imagine what cannot be verified. Any query about the subjective reactions of slaves is perilous. *But the question must be asked*" ("Paul Gilroy's Slaves," 9, emphasis added).

Indeed, the problem of the archive is one central to African diaspora studies. While there are many and competing archives, some of which I examine herein, a primary project of African diaspora studies has been to challenge those domi-nant and controlling archives, "the institutions that organize facts and sources and condition the possibility of existence of historical statements" (Trouillot, *Silencing*, 52).[19] Questions of evidence, legibility, authenticity, and power work as undercurrents that trouble scholars' attempts to recover lost stories in order to correct or simply disrupt the official historical record.[20] As Michel-Rolph Trouillot asserts, "Archives assemble. . . . They convey authority and set the rules for credibility and interdependence; they help select the stories that matter" (52). For scholars in African diaspora studies, the task is to revise not only what the archive looks like but what work it does in the present. Brent Hayes Edwards thus insists that we understand the archive as a "'generative system': in other words, a discursive system that governs the possibilities, forms, appearance, and regularity of particular statements, objects, and practices—or, on the simplest level, that determines 'what can and cannot be said'" (*Practice*, 7). As Edwards's intervention suggests, scholars of the African diaspora must at once acquiesce to the work of the archive and at the same time resist its dictates.

Indeed, the power of the archive to determine not only the stories that can be told but also the questions that we might ask is a fact that foils any attempt to recover that which not only did not make it into the archive but perhaps was never produced at all. As Hartman laments, "The task of writing the impossible (not the fanciful or the utopian but 'histories rendered unreal and fantastic') has as its prerequisites the embrace of likely failure and the readiness to accept the ongoing, unfinished and provisional character of this effort, particularly when the arrangements of power occlude the very object that we desire to rescue" (Hartman, "Venus," 14; she quotes Palmié, *Wizards*, 97). In the case of the free(d) mulatta concubine, Hartman's insight is particularly vexing, given Trouillot's assertion that the archive and thus our understandings of historical narratives are not endlessly capacious. The recovery or production of new facts does not necessarily eliminate silences. Rather, the new facts "will have to gain their right to existence in light of the field constituted by previously created facts. They may dethrone some of these facts, erase or qualify others" (Trouillot, *Silencing*, 49). At stake in inserting the free(d) mulatta concubine as an African diasporic subject into the archive, in insisting on her centrality to how we understand unfreedom and possibilities for freedom across a black Atlantic, is not only the specter of failure but perhaps more urgently in this case the question of what silences such a move might produce.

"But the question must be asked." The African mulâtresse's presence on the slave ship reminds us not only that captive Africans carried their own memories but that they witnessed things along the way. It is, at first, tempting to take this reminder too literally and too linearly. For example, the mulâtresse traveled from one place where Africans (and here I would like to place a small marker that I do not use "Africans" lightly) apparently defined the terms of the sexual and domestic unions between European men and local black and mixed-race African women, where travelers noted the spectacle of extravagant *folgars*, or "balls," to another place where the near-mythic institutions of quadroon balls and *plaçage* (extralegal contractual unions between free quadroons and wealthy white men, arranged by the women's mothers) would come to saturate representations of free women of color's sexual and domestic lives. Given that this movement follows the direction of the slave trade, the possibility that plaçage and quadroon balls may be reiterations of the practices of signares rooted in African cultural and social traditions is appealing in its romance of continuity. However, the impulse to seize on this connection risks a danger particular to reading and theorizing African diasporic subjects and traditions. David Scott thus describes an "anthropological problematic" that "attempt[s] to place the 'cultures' of the ex-African/ex-slave in relation to what we might call an authentic past, that is, an anthropologically identifiable, ethnologically recoverable, and textually representable past" ("That Event," 263). Scott's caution builds upon Edouard Glissant's warning that "one of the most terrible implications of the ethnographic approach is the insistence on fixing the object of scrutiny in static time, thereby removing the tangled nature of lived experience and promoting the idea of uncontaminated survival" (*Caribbean Discourse*, 14).

What Glissant's warning implies, and indeed what he produces and delineates, is that alternative and counterapproaches to history must in fact engage that "point of entanglement, from which we were forcefully turned away" (*Caribbean Discourse*, 26). To contend with the "point of entanglement" is also to refuse to capitulate to the dominant archive's (and, hand in hand, its historiography of African America) demand for a linear, progressive reading of history and a framing of diasporic movement and production from African origins to New World survivals or reimaginations. Thus, in his illuminating work on Brazilian Candomblé, J. Lorand Matory offers a "revision of diasporic cultural history . . . based on the premise that Africa is historically 'coeval' (Fabian 1983)—or contemporaneous—with its American diaspora" (*Black Atlantic Religion*, 39). Offering the metaphor of an "Afro-Atlantic dialogue" for understanding black diasporic cultural history, Matory posits that, rather than trace a linear history from African culture through its survivals in the Americas, a "dialogue metaphor" would emphasize the synchronous, "multidirectional" exchanges between Africans and African Americans (291). For Matory, such a metaphor "highlights the ways in which cultural artifacts, images, and practices do not simply 'survive' or endure through 'memory': they are, rather, interpreted and reproduced for diverse contemporary purposes" by numerous "actors" who possess "culturally diverse repertoires" and who inhabit a diversity of subject and power positions within the diaspora (291). And most importantly, such a metaphor emphasizes the stakes of engaging the "point of entanglement" against the dominant archive: "As if in a literal dialogue, such interpretations and reproductions [of the cultural artifacts, images, and practices] can also be silenced, articulated obliquely, paraphrased, exaggerated, quoted mockingly, or treated as antitypes of the legitimate self" (291).

It is against this context—diaspora's theorization of the uses and misuses of dominant archives and the evidence they offer—that the archival presence of the traveling African mulâtresse compels me. Rather than read her apparent linear and unidirectional movement from Gorée to New Orleans as evidence of

a parallel trajectory for understanding the ubiquity of the free(d) mulatta concubine across the diaspora, I consider how her presence engenders a theorization of the synchronicity of diasporic production and reproduction across black
Atlantic space and time. Her presence on board the slave ship further disrupts
dichotomous readings of the geographic relationship between Africa and the
New World. Her simultaneous parallel movement with and diametric difference from the captive Africans who most substantially define our understandings of diaspora is a simultaneity made both legible and unexplainable through
the dominant archive. Whereas traditional examinations of the figure presume
the inevitability and thus the coherent event of her appearance, I am interested
in how her appearance illuminates the incoherence of diaspora. I thus mine her
archive not necessarily to produce a new narrative of diaspora but rather to see
what else is there.

Ezili, Marasa, and "Another Realm of Discourse"

To see what else is there is not only to look more or look for more. It is to
see and listen differently, to be open to suggestions, elusive presences, and contrary evidence. If the traveling African mulâtresse disrupts repetitious visual and
written descriptions of the free(d) mulatta concubine, then Ezili Freda, the most
visible lwa (goddess) in the Haitian religious practice vodou, utterly confounds
them. My invocation of Ezili is central to this book's methodology. This turn
to an African diasporic religious practice as a counterarchive is, of course, not
without precedence. I draw upon the paradigm-shifting work of Barbara Christian, VèVè Clark, and Dayan, especially (and see also Gates, *Signifying Monkey*).
Christian and Clark are foundational in their insistence that theoretical perspectives on the lives of black people in general and black women in particular demand what Clark, developing a methodological theory rooted in vodou practice,
names "diaspora literacy." Following Christian, such an approach "acknowledges
the existence of an African cosmology, examines how that cosmology has been
consistently denigrated in the West, and explores its appropriateness for texts
that are clearly derived from it" (Christian, "Fixing Methodologies," 365). Thus,
in her examination of the rituals, practices, and writing of Haitian history, Dayan
explains the work of vodou: "I emphasize the intensely intellectual puzzlement,
the process of thought working itself through terror that accounts for what I
have always recognized as the materiality of vodou practice, its concreteness, its
obsession with details and fragments, with the very things that might seem to
block or hinder belief" (*Haiti*, xvii). For Christian, Clark, and Dayan, the beliefs
and practices enacted through African diasporic religious systems are neither

metaphorical nor fantastical but rather the rehearsal and application of black Atlantic subjects' intellectual and spiritual labor in theorizing their histories and presents. It is here, in the rituals and belief systems, where theory meets praxis.

While African diasporic religious practices produce a counterarchive, they also suggest a counterparadigm, an alternative methodology for reading the archive. Turning to the lwas and their representation in ritual signs of vodou, VèVè Clark considers how one in particular, that of the marasa trois (divine twins), points to "the transformation of cultural oppositions in plantation societies" ("Developing," 44). Clark's intervention, her assertion that those of us committed to theorizing diaspora from "an informed, indigenous perspective," to resisting the "binary nightmare" instrumental to the production and maintenance of slavery and its political, economic, and social legacies, is especially important to my invocation of Ezili here (42, 44). For Clark, "marasa consciousness" enables a transgressive and transformational move beyond binaries not in order to resolve or synthesize them but rather in order to "[dance] into another realm of discourse" entirely (44). The presence of the free(d) African mulâtresse who apparently boarded a slave ship of her own volition startles and then disappears. However, rather than attempt to reconcile her appearance in the archive, on the ship, with what we already know about the Middle Passage, rather than lament her disappearance into the landscape of colonial New Orleans, this book endeavors to follow her trace into "another realm of discourse," to search for echoes, iterations, even ghosts that, like her, intervene in the repetitive depictions of the free(d) mulatta concubine.

It is there, in "another realm of discourse," that Ezili makes her appearance. And while Dayan persuasively insists that Ezili, "a goddess born on the soil of Haiti who has no precedent in Yoruba or Dahomey," is part of the pantheon of lwas and "vodou practices [that] must be viewed as ritual reenactments of Haiti's colonial past, even more than as retentions from Africa" (*Haiti*, 58, xvii), I suggest that she is *also* something else.[21] Her identity, as visually represented in Haitian art and as verbally described by practitioners, flows from black through mulatta to white and thus forcefully evokes a potential theoretical framework through which we can read the black female subject in diaspora. Her manifestation at once invokes and disrupts binaries between black and white, civilized and savage, promiscuous and chaste, fertile and sterile, straight and gay, passive and regressive, concubine and mistress, silent and raging. At the same time, as Dayan insists we recognize, "in ritual performances this dichotomy is both entangled and blurred" (*Haiti*, 59).

Methodologically, Ezili thus performs two kinds of labor in this project. First, contemporary descriptions of the free(d) mulatta concubines in colonial Saint-Domingue echo those of the signares of eighteenth-century Senegal and the quadroons of antebellum Louisiana and would thus seem an obvious fit into the archive of the free(d) mulatta concubine. However, while such descriptions provide important historical and discursive context for reading Ezili, they cannot do much more than confirm the repetitive depictions of the free(d) mulatta concubine so pervasive in eighteenth- and nineteenth-century accounts. Ezili, on the other hand, intervenes because she enables a shift from reading the free(d) mulatta concubine from outside blackness to imagining how the figure looks from within an African diasporic perspective.

Second, Ezili draws and frames our attention to two intersecting problems of diaspora: translation and geography. As Edwards insists, "It is not possible to take up the question of 'diaspora' without taking account of the fact that the great majority of peoples of African descent do not speak or write in English" (*Practice*, 7). It would do well to add that neither should we presume standard notions of literacy. Indeed, there is a rich tradition in African American letters of turning to the vernacular in order to read and theorize black literatures (see Gates, *Signifying Monkey*; Baker, *Blues*; Clark, "Developing"). In employing a very specific and particular Haitian figure in the service of a geographically and temporally expansive theorization of diaspora, I endeavor to at once recognize Ezili's untranslatability and consider how her manifestation might suggest "a transnational dimension to black identity" (Hanchard, "Identity," 40; see also Matory, *Black Atlantic Religion*). As a goddess, Ezili enables an "entanglement and blurring" not only of racial and sexual binaries but also of the discrete boundaries between language, nation-states, and, most importantly, material and imaginative geographies.

It is in the entanglement and blurring of dichotomies that Ezili compels my reading of the free(d) mulatta concubine. The lwa appears multiply and variously to her serviteurs (devotees), but three iterations dominate at least her discursive representations: Ezili Freda, the gentle, seductive, and capricious mulatta goddess of love; Ezili Dantò, the black single mother who bears the scars of both the Haitian Revolution and Ezili Freda's jealousy; and Lasirèn, the siren, "a fleeting presence, never fully seen, hinting at something monumental," whose devotees describe her as white, black, and mulatta (Brown, *Mama Lola*, 223). Of these three iterations, it is Ezili Freda, the mulatta mistress, who is most familiar and most often described in the literature. Central to each of Ezili's incarnations is an embodiment of the economy of forced concubinage and powerlessness that framed the experiences of free(d) and enslaved black and mulatta women across the Atlantic. That is, while the goddess is specific to Haiti, those memories and events that she evokes in each of her manifestations repeat themselves over and over again across Atlantic spaces. In tandem, free and enslaved historical subjects represented as mulatta concubines and written and visual depictions of these women circulated and traveled within a circum-Atlantic space that reflected and enacted the racial and sexual economies that governed these women's lives. Dayan emphatically insists: "[Ezili] might more accurately be seen as the blunt recollection of what those who were abused first by the master and then by the mistress had come to know. This time, however, the rigors of knowing demand a reenactment that goes beyond imitation. The place of torture becomes the scene for a charade of love. The knowledge has to do with the costs and the perils of mastery: a grotesque distortion performed in Ezili's moves from deification to defection, her confounding of angelic and brute" (*Haiti*, 65). Dayan's argument is utterly convincing. And, and. The African mulâtresse who boarded the slave ship of her own volition is there, too. Whether and how she is remembered: that is a question.

Spiral: The Free(d) Mulatta Concubine across Time and Space

Indeed, Ezili's ability to "entangle and blur" binaries is perhaps most urgent in considering the temporality of African diasporic imagination and subject formation. By reading the Haitian goddess Ezili against the historical subjects represented in eighteenth- and nineteenth-century written and visual documents, I endeavor to resist thinking about the free(d) mulatta concubine as a relic of some "discrete past kept alive through narratives" (Trouillot, *Silencing*, 150). I also strive against using Ezili as mere metaphor and instead strive to attend to the interconnectedness of sex, gender, spectacle, geography, and terror in the work of African diasporic memory and history.

The book's structure and choice of objects of analysis reflect both my emphasis on the nonlinearity and multidimensionality of African diasporic geographies and my reframing of the archive. Thus, I've assembled a diverse array of archival sources that span African diasporic time and space. These sources include eighteenth- and nineteenth-century letters, petitions, and travelers' narratives from Senegal, colonial Saint-Domingue, and the United States; nineteenth-century New Orleans newspaper accounts and African American literature; and twentieth-century popular representations (culled from oral histories, guidebooks, religious iconography, and ethnographies) of the free(d) mulatta concubine from Senegal, Haiti, and the United States. I place objects from disparate contexts against one another in order to emphasize how black subjects, in order to envision the possibility of freedom and agency, must inhabit multiple imaginative and physical landscapes simultaneously. Following Clark's invocation of "marasa consciousness," my book unfolds in a spiral-like fashion, with each chapter considering a recurring problem in representations of the free(d) mulatta concubine across black Atlantic time and space.

Chapter 1 begins by considering the problem of the dominant archive in authenticating African diasporic geographic understandings of history and memory. In a comparative analysis of twentieth-century ethnographic descriptions of the Haitian vodou deity Ezili Freda and eighteenth-century male European travelers' descriptions of the famous signares of the Senegalese island entrepôts Gorée and Saint-Louis, I examine how the dominant archive presents the free(d) mulatta concubine as an object of desire and consider what such representations can teach us about how black subjects imagine and understand freedom. Attending to questions of geography, memory, gender, sexuality, ritual, and liminality, this chapter establishes two core themes that run throughout the book. First, it theorizes temporal geographies of diaspora in order to resituate how we understand the experiences of freedom and slavery in the black Atlantic. Second, it (re)constructs an archive of the free(d) mulatta concubine that emphasizes how black subjects *within* diaspora imagine and theorize a figure who is most often read as a stereotype produced from a patriarchal, white, and male desiring gaze *outside* black subjectivity. In prioritizing imaginative landscapes and geographies over official histories, this chapter offers a methodology responsive to the field's calls to challenge, resist, and revise the dominant archive of African diasporic histories.

Next, noting the dominant archive's obsession with the sexual lives of free(d) mulatta concubines, the second chapter examines the question of privacy in reading the authority and freedom of these women. This chapter explores how the very descriptions that document and legitimize the constant surveillance of free(d) women also subject themselves to disruptive readings that allow us to glean how women marked as free(d) mulatta concubines may have negotiated and resisted that surveillance. On the one hand, to read this archive is to capitulate to the voyeurism that violated these women's authority over their bodies. At the same time, the dominant archive's refusal of privacy to these women produces a space to examine how these women processed and navigated that same violation. In its examination of privacy, intimacy, and unfreedom, this chapter thus invites scholars to reflect on the replication of violence and terror our own efforts to recover histories might engender.

The third chapter moves from the intimacy of libidinal relations to considerations of family, kinship, and motherhood. My examination centers on two eighteenth-century documents. The first is an oft-cited but little-examined published work, *L'Affrique et le peuple affriquain* (1789). The book includes a petition from the free(d) men of color inhabitants of Saint-Louis, Senegal, to the French

Estates-General, as well as a three-hundred-page appendix written by the book's author, Dominique Harcourt Lamiral, a French commercial agent. The second document is an unpublished letter from a free(d) black woman living on Gorée in 1737. While this remarkable letter is easily accessible in the French colonial archival repository, the historiography of the island appears to have ignored it. I argue that these two documents, read together, reveal the centrality of kinship in black diasporic claims to authority and autonomy. Furthermore, central to both documents' assertion of kinship are claims to discursive and bodily possession of the free(d) mulatta concubine. And while the appearances of these two documents are inextricable from the material histories of eighteenth-century Saint-Louis and Gorée, the stakes of possession, gender, kinship, and authority once again echo across diasporic time and space, this time in the iconography of a second iteration of Ezili, her sister Ezili Dantò, the scorned and mutilated dark-skinned single mother–warrior to Ezili Freda's mulatta love goddess. At stake in this chapter is not only how the archive shapes our ability to see and recognize self-possession in Atlantic spaces as diasporic acts but also how practices of self-possession may limit as much as open possibilities for family and kinship across a black Atlantic.

Chapter 4 returns to the question of diasporic geographies in order to attend to two theoretical pressure points central to my project: first, the status and privilege of free(d) mulatta subjects against the precariousness of their freedom; and second, the critical differences between African and American slave societies against the persistent echo and repetition in transatlantic representations of the free(d) mulatta concubine. I juxtapose two works whose mid-nineteenth-century publication dates and revisions of black Atlantic free(d) mulatta concubines belie the limits of their comparability. *Esquisses sénégalaises* (1853) offers written and visual descriptions of the signares from the perspective of an orphaned and French-educated son of a Senegalese mother and a French father, Father David Boilat. The second object of analysis in this chapter is a U.S. antebellum narrative written by a free woman of color from the North, Eliza Potter's *A Hairdresser's Experience in High Life* (1859). I contend that both writers produce subversive geographies of the places about which they write and center revisions of the free(d) mulatta concubine in these geographies. However, rather than emphasize the similarities between Boilat and Potter, I explore the specific and distinctive contours of each work. This chapter centers itself inside the paradox of the echo traced throughout this book: that in order for it to resonate, to sound and feel familiar, the echo must move across an uneven, expansive, and utterly strange terrain. Rather than attempt to resolve this paradox, chapter 4 inhabits it, exploring its consequences and possibilities for imagining not only the possibilities and limits of freedom across the black transatlantic but also the limits of the notion of diaspora itself. As another turn in my book's spiral structure, my examination of how Boilat and Potter each enacts a geographic engagement with and deconstruction of the free(d) mulatta concubine as historical subject and imaginative object returns to and expands the first chapter's delineation of African diasporic geographies.

Across all four chapters, the movement of the unnamed African mulâtresse from Gorée to New Orleans aboard the slave ship *La Galathée* propels my own tracing of this spiral. As the following chapters unfold, as I trace the free(d) mulatta concubine's spiraling presence across diaspora, I leave behind here the one subject who physically traveled across diasporic space. For this project is not about her specifically; rather, I am compelled by the simultaneous possibility and improbability of her shared diaspora-ness with the captive Africans held on board. Probing the experiences of captive Africans thrust into the Middle Passage, Stephanie Smallwood tells us, "In one another's eyes they saw the reflection of their own traumatic alienation" (*Saltwater*, 121). What would these same captives have seen of themselves within the face of the free(d) mulatta concubine? What did her presence say of freedom and its theft and possibilities to them? It is with these questions that I begin.

CHAPTER I

Echo and the
Myth of Origins

> Echoes are delayed returns of sound; they are incomplete reproductions,
> usually giving back only the final fragments of a phrase. An echo spans large
> gaps of space (sound reverberates between distant points) and time (echoes
> aren't instantaneous), but it also creates gaps of meaning and intelligibility.
> —JOAN SCOTT, "Fantasy Echo"

In 1789 Antoine Edmé Pruneau de Pommegorge, a former advisor to the
governor of Senegal, published his *Description de la Nigritie*. The opening pages
of his travel narrative offer a description of the island of Saint-Louis, located
at the mouth of the Senegal River, and its inhabitants, "métisses, métis, mulattos, mulattas, quadroon men, quadroon women and free Negro women with all
of their captives."[1] Saint-Louis and its more famous counterpart, Gorée Island,
located just off the coast of Senegal, played crucial roles in France's interests in
West Africa, serving as "thriving, cosmopolitan ports" from the era of transatlantic slavery through the securing of European colonial rule (Jones, *Métis*, 4).
Pruneau, who spent twenty-two years in West Africa, continues his description
of the island's inhabitants by noting that "in general, the women of this island are
strongly attached to the white [men] and care for them as no one else when they
are sick."[2] He explains how these women—free Negro, mulatta, and quadroon—
own slaves who sell salt in order to procure gold for their mistresses; in turn, the
women "use some of the gold to make jewelry and the rest to purchase fabric for
clothing," for according to Pruneau, the women "love, like everywhere else, their
finery."[3] Pruneau then proceeds to detail the women's elaborate toilette:

> They wear an artistically arranged white handkerchief on the head, over which
> they affix a small narrow black ribbon, or a colored one, around their head.
> A shift *à la française*, ornamented; a bodice of taffeta or muslin; a skirt of the

same and similar to the bodice; gold earrings; anklets of gold or silver, for they will wear no others; red morocco slippers on the feet; underneath their bodice a piece of two ells of muslin, the ends of which dangle beneath the left shoulder. . . .

The women being thus escorted when they go out, they frequently encounter a *griot*. . . . [I]n such instances he does not lose the opportunity to precede them, declaiming their praises with all the exaggerations he can think of, and some immodesties which they know, the women being so flattered that in the rapture excited by this adulation they often fling some of their garments to the singer when they have nothing left in their pockets to give him.[4]

While never naming them as such, Pruneau describes a group of women who would become famously known as signares, "wives of [French trading] company personnel who accumulated colossal personal fortunes and rose to play important roles in the economic and social lives of such colonial enclaves as Saint-Louis, Gorée and Fort Saint James" and who, despite their varied positions on a black/white racial schema (as evidenced by Pruneau's introduction), are most often and most persistently depicted in scholarly and popular histories as mulattas (Barry, *Senegambia*, 76). Products of the European incursion into West Africa and but one articulation of the pervasive conjugal unions between white European men and black African women, the signares, symbolically and inextricably attached to Saint-Louis and Gorée, have acquired a uniquely iconic status within an African diasporic landscape.[5]

An ocean and a world away, nearly two hundred years after Pruneau's report on the signares, Jewish American filmmaker and vodou initiate Maya Deren published her description of the sacred rites of the lwa Ezili, the "Vodou love spirit" (Brown, *Mama Lola*, 3). In contrast to Pruneau's documentation of the quotidian practices of the signares, a group of women whose lives left a trail of evidence in official colonial archives, Deren describes a goddess as she manifests herself within a ritual ceremony, a divine figure whose presence is as richly documented in its own official but counterhegemonic archive. Whereas Pruneau describes historical subjects as they go about their everyday routines, Deren documents a goddess's physical manifestation in sacred ritual; here, Ezili's physicality is apparent in the comportment, actions, and words of the human she possesses. The geographic, temporal, social, and ontological differences between Pruneau's and Deren's accounts are thus vast and profound. Across this chasm, there sounds an echo.

Like Pruneau, Deren first describes her subject's attachment to finery, recalling how "Erzulie moves in an atmosphere of infinite luxury, a perfume of refinement, which, from the first moment of her arrival, pervades the very air of

the peristyle, and becomes a general expansiveness in which all anxieties, all ur-
gencies vanish" (*Divine Horsemen*, 139).[6] Because Deren is describing a goddess's
physical manifestation, the attendant objects and movements she delineates are
provided, performed, and witnessed by the people who serve her; they are material, not imagined. As with that of the women in Pruneau's account, Ezili's
toilette is central to her legibility:

> Her first act is to perform an elaborate toilette for which the equipment is al-
> ways kept in readiness in the hounfor or the private chapel. . . . The enamel basin
> in which she washes is neither chipped nor discolored; the soap is new, still in
> its wrapper; there are several towels, probably embroidered; and a special comb,
> mirror and even tooth-brush have been consecrated for her. She is provided
> with a fresh white or rose silk handkerchief which she arranges carefully around
> her hair. Perfume is imperative, and there may be powder as well. A white or
> rose dress of delicate cloth, with lace or embroidery, has been kept in readiness
> for her. And finally, she is brought not one necklace, but several, of gold and
> pearls, along with ear-rings and bracelets and her three wedding-bands. (Deren,
> *Divine Horsemen*, 139)

And again, just as Pruneau's portrayal of the signares details the public adulation enjoyed by the women, Deren's description ends with the adoration Ezili
encounters as she walks amongst her devotees:

> The very process of this creative transformation becomes so significant that
> whether it is a large audience or a small family who await her, or how long they
> may have to wait, ceases to be of any consequence. . . .
>
> Thus attired, powdered and perfumed, she goes out into the peristyle es-
> corted by several of the more handsome men, her favorites. There she may make
> the rounds, greeting the men guests effusively, but extending only the little fin-
> gers of each hand to those women who are not special devotees. (*Divine Horse-
> men*, 140)

Like the signares, Ezili inhabits both her present and the archive vain, pampered, frivolous, sensual, and powerful.

Both Pruneau and Deren describe figures who either historically or imaginatively inhabit a spectrum of racial and social categories but are most famous
to those outside the communities that know them as free, seductive mulattas
with full power and authority over their sexual bodies. Within this context, the
resonance across time and space between these two descriptions is striking. The
attention to detail in both descriptions mirrors each subject's obsession with her
toilette. Both descriptions emphasize the role luxury and refinement play in each

figure's comportment, drawing specific attention to how each adorns her head with a "white handkerchief," wears clothing intricately embroidered or ornamented, and insists on gold jewelry as an accessory. Each figure's arrival on the scene is met with adulation and devotion. Both Pruneau and Deren describe free mulatta women who, reveling in adornment and riches, command attention, service, and praise from and within black folk communities.

The echo between the signares and Ezili sounds not only in representations of their vanity and relationships to the communities they serve but also in each representation's complex relationship to prevalent understandings of its subject. (And here, it matters that while Pruneau and Deren had very different relationships to their subjects—one a government official imposing European authority on the protocolony Senegal, and the other an outsider filmmaker who would become a participant-observer devotee of vodou in contemporary Haiti—both write to audiences outside the communities they describe.) Both Pruneau's and Deren's descriptions are canonical in the historiography of their respective subjects, and yet both descriptions offer the possibility of subverting the very stereotypes they appear to invoke, that both the signares and Ezili are most legible as seductive, vain, pampered mulattas. Thus, against the hyperstatic representation of the signares as mulattas, Pruneau neither calls these women signares nor fixes them as uniquely mulatta. Indeed, while his opening pages describe the range of racial classifications inhabited by the free women of Saint-Louis, the paragraph in which he describes their attachment to white men and their elaborate toilette and dress introduces the subjects as specifically "négresse," stating that "the majority live in great luxury, and most of these Negro women own thirty to forty slaves."[7] Likewise, Deren's attention to Ezili's gestures, "careful, unhurried accumulation of costume," and "elaborate toilette" is so exquisitely detailed that one misses that left unspoken is an explicit description of Ezili's color (*Divine Horsemen*, 140, 139). Instead, throughout *Divine Horsemen*, Deren's descriptions of Ezili stand out in the lwa's public archive for their silence on the racial and color status of this goddess, each of whose multiple incarnations in the vodou pantheon is marked by specific, if fluid, racial signifiers.[8] While Deren's silence regarding Ezili's visual appearance underscores the lwa's resistance to fixed racial legibility, Deren's description here of the Ezili she calls the "Goddess of Love, the muse of beauty" is surely that of Ezili Freda, most often represented and described by practitioners and scholars as a "white" mulatta woman (Deren, *Divine Horsemen*, 138).[9]

Not only is the echo discursive, with descriptions of both figures repeatedly emphasizing the beauty, elaborate toilette, and powers of seduction of both women, but it also resonates geographically and materially. It matters that the signares and Ezili are each attached to the most diasporic of places: island entrepôts, slave ports, ontological portals that witnessed (indeed produced) the dispossession and repossession of black bodies and persons. It matters that neither Saint-Louis nor Gorée nor Saint-Domingue was home to black people before the incursion of Europe into Africa.[10] It matters that in their access to and control over wealth, the signares and Ezili disrupt and have the potential to subvert the racial and sexual economies of capital and power dominating their respective milieus. It matters that each figure's racial legibility is central to understanding her social, economic, and political significance, as well as the place she inhabits. And it matters that the facts on the ground of each figure's appearance both substantiate and complicate her discursive stereotyping. The echo, then, is not simply about what might otherwise be a persistent universal investment in an ethereal hyperfemininity. Nor can we begin and end with an understanding of how this echo reflects white male colonization and objectification of African and black women's bodies. Rather, the echo's resonance across spaces—material, geographic, and discursive—demands that we attend to other possibilities for its origins and its tenor.

This chapter thus begins with this echo in order to unpack the questions of origins and evidence as they emerge across African diasporic histories and memories. At stake in this chapter are this resonance and the questions it raises for understanding the multiple ways geography, visibility, and sexuality intersect in African diasporic memory and history. I contend that visual and written representations of the free(d) mulatta concubine as historical agent and as divine subject echo within each other and across African diasporic time and space. This echo invites us to consider how captive Africans passing through places inhabited by the free(d) mulatta concubine, thrust against the limits of possibility, belonging, and being, may have seen, imagined, remembered, and theorized these women's experiences of freedom.

Presence

Of course, as echoes do, so too does this one falter, fracturing across the distance it must travel. While both the signares and Ezili Freda were notorious for their sexual relationships, the shape and purpose of these relationships differed significantly. The signares' serially monogamous relationships with European men followed the material and physical needs and dictates of the men's arrivals to and departures from the islands. Ezili Freda, on the other hand, appears a capricious, demanding, and promiscuous wife who holds full authority over her sexual and conjugal choices. As Leslie Desmangles explains, "Her life as depicted in Haitian mythology abounds with scandals which, by normal standards of morality, would be considered disgraceful conduct. Her partners in spiritual *plasay* (concubinage) include not only her male devotees, but many lwas as well" (*Faces*, 132–33). And while the signares, like Ezili Freda, occupied superior status positions with regard to those who served them, those who served the signares did so out of force, coercion, or legal obligation. Those who serve Ezili Freda do so from a place of sacred devotion and divine compulsion. (At the same time, it matters that vodou devotees, who call themselves "serviteurs," understand their relationship to the lwas to be one of service.) Finally, the echo in the clothing, the headscarf, and the love of finery and gold jewelry has a distinctive historical context for each figure. For the signares, the official record, largely dependent on eighteenth-century European narratives, characterizes their distinctive dress and vanity within simultaneously culturally exotic and completely familiar terms: while their mixed style of clothing was rooted in African and Islamic traditions, the elaborate investment in the style itself reflected a universal femininity. The signares were "women like everywhere" (Lamiral, *L'Affrique*, 48). Ezili Freda's vanity, on the other hand, is rooted in the notorious and subversive sartorial extravagance of Saint-Domingue's free women of color. Explaining dress as a site of rebellion and subversion in colonial Saint-Domingue, Jean Fouchard describes how "African creoles and house-servants who, with their tendency to imitate the master's fashion in dress, devoted their meager resources to clothing themselves . . . embellishing their clothes with colored buttons and with trimming, the *insolent luxury of the menial condition*" (*Haitian Maroons*, 42, emphasis added). And Colin Dayan insists that we recognize that with Ezili, "the elaborate dress and the details of service articulate a specific experience of Saint-Domingue that goes beyond the scattered scriptural, classical, and West African materials assembled in the manifestations of Ezili" (*Haiti*, 58). In isolation, such fractures signal that Ezili and the signares are not the same subject, their similarities coincidental rather than evidential.

And again, as echoes do, so too does this one reverberate in multiple directions. Between Pruneau's description of the signares in eighteenth-century Senegal (and its own repetition across eighteenth- and nineteenth-century French and British accounts of Gorée and Saint-Louis) and Deren's encounters with a lwa in twentieth-century Haiti (frequently cited by and thus foundational to a wealth of scholarship on vodou) lies a veritable canon of travelers' descriptions of the free(d) mulâtresse of colonial Saint-Domingue. Eighteenth-century European and U.S. travelers' accounts of the colony's free women of color did not merely note but in fact "dwelled" upon and anguished over "their exquisite taste, their love of finery, and their special attachment to lace, linen, silks and gold" (Dayan, *Haiti*, 174). As Doris Garraway explains, "In nearly every published description of Saint-Domingue, the mulatto woman was figured primarily as a libertine whose sole occupation was to perfect the art of pleasure" (*Libertine*

Colony, 230–31). Within these colonial narratives, and despite the contemporaneous reputation of mulatta women as "economically prudent, thrifty, and even entrepreneurial ... more independent and financially much better off than white women" (235), at stake in the depiction of the free(d) mulatta's vanity, sensuality, and wealth was the threat she presented to the "stability of France's hold on its most valuable colony" (Clark, *Strange History*, 49).

So central was the Saint-Dominguan free(d) mulatta concubine to the formation of nation in the New World that it is *her* particular presence that traipses across American time and space. Dayan thus considers how the echo of the free(d) mulâtresse in colonial Saint-Domingue sounds itself in contemporary representations of Ezili and illuminates Haitian people's understandings and theorization of classed, racialized, gendered, and sexualized power dynamics in that place under colonial rule and since independence. Indeed, as should be transparent throughout this chapter, Dayan's analysis of Ezili in Haiti opens up the possibility for and guides my own exploration of the echo between this goddess and the free(d) mulatta concubine across a black diasporic time and space.

Whereas Dayan probes the dimensions of the free(d) mulâtresse of colonial Saint-Domingue's echoes across historical and contemporary time in Ezili, Emily Clark excavates the route dominant colonial narratives of the free(d) mulatta concubine in colonial Saint-Domingue traveled across the Americas, tracing how the threat posed by the free(d) mulatta concubine and the rhetorical discourse of that threat followed refugees of the Haitian revolution into the United States, crossing national, cultural, and linguistic borders, landing primarily and most profoundly in nineteenth-century New Orleans.[11] However, as Clark carefully delineates, antebellum New Orleans was not colonial Saint-Domingue, and the social, legal, and economic systems that structured freedom, race, gender, and sexuality had distinctive consequences for the women who may have moved across the same routes as the travelers' narratives. As Clark's excavation reveals, not only do travelers' depictions of the Saint-Domingue mulâtresses reappear in descriptions of New Orleans's quadroon women, mirroring the migration of refugees from revolutionary Saint-Domingue to New Orleans, but so too do they distort our ability to see the mundanity and the geographic and national specificity of the lives of the antebellum North American city's free women of color.

Dayan and Clark thus illuminate the stakes of the free(d) mulatta concubine's echo within American spaces—across time and material realms in Dayan's analysis, and across physical and national place in Clark's examination. Against their interventions is the question of how the historical presence of the signares in African ports both extends and disrupts geographies of the free(d) mulatta concubine that center an American context even as those American geographies challenge dominant readings of the figure. Indeed, it is the very historicity of the signares, the measurable fact of their existence, against Ezili's divine manifestation that allows us to speculate on this echo in the first place. That is, if the signares were goddesses, if they were another diasporic manifestation of a female deity marked by her connection to wealth, water, and sensuality, then they might be evidence for what we already know, that African diasporic religious practices circulate across the Atlantic. But for their historical presence, the signares could be understood as one more variation on an African diasporic religious archetype, a manifestation of Osun, Yemaya, Mami Wata, and Ezili, all goddesses in diaspora associated with water, business acumen, wealth, and sensual femininity.[12] Instead, the signares' historical presence—on an island entrepôt and in a slave society where their ability to mediate commerce and power over waterways has commanded awe and astonishment across centuries—demands a reassessment of the persistence of the free(d) mulatta concubine in black Atlantic memory and practice that attends to how these women, from all accounts powerful traders who not only held household slaves but through their position as intermediaries played significant roles in the transatlantic economy of slavery, fit into and shape our understanding of an African diaspora produced by this very economy.

Spiral

Given that the signares and Ezili inhabit key stops in what was a French Atlantic triangle, the possibility that Ezili is a remembering not only of Saint-Domingue's mulattas, as Dayan argues, but also of the signares is seductive in its promise of an account of what captives passing through Saint-Louis and Gorée, chained and bound for the Americas, saw and chose to remember. Certainly, both the signares and Ezili tell origins stories central to diaspora's belongings. The signares figure prominently in academic and popular histories of eighteenth-century Saint-Louis and Gorée as black and mixed-race African women who engaged in sexual relations and relationships with European men. However, the signares were by no means unique; seventeenth- and eighteenth-century travelers' narratives frequently describe Luso-African communities (those formed through the initial contact between Portuguese traders and African societies) across the coast and into the hinterland of West Africa.[13] Prominent mixed-race women traders appear in Portuguese documents as *senhoras* more than a half-century before the appearance of the signares in French correspondence. Attached, however, to Gorée, a place that has achieved near-mythic status in representations of African diasporic history, the signares, as specifically named and geographically placed subjects, enjoy a particular if notorious celebrity in academic and popular histories of the two islands. And while scholarship acknowledges that this group of women descended from neighboring African communities and occupied a range of racialized positions, contemporary guidebooks to both islands consistently represent the signares as beautiful mulattas and half-caste women, marvel over the women's sensuality, and reproduce stock visual depictions of the signares as seated, solitary figures whose elaborate dress and ornamentation often stand in for the economic histories of the islands.

In contrast to the apparent stasis of the signares, Ezili's fluid presence precludes fixing. As Dayan argues, vodou enacts "rituals of memory [that] could be seen as deposits of history" (*Haiti*, 35). From within these rituals emerges the lwa Ezili, who appears to her serviteurs (devotees) in multiple guises, depending on the rite being performed.[14] As Ezili Freda, she is, as reported by her Haitian devotees in ethnographic interviews, a variously white or a white mulatta woman, perfumed and powdered, "fancy ... very glamorous" (Alourdes, a Haitian manbo [vodou priestess], in Brown, *Mama Lola*, 248), a "hot pepper, prostitute, *bousen*, hot girl" (George René to Marilyn Houlberg in "My Double," 298).[15] Ezili Dantò is "from Africa ... the one who help my country to fight with the white people. She helped them to win that war" (Maggie, Alourde's daughter, in Brown, *Mama Lola*, 229). Ezili Dantò is also a dark-skinned single and fiercely protective lesbian mother bearing facial scars who, after being wounded during the Haitian revolution, "was going to talk, to tell something, and then they go over and cut out her tongue because they don't want her to talk" (229).[16] As Lasirèn, well, "if you see her with your eyes in the sea, she's white; when you dream her, she's black" (Alourdes, 223). She is the mermaid who takes people beneath the sea, back to Africa (223). In these and other incarnations, Ezili, as Dayan has eloquently argued, embodies the histories of women in colonial Saint-Domingue: she is the elite white mistress, the mulatta concubine, the subjugated black woman. Always, her sexuality is central to her significance. The geographic specificity of Ezili is particularly evident in her embodiment as Freda: both devotees and scholars describe her variously as white and mulatta, where the fluidity in her racial marker both signifies white Creole mistresses *and* free(d) mulatta concubines and suggests a resistance to translation across racial orders.[17]

While the signares and Ezili appear to inhabit the archive differently—one more repetitiously, one more disruptively—contemporary representations of both invoke origins stories of the places they inhabit. Their history told almost exclusively through a textual record produced by white European male subjects, the signares tell a revised origins story of the trade in humans. As they do with the free(d) mulâtresses of colonial Saint-Domingue, French documents articulate anxious concern regarding the signares' ability to profit from their sexuality. A 1763 memo written by French botanist Michel Adanson, who spent several years on the island of Saint-Louis, with frequent visits to Gorée, "excoriated the corrupt practices of officials associated with signares, which were grossly unfair to lower-ranked French employees (Brooks, *Eurafricans*, 211)."[18] And like Pruneau, eighteenth-century European travelers to the islands rarely failed to offer extended descriptions of the women's beauty, wealth, and status. What is missing from the historiography—although not necessarily the archive, of course—are the perspectives of the women themselves and the perspectives of the indigenous and diasporic Africans—captive and free—who may have encountered these women. Given this archive, it comes as no surprise, as James Searing notes, that scholarly and popular representations of Gorée and Saint-Louis "focus almost entirely on French life and activities on the islands, and on French relations with the signares. . . . These works are full of descriptions of the charm and fecundity of the signares and the libertine life of European traders" (*West African Slavery*, 224n2). Often disappeared from such accounts are black African women, the black African male chiefs, and black and mulatto male merchants who actively participated in and benefited from the trade, as well as the raced and gendered power relationships between Europeans and Africans and within African communities that complicate assertions of voluntary concubinage between male European strangers and local African women.

Exemplary of this revised origins story is this description from the 1985 UNESCO guide, *Gorée: Island of Memories*:

> A single launch is the only link between Gorée and the mainland. At its leisurely pace it bears the visitor away from the hooting, shouts and all the hubbub of the modern city of Dakar. The short crossing to the island is a precious interlude of peace and quiet, a brief but intense experience of detachment. On landing, one is in another world, a world that belongs to the past, and images are telescoped: the opulent *signare* side by side with the slave, and bales of tobacco from the Americas piled up on the quay. (18)

Here, the Europeans responsible for the transatlantic trade in humans are absent. The signare in her opulence stands in for all of the parties responsible for the tremendous wealth acquired through the theft and enslavement of captive Africans. Through the signare, a history of theft, rape, captivity, and torture is rewritten: the terrifying journey from the hinterland to the last stop before embarking on the Middle Passage is erased by a "precious interlude of peace and quiet"; the brutal and unequal collusion between European and African traders is eclipsed by the "opulent signare," who appears safe at home on an African continent. The unmarked slave is a necessary but unremarkable part of the story told in the otherwise vividly drawn portrait of the signare and "bales of tobacco from the Americas piled up on the quay." This is the revised origins story, first suggested by eighteenth-century European travelers who emphasized the signares' dangerously seductive influence over French officials and personnel, then illustrated by nineteenth-century ethnologists, and finally reified in twentieth-century guidebooks hoping to increase tourists' pilgrimages to the island.[19] While the families and descendants of the signares hold their own archives—family photos and stories, especially—that counter the hyperstasis of visual and written representations of the women, the official story, produced, published, and circulating across time and space, is the one that endures, each iteration further solidifying and embellishing this revised origins story.[20]

Ezili's archive has a different trajectory. Representations of Ezili translate her devotees' religious and bodily experiences of the goddess into a visual iconography illegible to a colonizing eye. Ezili's archive includes vèvès (sacred signs marking the crossroads and used to invoke the lwas) drawn on the ground and wiped away, paintings on the walls of people's homes, ritual enactments enclosed in secrecy, cluttered altars in private rooms, intricately detailed and decorated ritual flags, and devotees' remembered accounts of possession by and marriage to the goddess. Visual representations of her physical being that depict her as the Virgin Mary or the black Madonna underscore vodou's syncretism and the history of its practitioners' subversive resistance to religious persecution. And while Ezili's multiple incarnations within vodou are at once diverse and specific, so too are they "entangled and blurred" (Dayan, *Haiti*, 59). Emblematic of the simultaneous diversity and persistence of her archive is that the iconography for Ezili nearly always includes a heart.[21] For Ezili Freda, the gentle Rada spirit, the heart is whole, jeweled, and ornate, an *M* intersecting it to signify her status as mistress. A sword pierces the heart of the wounded, devoted mother Ezili Dantò and her fierce Petwo sister Ezili-je-wouj. And "Ezili of the Waters" Lasirèn, whose manifestation disrupts the Rada/Petwo dichotomy, materializes wearing a heart pendant around her neck, or appears with one of her sisters' hearts placed near her.[22] Across these representations, central to the history Ezili tells, is, as Dayan insists, a story of love and possession.

Indeed, insisting that in Ezili "a goddess was born on the soil of Haiti who has no precedent in Yoruba or Dahomey," Dayan, as noted above, argues that Ezili's archive, full of submission, hopeless and scorned devotion, fierce love, brutality, and betrayal, reenacts a history of the experiences of Haitian women (*Haiti*, 58). History points not to a fixed moment in the past but rather to an ongoing process that underscores the simultaneous changing/unchanging circumstances of Haitian women before, during, and since the revolution. That is, in contrast to a nearly hyperstatic archive that freezes the signares in a protocolonial moment, the fluidity and ephemerality of Ezili's archive, in its representation of a collective recollection, insists on a recognition of the simultaneity of a group's understanding of its past and what Trouillot names the "continuous creation" of its history: "They do not succeed such a past: they are its contemporaries" (*Silencing*, 16). If vodou is rooted both in captive Africans' remembered spiritual knowledges and practices and in black subjects' responses to the brutalities of racialized slavery, so too is it continuously reproduced by the specificities of Haitians' experiences of and responses to the particularities of the unfolding of their history in the wake of persistently oppressive European and U.S. responses to its continued struggle for independence.[23] Thus, while Ezili travels across North American spaces, served not only by a Haitian diaspora but also by a racially and geographically diverse group of vodou practitioners, and even mutates into contemporary representations of the voodoo queen Marie Laveau in New Orleans, she is most decidedly a Haitian goddess. Just as the signares, black and mixed-race African mistresses and concubines of European men, achieved their singularity because of their attachment to a specific geographic location, Ezili, a goddess with analogies to but no equal in other religions and myths, is singular because she literally arises from the ground of Haiti.

And there is this. As much as Ezili is undeniably Haitian, so too is she decidedly diasporic. Across and within each of her various guises, she carries with her remembered Fon/Ewe, Yoruba, and Kongo goddesses and gods. Scholars persistently route her to the Yoruba *òrìsà* (deity) Òsun. Most popularly connected to water, wealth, and fertility, a goddess whose ritual objects and characteristics include a "fan, mirror, brass (gold, copper, coral, yellow, money), honey, pumpkin, peacock, vulture, beautiful hair, comb, [and] perfume," Òsun is a divinity whose palpable resonance in Ezili persists across time and space (Murphy and Sanford, *Òsun*, 7). Ezili's manifestation as Lasirèn is perhaps most obviously diasporic, as this version of Ezili, the water goddess who "hovers large and dark and silent just below the surface of the water, a place Haitians call 'the back of the mirror'" (Brown, *Mama Lola*, 223), finds her echo in Mami Wata, the West African mermaid whose appearance cuts across nations and ethnic groups and whose discernible roots in global trade encounters driven by European interests reflect a uniquely African diasporic experience.[24] Thus Karen McCarthy Brown speculates, "Lasyrenn may have roots that connect, like nerves, to the deepest and most painful parts of the loss of homeland and the trauma of slavery" (224).

In another turn, Ezili's very name reminds us of a specifically diasporic injury, the ungendering of the black body. As Guérin Montilus posits, "The remote island of *Agonve* in *Azili* lake at the southern border between Dahomey and Nigeria, sent to Haiti their male *vodun Azili*, the mythical landlord and generator of this lake. This *vodun Azili* probably migrated through a branch of Agonlinu at Quidah in ancient time. *Vodun Azili* became the beautiful mulatto woman *Ezili-Fweda*, called after the former name of Ouidah" ("Africa," 77). In isolation,

Ezili's transformation from male to female is neither necessarily traumatic nor reflective of injury. However, it is not in isolation. As an instructive tradition of black feminist work has made clear, ungendering is constitutive of the trauma of black female subjection and subjectivity.[25] In her persistence and transformations, then, Ezili in all her incarnations, including that of the elite mulatta mistress, suggests an origins story grounded in diaspora.[26]

The dominant archives of the signares and Ezili thus appear to tell two interrelated but nonetheless distinct origins stories. Each figure derives her meaning from her specific location in time and place. Each functions in a distinct, contested, and dynamic economy of sexuality, race, and power. One is a historical subject presented in official and popular histories as possessing material wealth and agency; the other is a goddess served by dispossessed diasporic subjects in order to imagine or invent possessing power, autonomy, and wealth. At the same time, each figure echoes across time and space into the other, each figure's diverse and multiple manifestations contesting the authority and stability of the other. The signares contest the foundational origins story signaled by Ezili, that the free(d) mulatta locates her origins exclusively in the sexual and racial violence of American slavery. Rooted to local social networks, grounded in indigenous cultural traditions of women as traders and healers, the signares disrupt the notion that the free(d) mulatta concubine's apparent autonomy and agency in a slave society derived exclusively or even primarily from her sexuality.[27] The signares thus complicate an origins story rooted in subjection, sexual violence, and marginalization. Likewise, Ezili disrupts the origins story told by the signares. In contrast to the "opulent signare," Ezili, in her multiple divine manifestations as elite and subjugated and her geographic presence in a place at once a beacon for black people and an admonishment regarding the price of self-liberation, demands an account of the costs of the trade. Her embodiment of a "women's history of Haiti" remembered and reenacted by black subjects invites us to read against the official record's efforts to render captive Africans into unthinking objects and instead to imagine how that unmarked slave noticed by the UNESCO guide may have made meaning of what she or he saw on the quay. Indeed, the ritual and sacred devotion of Ezili's own serviteurs begs us to consider a relationship between the unmarked slave and the opulent signare beyond that defined by wealth, capital, and commodity; after all, in the UNESCO guide, they stand "side by side."

Finally, the signares and Ezili complicate the origins story told by the other because the echo between them spirals, refusing a single, coherent, verifiable account. Indeed, it is the presence of Ezili that invites us to consider the echo not as a back-and-forth or even a circular reverberation but rather as a sonic spiral. VèVè Clark's formulation of "marasa consciousness" and Kaiama Glover's atten-

tion to the aesthetic and theoretical concerns of Haitian Spiralism (a Haitian
literary movement that emerged in direct response to and "determined to engage
absolutely with the quotidian violence that plagued Haiti during the Duvalier
régimes" (Glover, *Haiti*, 20) are instructive. Grounding her analysis of the ritual
signs for vodou's divine twins, the marasa trois, in her extensive fieldwork, Clark
develops a theory of "marasa consciousness" in order to invite scholars of the
African diaspora to "imagine beyond the binary." Asserting that "representations
of African diaspora history and culture have assumed a binary formation," and
recognizing how captive Africans resisted and transgressed the "binary nightmare of slavery . . . on several levels of experience," Clark offers: "Those of us
accustomed to the Hegelian dialectic would seek in comparable environments
resolution of the seemingly irreconcilable differences: slave/master, patriarchy/
matriarchy, domestic/maroon, rural/urban, and the like when the marasa sign,
like others produced in agrarian societies, has another more 'spiralist' agenda
in mind" ("Developing," 42, 45, 43). Furthermore, as Clark notes, "The 'spiralist'
agenda to which I am referring has been transferred" to a specific Haitian literary tradition made most famous by "one of Haiti's premier authors in Creole and
French," Frankétienne (59n21). Glover explains that for the writers in this tradition, the spiral "is operational on many levels," including in its centrality to the
natural world. So foundational is the spiral to Haitian culture that it "decorates
the entire length of the *poteau-mitan* (the wooden post that stands at the center
of every Haitian vodou temple [*peristyle*] around which all ceremonies revolve)
and, as such, is an integral element of Haiti's most fundamental belief system"
(Glover, *Haiti Unbound*, viii). Glover's analysis of the aesthetic and theoretical
interventions made in Spiralist writing illuminates how these writers, in reflecting a simultaneously specifically Haitian and more broadly New World way of
being, create characters who are "irredeemably fragmented and multiple" (242).
Most significantly, "these unsettled and irregular beings ultimately . . . assert the
unrepresentability of being in general and of the subaltern in particular" (242).
Both Clark and Glover thus emphasize both the spiral's simultaneous specificity
to Haitian culture, history, and geography and its centrality to theorizing African diasporic memories, identities, and practices. As simultaneously a Haitian
entity and an African diasporic goddess, then, Ezili's echo across the Atlantic,
into and out of the signares, cannot help but spiral.

Attending to the sacred dimensions of the echo of the free(d) mulatta concubine in diaspora offers direction for both a rereading of the origins stories told
by official documents and a speculation of other possibilities in theorizing the
echo's dimensions. Indeed, tracing the spiral's twists and turns with an attentiveness to the sacred illuminates the official record's capacity to yield fractures to its
own authority. For example, if we can speak of influence and sources in imag-

ining the free(d) mulatta concubine across the Americas, then surely Moreau de Saint-Méry's classic account is foundational. Often cited and quoted, both emblematic and influential, Moreau's description of colonial Saint-Domingue's free(d) women of color is most striking in its invocation of the language of the sacred in describing the free(d) mulatta. He marvels: "The entire being of the Mulâtresse is given to voluptuousness, and the fire of this goddess burns in her heart to be extinguished only with her life. This cult is her whole law, her every wish, her entire happiness. There is nothing that the most inflamed imagination can conceive that she has not foreseen, divined, accomplished. Charming all the senses, surrendering them to the most delicious ecstasies, suspending them by the most seductive raptures: that is her sole study."[28] Moreau's simultaneously scornful and reverent description exemplifies the repetitiousness of eighteenth-century depictions of the free(d) mulatta concubine across the Atlantic.

However, what seeps through is the persistence of a sacred lexicon in the figure's representation.[29] On the one hand, the free(d) mulatta concubine's evident self-centeredness in her physical beauty, which pervades Moreau's description, finds its own echo in Deren's description of Ezili. As Dayan theorizes, the echo of Moreau's mulatta women in Ezili is precisely in her vanity and seductiveness: "Served by her devotees with the accoutrements of libertinage—lace, perfume, jewels, and sweets—this spirit carries the weight of a history that testifies to the unity of a profligacy and virtue, thus making a mockery of piety" (*Haiti*, 58). What strikes me this time, however, is not the echo in the women's vanity, sensuality, and materialism. Most profound in this iteration of the echo is the very lexicon of Moreau's description ("goddess," "cult," divination, "rapture"), one that invokes the sacred and otherworldly dimensions of these characteristics and practices embodied by historical subjects in an especially brutal slave society. And while Moreau's racial, gender, class, and historical status demand that we read his descriptions with measured suspicion, that the ritual of the free(d) mulâtresse's "voluptuousness" reappears in black Haitians' remembering and reenactment of history invites us to consider sincerely Moreau's invocation of the language of the sacred. In turn, Moreau's description invites us, too, to attend to the presence of the sacred in the rituals of adornment and promenade documented by Pruneau. Thus, in addition to considering Ezili a sacred reenactment of a decidedly nonsacred encounter between Europe and Africa, white and black, master, mistress, and captive, the pervasiveness of ritual and the allusive references to some notion of the sacred in at least three turns of the spiral invite us to read each of these iterations—historical subjects and divine goddess—as evidence of the centrality of the sacred and ritual in otherwise quotidian diasporic practices, strategies of being in the face of the most profane of events, the very calculated and brutal transformation of persons into chattel property.

I suggest that we consider that while the occurrence of the free(d) mulatta concubine across diaspora may be the most expected of consequences of the incursion of Europe into Africa and the Americas, how she inhabited that presence was evidently most unexpected by the white men who desired her. We might then consider her presence, her being in these places, to be not merely reactive but also something else. That is, if the presence of the sacred, evident and embodied in her rituals of dress, comportment, and solicitation of praise, reverberates in this echo, then we must recognize an origins story for this presence aside from one that privileges a desiring and possessive white gaze. As Steeve Buckridge's work explains in his examination of the roots and routes of the uses of dress as a site of "resistance and accommodation" in eighteenth- and nineteenth-century Jamaica, across cultures on the African continent "the ritual of dress is performance in nature: dress is not only the core but also the medium through which the human body is redefined over and over" (*Language*, 20). To pause in the echo's reverberation here—on the ritual of dressing oneself, of preparing for one's own display in public—as performance is to do, again, more than one thing. It is first to foreground attention to how free(d) women of African descent *themselves* imagined and performed their entry into the public social spaces otherwise produced by the machinations of European material and sexual desires. It is also to speculate on what captives passing through these spaces inhabited by these women, the signares, may have seen, witnessed, theorized, and carried with them across the Middle Passage.

We might first consider a sacred practice explicitly attached to the signares across contemporaneous accounts: their use and purchase of gris-gris. Describing the syncretic religious practices of the signares' ethnic group, Mamadou Diouf explains, "not only were the Catholics of the Four Communes circumcised at birth, but gourmets as well as mulattos celebrated Muslim religious holidays and carried amulets, gris-gris (charms) and talismans made by marabouts, containing verses from the Koran. The available sources mention that the greatest sources of revenue for marabouts were the signares and mulatto women, who paid them for making gris-gris, telling fortunes, predicting the future, protecting them against the evil eye, providing love potions, and so on" ("French Colonial Policy," 682). As Diouf argues, the habitants' syncretic religious practices were the central feature of a "profound cultural reconstruction that expresses a hybrid culture peculiar to groups of *habitants* and *originaires*" (672). While Diouf's emphasis is on the body civic and the citizenship of men in the public space, he notes in his analysis of the development of Christian and Muslim architecture on both islands that "both Muslim and Catholic forms of worship asserted themselves over genies and ancestral spirits, which from then on retreated into private space, obscure regions of the memory of the seaside (Gorée,

Dakar, Rufisque) and of the river (Saint-Louis)" (678). What Diouf's analysis thus opens up is a space to consider that private space of "genies and ancestral spaces," to consider the private intimate spaces on Gorée and Saint-Louis as spaces inhabited by the sacred.

And it is important here that I am not saying that the private, intimate spaces on the islands are inherently or necessarily sacred. Nor do I want to reify the patriarchal gendering of and fictional divisions between public and private spaces. What I do want to consider is why the signares may have invested so heavily in gris-gris, talismans from the marabouts. What might such adherence to an indigenously syncretic spiritual economy suggest about the signares' own sense of security and self-possession, for example? And if we consider the presence of the sacred in the most private and intimate of acts, be it the washing, perfuming, and dressing oneself before going out or the seduction and sex itself, how might that consideration impact our understanding of how these intimate acts engendered the possibilities for subjects marked African, female, and black or mulatta to acquire not merely wealth but, more importantly, a status that offered them some kind of protection from the sexual violence otherwise mundane in an Atlantic slave port? For as many times as contemporary sources and modern historiography mark these women as prostitutes and concubines, travelers' accounts written by the very subjects whose heteropatriarchal gaze would otherwise assert possession over these women are careful to point out that these women, notwithstanding their geographic and racial belonging, were modest and chaste to a point threatening to what one might otherwise think.

By considering the sacred, then, we might examine the sexualized relationships between the signares and European men not only in terms of the commercial transactions that produced the women's wealth but also in terms of the organization and production of knowledge such transactions signal. Dominique Harcourt Lamiral, a French commercial agent assigned to Saint-Louis in the late eighteenth century and whose volume I explore in more detail in chapter 3, offers an anecdote that illuminates how knowledge production and the sacred may have intersected in the signares' experiences of sexual violence. After detailing the rape of young female captives by Moorish traders and the successive entrance into signareship by these young girls, who were purchased as domestics by French men, Lamiral asserts that the young girls and women "do not believe themselves to have been deflowered.... They say, jokingly, and this opinion is generally received, that they have three virginities; that which the Moors took by force, that given out of friendship to their friend, and that which their husband bought."[30] The signares translate the trauma of captivity and rape into a source of discursive authority over their sexual bodies. When Lamiral details the sexual violence endured by such subjects as they move / are moved through captivity into signareship and explains the subjects' reframing of virginity by insisting that they have three virginities, we should consider how such a motto signals an insistence on the part of the women to define the terms through which others understand their sexuality and their control of their sexuality. Their knowledge production insists on producing a worldview that recognizes the horror of their experience while it also forces their witnesses to accept the women's terms of that worldview. That such a revision is not transformative of the material experience of being captive and marked African and female cannot be overemphasized. However, what I am suggesting is that it is important that we acknowledge and consider the tactical disruption of the dominating heteropatriarchal discourses about gender, sexuality, desire, and value.[31]

Thus, rather than speculate about the amount or absence of power held by the individual women thrust into these sexual relationships, what I am working through is the question of how the sexual relationships were understood by the women. It is to think about how the *privacy and intimacy* of the act, rather than the sexual acts themselves, and how the sacredness attached to that space may have offered a space for (re)defining not just one's place in the social order but the very social order itself. As noted earlier, the signares as African businesswomen who acquired and wielded wealth and power through their relationships with European men were not anomalous. They had precedent and predecessors along the west coast of Africa. What stands out on Gorée and Saint-Louis, however, is evidence of both intergenerational matrilineal transfers of wealth and power and the openness of this special class of women to newly produced signares. As George Brooks explains, not all women involved with European men on Gorée and Saint-Louis would have been considered signares: "Compared to the few women who achieved the status of signare, there would have been many Eurafrican and African girls who—due to their youth, lack of resources, or slave or grumete status—could establish liaisons only with artisans, soldiers, and sailors. . . . After perhaps several liaisons curtailed by the deaths or departures of lovers, enterprising women might accumulate sufficient resources and experience to parlay a marriage with a privileged company official and become a signare" (*Eurafricans*, 212–13). Thus, while signareship was accorded to only elite women, the *possibility* of acquiring that status was available to all "girls and young women" on the island (212). What I am suggesting here is that the possibility of becoming a signare may have itself been something sacred. And it was sacred not because of the wealth or status it afforded but because of the possibility of protection from the sexualized violence otherwise ubiquitous in a slave society that it promised.

In these places, Gorée and Saint-Louis, whose island geographies underscore their liminality as "contact zones," the echo's utterance opens a space for imagining an origins story told from within the space and process of dispossession (Pratt, *Imperial*, 7). It is in these places that we might consider the ritual and performance of dress so central to depictions of the free(d) mulatta concubine across the Atlantic not simply to have originated in a pre-European contact Africa to be transformed in the Americas but also to have acquired a meaning specific to African women's experiences of European incursion. The echo's utterance in these places, enacted in the rituals of dress, comportment, adornment, and praise performed by free(d) black and mulatta women close to and still in contact with the local African societies that produced the significance of these rituals in the first place, is as much witness as it is evidence. Its persistence suggests an account of how these women, free in status and movement, exercising control over their sexual(ized) bodies, holding their own captives as household slaves, and participating in the transformation of other captives into commodities for the transatlantic economy, may have used their rituals of dress as sacred performance to engender, protect, inhabit, or otherwise navigate the dimensions of their freedom in these utterly diasporic spaces.

The stakes of making meaning of the echo's utterance on this side of the Atlantic, in these places of unbelonging, are made clear in Olaudah Equiano's description of his first encounter with the African coast after his kidnapping and transport from Ibo-land, where he conveys the moment of recognition of his dispossession:

> The first object that saluted my eyes when I arrived on the coast was the sea, and a slave ship, which was then riding at anchor, and waiting for its cargo. These filled me with astonishment, that was soon converted into terror, which I am yet at a loss to describe, and much more the then feelings of my mind when I was carried on board. I was immediately handled and tossed up to see if I was sound, by some of the crew; and I was now persuaded that I had got into a world of bad spirits, and that they were going to kill me. Their complexions too, differing so much from ours, their long hair, and the language they spoke, which was very different from any I had ever heard, united to confirm me in this belief. . . . When I looked round the ship too, and saw a large furnace or copper boiling and a multitude of black people, of every description, chained together, every one of their countenances expressing dejection and sorrow, I no longer doubted of my fate; and, quite overpowered with horror and anguish, I fell motionless on the deck and fainted. When I recovered a little, I found some black people about me, who I believed were some of those who brought me on board, and had been receiving their pay: they talked to me in order to cheer me, but all in vain. I asked them if we were not to be eaten by those white men with horrible looks, red faces, and long hair. (*Interesting Narrative*, 32–33)

Equiano's account underscores what we should know but can barely (if at all) imagine: the slave entrepôts along the west coast of Africa were sites of terror bordering on the marvelous for the captive African brought to them. As importantly, Equiano's account reminds us that the captives forced through these spaces observed, considered, and made meaning of the traumatic entry to the slave entrepôt: his expectation that he would be boiled and devoured is neither fantastic nor paranoid but instead terrifyingly logical. And while his physical being may have survived, he and other captives experienced an ontological trauma, a "kind of total annihilation of the human subject" (Smallwood, *Saltwater*, 61).[32] And finally, his account offers evidence that captured and bound Africans made meaning of not just what but also whom they saw: he most certainly had "got[ten] into a world of bad spirits."

And given that the landscape and the objects and people inhabiting it instilled terror in the captive Africans brought to it, we must ask what they might have seen and thought when catching a glimpse of the signares, whose public presence engendered a consistent and detailed wonder and attention from European men. According to Brooks, on Gorée at least, captives bound for the Americas filled labor needs on the island that would have placed them in public spaces, surely in view of and able to view some of the social life on the island: "The loading and unloading of pirogues and other vessels, the transporting of foodstuffs, water barrels, and merchandise around the island, the breaking of stone for construction, and other rough labor was done by the trade slaves held in the fort awaiting embarkation. These individuals worked two by two, wearing iron collars linked by chains five to six feet in length" (*Eurafricans*, 209).

While laboring thusly, did the captive Africans notice that these women, all free and apparently at ease in their luxury, occupied a range of skin tones that ranged from a familiar blackness to a fantastic whiteness? Did they hear the women speak to one another or their own captives and recognize or decipher familiar sounds and cadences? Did the captive Africans differentiate the possible ethnic and national origins of the signares from those of the utterly alien Europeans? Did they surmise, speculate, or otherwise know the sources of the signares' freedom and apparent bodily security and integrity?

Surely, as Equiano's account indicates, the place of embarkation for the captive Africans was, in its terror, without parallel. These same subjects would disembark in another place also without compare in its singular terror. While Saint-Louis and Gorée, on the one hand, and Saint-Domingue, on the other, were both slave societies produced by the same racialized, gendered, and sexualized system of theft, captivity, brutality, and profit, little would translate from one side of the Atlantic to the other. To be a free(d) woman of color in a West African slave entrepôt was again not the same as to be a free(d) woman of color in an American place. To be held as a household slave in Gorée and Saint-Louis would not help one survive as any kind of slave in the Americas, perhaps most especially in Saint-Domingue.

But this one thing, the desire of European men for African women and the consequent (but absolutely not certain) and likely perilous possibility for these women to somehow navigate this desire, this one thing would remain constant. And it must be remembered too that the signares, or women like them, would not have been the only free or freely moving subjects who appeared familiar to the captives. The captives had, after all, been brought to the coast by men who looked (even if they did not speak) like them. We know from the official archive that African men, black and mixed race, free and captive, also labored aboard slave ships that moved throughout the triangle. And perhaps most importantly, we should know that the captive and free(d) subjects *saw each other*. Thus Searing explains, "Gorée was the site of a number of important rebellions and attempted escapes between 1750 and 1776" and describes two specific instances wherein the threat of revolt of captives held on the island depended upon or was exposed by the free(d) inhabitants on the island (*West African Slavery*, 109). In 1777 "the French narrowly repressed revolt by the prisoners from Kajoor (held in a conflict between the French and their African trade partners), which had been prepared with the help of some of the inhabitants of the island and the village of Dakar" (110). And Pruneau himself described a "slave revolt that occurred on Gorée and the slave ship *Avrillon*, between 1749 and 1751"; as Searing explains, "The French learned accidentally of a well-planned revolt from a child who had been placed in the slave pens as punishment for petty theft" (147, citing Pruneau, *Description*, 114–17). While the French aborted the revolt and executed two of its leaders, despite "being warned about the danger, the captain of the slaver *Avrillon* took no extra precautions with his dangerous cargo. The same 500 slaves revolted again at sea ... killed seven whites on the ship, including the captain, and they were not subdued until 230 had been killed, after the ship's crew turned the ship's guns on the revolting slaves" (147–48). While the captives' extraordinary organization in this case was due to their "unusual social status" as "warriors who had fought for the recently deposed Geej king," their desire for freedom was not unique (147). The record shows, then, not only that captive and free(d) Africans saw each other in these places and encountered that recognition variously but also that captive Africans were never passive subjects and in fact enacted relationships with free subjects, successfully or not, to engineer resistance to and revolt against their captivity.

It should be remembered, then, that a diversity of individuals acted and responded in these places. And here I am concerned with the spectacular visibility of the free(d) mulatta concubine, whose presence repeats and moves across an

African diasporic imaginative and spiritual landscape. Thus, this thing might be remembered, that in this place, this site of unbelonging and terror, in this place there was, somehow, possibility. And it may be that the freedom performed in these sacred rituals of dress, comportment, adornment, and praise signaled to the observant (and how could they not be) captive Africans that to be free would now have to mean something entirely different from what it had meant before capture, that the very possibility of freedom was now contingent on one's sexual desirability, that to be free could never again (if it had before) come without cost and obligation. And this new understanding of freedom was something to remember.

Evidence

The echo between Pruneau's and Deren's descriptions thus tantalizes in its suggestion of a linear, traceable relationship between what was seen and what is remembered across the centuries-old transatlantic chasm inhabited by African diaspora. However, the official evidence of records kept and preserved belies the seduction of such a reading. For example, while Saint-Domingue accounted for just over 80 percent of disembarkations in the French Atlantic slave trade, less than 7 percent of these captives embarked at ports in Senegambia, including Gorée and Saint-Louis. The majority of slaves arriving in Saint-Domingue came from west-central Africa, followed by the Bight of Benin (Geggus, "French Slave Trade," 136, Table IV, 138, Table VII). Furthermore, although Senegambia accounted for nearly half of the captives in the French slave trade overall during the second half of the seventeenth century, as the volume of the trade increased over the course of the eighteenth century, the proportion of captives taken from Senegambia decreased.[33] These demographics for captive Africans brought to Saint-Domingue make it appear unlikely that the captives who did pass through Gorée and Saint-Louis, whatever they may have seen and witnessed, would have had a significant impact on religious practices on Saint-Domingue (a fact supported by the consensus that vodou reflects Fon/Ewe, Kongo, and Yoruba religious practices). The possibility that Ezili may be a remembering or reenactment of the signares thus appears unlikely given such evidence.

Still, despite the apparent absence of a quantifiable historical connection between the signares and Ezili, the resonance between Pruneau's and Deren's descriptions pulls as if at a loose thread. It pulls because there persists a core tension between theorizing and living diaspora: that between the impossibility of return and the intractability of the desire to return to intact beginnings. As Dionne Brand so evocatively writes, this imagined point of return is "that place where our ancestors departed one world for another; the Old World for the New. The place where all names were forgotten and all beginnings recast . . . the creation place of Blacks in the New World Diaspora at the same time that it signified the end of traceable beginnings . . . a site of belonging or unbelonging" (*Map*, 5–6). And while, as Brent Hayes Edwards insists, "there is never a first diaspora: there is never an originary, single dispersion of a single people, but instead a complex historical overlay of a variety of kinds of population movement, narrated and valuated in different ways and to different ends," there persists in diaspora, evidenced in creative work across African diasporic time and space, a desire to return to that place of "belonging or unbelonging," that moment before permanent rupture ("Langston Hughes," 691).

That desire is in part predicated upon the insufficiency of the archive to account for one's beginnings, one's lost belongings. At the same time, it is this very impossibility of isolating the point of origins in diaspora that makes possible claims for beginnings. Thus, Stephanie Smallwood's reminder about origins echoes Edwards's caution and also signals a weakness in the official record's claim to evidence: "Although it is true that most ships obtained their entire cargo from only one or two ports, an equally important point is precisely that these were ports: collection sites, central places to which goods—in this case, people— flowed from afar and were collected for shipment" (*Saltwater*, 104). Furthermore, as Rebecca Scott and Jean Hébrard explain, on the West African side of the Atlantic, traders inventoried captives in "generic phrase[s] like 'captifs jeunes pièces d'Inde sans aucun défaut' (young captives *pièces d'Inde* without any flaws). *Pièce d'Inde* was a unit based on the exchange value of a bolt of printed cloth from India, the cost of a healthy male captive between the ages of fourteen and thirty-five. Individual names and ethnic affiliations generally went unrecorded" (*Freedom*, 7–8). According to Scott and Hébrard, it was in the Americas that "ship captains began to vaunt the 'nationalities' of those whom they would sell. . . . In some cases, such 'national' markers were simply a rough-and-ready indicator of the African ports of call of a slaving vessel" (8). Thus, even the most meticulous of inventories taken at the point of embarkation, even the most careful scouring of official documents, could not make legible or otherwise quantifiable the cultural, social, and ethnic histories carried by (and made lost to) those persons made commodity.

It is through these fissures in the dominant narrative that the echo's trace resonates most compellingly, inviting us to listen, to witness as it fills those spaces even as it draws attention to and deepens these "gaps of meaning and intelligibility." Indeed, to engage in this echo's pull is at its core a geographic act—the echo between the signares and Ezili sounds across time and space, the sound of an echo requires the materiality of place and location. Brand's meditation on geography and diaspora illuminates the stakes of this geographic act:

> The Door of No Return is of course no place at all but a metaphor for place. Ironically, or perhaps suitably, it is no one place but a collection of places. Land-falls in Africa, where a castle was built, a house for slaves, *une maison des esclaves*. Rude enough to disappear or elaborate and vain enough to survive after centuries. A place where a certain set of transactions occurred, perhaps the most important of them being the transference of selves. The Door of No Return—real and metaphoric as some places are, mythic to those of us scattered in the Americas today. To have one's belonging lodged in a metaphor is voluptuous intrigue; to inhabit a trope; to be a kind of fiction. . . . It is to apprehend the sign one makes yet be unable to escape it except in radiant moments of ordinariness made like art. To be a fiction in search of its most resonant metaphor then is even more intriguing. So I am scouring maps of all kinds, the way that some fictions do, discursively, elliptically, trying to locate their own transferred selves. (*Map*, 18–19)

Brand's insistence that the site of dispossession is "no place at all but a metaphor for place" reveals the simultaneous materiality of the slave coast entrepôt and its no-less-consequential imaginative dimensions. To "scour maps . . . elliptically," to search for the original utterance of the echo, is not to hope to actually find it but rather to figure out how not to be lost in and along the routes it travels, meanders, bounces back.

As well, Brand's insistence that "to be a fiction in search of its most resonant metaphor is even more intriguing" underscores the central paradox in excavating and evaluating evidence in diaspora on which I am pressing here: for all its ability to provide quantifiable statistics about slave trade voyaging points of departure, sites of captive acquisition, places of landing and disembarkation, number of chattel lost to disease, abuse, pirates and privateers, and calculated actuarial risks, the official record not only does not tell the full story but does not tell the important stories. The evidence that matters is precisely the evidence that is not there. And still, one demands evidence. An African diasporic literary and intellectual archive thus overflows with suggestions and prescriptions for dealing with the impossibility of producing adequate and legitimate evidence: offered in lieu of documents are speculation, memories, stories, bodies in performance and in agony. The search for submissible evidence, the effort to produce such evidence, is itself a sacred ritual central to being and thinking in diaspora, in blackness. And essential to this ritual is a resistance to, a subversion of, dominating ideas of what this evidence may look like. Brent Hayes Edwards's assessment of Thelonious Monk's "Evidence" is suggestive of this ritual of resistance; what he says about Monk's piece should be read as instruction: "'Evidence' is remarkable because it moves by distillation and subtraction rather than by extrapolation or augmentation" ("Evidence," 52). Brand declares unequivocally, "Any wisp of a dream is evidence" (*Map*, 19).

Ritual

Following Clark's argument that "marasa states the oppositions and invites participation in the formulation of another principle entirely" and her exhortation "to read the sign as a cyclical, spiral relationship," we might consider how the insufficiency and unreliability of the evidence proffered by the official archive invites us to explore other geometric and geographic routes of memory and diasporic practice traveled and signaled by this echo ("Developing," 43). The signares' entrenchment in their geographic location alongside the apparently negligible number of ships carrying captives directly from Gorée and Saint-Louis to Saint-Domingue would seem to preclude the very thing these echoes offer evidence for—the exceeding of their boundaries. But what if we consider each of these manifestations of the free(d) mulatta concubine in diaspora not exclusively as a product of the transatlantic slave trade and white patriarchal heterosexual desire but also as a product of a diasporic practice? What if we think about what repertoires, memories, and traditions shaped and informed how black women navigated sexualized power relationships with conquering white men across diaspora?

A 1966 guidebook for the island of Gorée, which happens to be the African place closest in distance to the Americas and a place located between Saint-Louis and Haiti, offers a description from which the signare emerges as a ghostly subject who at once intercepts and amplifies the echo between Pruneau's and Deren's descriptions. Appearing six years after Senegal's independence from France, authored by a Senegalese writer, and published in Dakar, the guidebook's description intersects with Gorée's place in an African diasporic imaginary to produce not a synthesis or reconciliation of the oppositional narratives between the official archive of Middle Passage routes and transactions and the recalcitrant echo between the signares and Ezili but rather a third way of reading the echo. This third way of reading, following Clark's "marasa consciousness" methodology, reveals that, more than something remembered, what perhaps is most important about the echo is that it reflects a speculation, a possibility of being in a history and existence otherwise marked by violence, displacement, and longing.

Of course, as I note above, between Pruneau's and Deren's descriptions there exists an abundance of depictions of the free(d) mulatta concubine and her attention to wealth and femininity across diasporic time and space. In addition, representations of the signares and Ezili vary across more than three hundred years of written records of both; I do not want to suggest that either subject's representation is static or fixed in appearance or meaning. Indeed, textual depictions of the signares variously represent them as wives, prostitutes, mistresses, opportunists, ladies; black, mulatta, quadroon; free and freed subjects. These variations sometimes reflect the writer's own prejudices, but they also reflect the diverse social positions of the women living on the islands: not all women cohabited with European men, and not all women who did so were signares. Visual representations, however, vary less so in their frame and tone. As a goddess, Ezili is perhaps even more fluid and elusive in her representation, with devotees' descriptions of her reflecting resistance to and subversion of rigid and fixed categorization. She is variously and all at once mulatta, black, white; beautiful and scarred; vain and capricious; a fiercely protective single mother; promiscuous and diverse in her sexuality even as she demands fidelity. And finally, both the signares and Ezili inhabit highly visible places in contemporary black imaginaries. To settle on this 1966 guidebook as the point of departure for tracing the echo's move into what Clark might call "another realm of discourse" is thus, in many ways, arbitrary (Clark, "Developing," 44).

However, I have chosen this example deliberately because it inhabits multiple temporalities, underscoring the past's persistent intrusion upon the present. The signare appears in a guidebook produced by and in the service of a newly independent black Senegal, yet the description depends on the observations of European white male colonial/colonizing gazes. The visual depictions of the signares that appear in this guidebook are reproductions of mid-nineteenth-century illustrations by French artists, many of them reappearing in a late nineteenth-century French encyclopedia explicitly produced for the benefit of France's colonizing enterprise in Africa, Colonel Henri Frey's 1890 *Côte Occidentale d'Afrique*. And finally, this guidebook attaches its portrayal of the signare to eighteenth-century maritime, transatlantic architectural spaces that are reimagined to meet the desires of a twentieth-century traveling tourist. As I consider in detail below, the signare in this guidebook is as much timeless and ephemeral as she is grounded and attached to the specificity of Gorée's geography. The signare in this guidebook thus offers an apt subject not only for mapping and reading the origins story suggested by the echo between Pruneau's and Deren's descriptions, between a historical subject embedded in eighteenth-century Saint-Louis and a supernatural subject encountered in twentieth-century Haiti, but also for attending to diasporic practice as ritual and rehearsal.

Gorée: Guide touristique offers forty-six pages of brief descriptions of key elements of Gorée's history and contemporary significance alongside black-and-

FIGURE I.
*Signare en grand costume
(Aquarelle inédite de
Darondeau).* Colonel
Henri Frey, *Côte
Occidentale d'Afrique:
Vues, scènes, croquis (Paris,
1890),* reproduced in
Babacar Seck, *Gorée:
Guide touristique* (Dakar,
Senegal: SAFER, 1966).
Lending library, Michigan
State University Libraries;
digitization, Wayne State
University Libraries.

white photographs and illustrations. In this context, the guidebook introduces the reader to the signare with a full-page portrait facing a written description, the portrait a reproduction from Frey's 1890 encyclopedic book on West Africa (figure 1). The guidebook's caption for the portrait reads, "'Signare' half-caste of origin more or less Gascony, Brittany or Normandy." The text facing the page opens by directing the reader to "admire the velvety skin of the young half-caste: it ranges from the color of cream to that of coffee dashed with milk."[34] The words linger on the clothing and adornment of a single seated, poised, and apparently timeless beauty:

> With her Andalousian complexion, her delicately blue-stained lips, her jet-black hair that frames two melodious curls of gold filament, her hairstyle, which she calls Dioumbeul, standing several centimeters in the air. Made of flamboyant madras scarves, simple Senegalese scarves with small blue and white squares, or white satin embroidered with fiery red roses, these strange head-dresses shaped like sugar-loaves are wrapped around the head by a narrow black or colored band. This monumental "dioumbeul" offers the allure of a triple-crowned papal tiara, as a garland embroidered with gold fringe spirals it three times. A

long white blouse of fine linen [is] fashionably cinched by means of a cotton loincloth formed by gathering woven bands of thirty centimeters wide and embroidered by wool thread where dominate blue, red, yellow, green, and golden yellow. The European loincloths are painted with diverse motifs or stripes. All of the pieces of fabric fall to the ground, sweeping across red and yellow Moroccan slippers. Another piece of fabric, often very fine, thrown carelessly over the shoulders, confers a vaguely Roman silhouette. The hands of these mulattas, their arms, their ears, and their breasts scintillate with artistically worked gold jewelry.[35]

Here is a description of a beautiful young girl whose every inch of physical appearance signals her ethereality. Her devotion to her physical appearance is marked by opulence, cosmopolitanism, and sensuality—sight, taste (the sugar loaf), touch (the weight of the fabrics), even smell (one imagines the scent of baking bread) and sound (melodious). From her French origins to "her Andalousian complexion," "her delicately blue-stained lips," "her jet-black hair that frames two melodious curls of gold filament," to her elaborate headwrap, consisting of Senegalese and Indian (madras) materials, her "Moroccan slippers," and her "vaguely Roman silhouette," the signare in this guidebook is otherworldly.

The exquisitely detailed text, facing a clearly defined portrait of its subject, suggests the inscrutability of the visual representation: without the interpretive work of the textual explication, we cannot know or appreciate what we are seeing. On the one hand, the black-and-white illustration seems straightforward: a young woman sits on what appears to be the ledge of an exterior wall of a concrete or adobe building, her back aligned with a vertical column. Her head is adorned with a conically shaped wrap, and she wears two earrings and a necklace. She is covered from head to toe in printed cloth. In the background stands a cluster of palm trees. The image is crisp. Nonetheless, the written text facing the image instructs the reader how to read the signare: for the outsider, the visitor to this place, the otherwise anonymous subject is made legible only through the exquisite detailing of her appearance. Between the image's apparent straightforwardness and the textual mediation of the image's signification—telling the reader not only what to see but how to see—the signare emerges as a ghostly subject, tangible only through the guidebook's mediating text.

To suggest that this signare is a ghost is to recognize her simultaneous presence as a historical and mythic subject. Heavily documented in the archive by European men who express their desire for and revulsion toward these women—describing them as prostitutes in some places, seductive and exceedingly modest in others—the signares are startlingly silent in the archive, often only speaking for themselves, as Mark Hinchman argues, through the architectural evidence of their still-standing homes and the paper trail of probate deeds listing their material possessions and property accumulation ("African Rococo," 90–91). And while the historical record is clear on both the existence of these women and the roles they played as the islands' most prominent inhabitants, the geographic, ethnic, and social roots of the women "remain obscure" (Searing, *West African Slavery*, 100). Searing posits, "It is likely they were formed by three separate currents of emigration to the islands. Free women traders from the mainland, like those described by La Courbe, expanded their commercial activities by 'marrying' Atlantic merchants and establishing themselves as *signares*. Secondly, it is likely that some of the Afro-Portuguese *signares* based on the mainland migrated to the islands and reestablished themselves as intermediaries in the Atlantic trade, and that this group gave its name to the *signares*. Thirdly, European sources suggest that some *signares* were slave women chosen as mistresses by Atlantic merchants from the female slaves that the slave trade brought to Saint Louis and Gorée" (100). Searing's willingness to speculate on and not to provide the specifics of the "European sources" that "suggest" the signares' origins in bondage is telling; it is suggestive not of Searing's scholarship but rather, and again, of the limits of the archive in telling the stories of the very subjects produced by the European transatlantic trade in humans and the attendant ritual of speculation.[36] In the historical archive, then, the signares appear suddenly, as if they were always already there, powerful free mulatta concubines whose possible origins as enslaved sexual objects constitute what Avery Gordon calls that "seething presence," their origins "something lost, or barely visible, or seemingly not there to our supposedly well-trained eyes" (*Ghostly*, 8).

Indeed, the guidebook produces a subject that seems to haunt the very place promoted by the guidebook as a tourist destination. While it does not explain the signares, the guidebook includes two other illustrations that depict the women: *La maison des esclaves en 1839* (The house of slaves in 1839) and *À gauche la maison des esclaves, à droite le musée historique vers 1807* (On the left the house of slaves, on the right the historical museum around 1807) (Seck, *Gorée*, 15, 13). The first illustration, dated 1839, depicts a house and courtyard that bustle with activity. On the top floor of the house is a figure looking out a window, another descends the exterior stairs, another wears what appears to be a conical head covering, the fourth is a clearly marked bare-headed African woman with a baby wrapped on her back, and to the far right, seated on the wall, are two male figures. On the first floor of the house, which includes the courtyard, two groups cluster. At far left is a seated woman who in dress and bearing appears to be a signare and two standing men, both of whom wear turbans and who are dressed in loose-fitting shirts, belted at the waist, atop flowing bottoms akin to gauchos or culottes. To the far right are two more clearly defined signares, one of them watching a female servant or slave pound yam; this signare has a child standing by her side. The signares are presented as part of a community, part of the social activity on the island. At the same time, they stand apart, supervising the labor central to the slave society. The second illustration offers a telescoped perspective looking down a street in Gorée. On the left is *la maison des esclaves*, presumably the reverse shot of the first illustration. Leaning over a balcony are two figures, their barely discernible head coverings and clothing marking them as signares. They look down into the street, where another figure, difficult to discern, gazes back at the women. In contrast to the solitary figure portrayed in the guidebook's *Portrait de signare*, in the guide's illustrations of the island's typical architecture the signares are threaded into the social fabric of Gorée, clearly a visible part of the island's communal life. They see and are seen by the other subjects who move about the island.

Thus, within the interstices of the guidebook, in pages tucked between an entry that describes how "Gorée was advantageously located for the worst as it was for the best, was the revolving patch of these disgraceful transactions between nations said to be, in this era, civilized," and a passage that describes the 1944 official decree that proclaimed Gorée an important historical site, appear the signares, unmarked figures who populate the illustrations depicting two key buildings on the island (Seck, *Gorée*, 12, 16). They are background figures, embedded in the island's architecture. The guidebook's other references to the signares, brief in their length and tone, call attention to the signares' inextricability from Gorée's architectural evidence of its transatlantic past: in its entry "Le Musée de Gorée et l'I.F.A.N.," the guidebook informs the visitor that the "romantic building that houses the Gorée Museum of IFAN [Institut Français d'Afrique Noire] held captives for thirty years, from 1777 to 1807, and belonged to the rich signare Victoria Albiri."[37] In its introduction to its guided tour of "visite de points remarquables de l'île" (noteworthy sites on the island), the guidebook restates its definition of the signares contained in the above described caption for the *Portrait de signare*, this time within the context of the island's decay, describing how "in 1936 nothing remained on the island except homes falling into ruins, where lived approximately five hundred Goréens. These were the descendants of the 'signares,' half-castes of origin more or less Gascon, Brittan, and Normand."[38] And finally, there is "the house where Mother Superior Javouhey lived, on the corner of Boufflers Street and Dongeons Street. ... Boufflers Street, the main arterial road on the island, recalls the memory of the illustrious Chevalier Stanislas de Boufflers. Many 'signares' cried at his departure from Gorée, especially Anne Pepin. One even recounts that the sand of his last steps on the beach was retrieved and kept in small bags, in hopes of his return."[39]

In a guidebook that focuses almost exclusively on the European history of this island off the coast of West Africa, the signare becomes the sole representative of the closest approximation of an indigenous African identity. At the same time, the extensive text detailing the signare belabors her exotic presence, lingering over every detail of the woman's physical appearance. We are invited to salivate over her extraordinary beauty, vanity, and wealth without being provided any concrete historical context. The guidebook locates her origins in far-off France with no explanation as to why or when she arrived in Gorée. Once we are attuned to her presence, we see her everywhere in the guidebook and by extension on Gorée. Indeed, in the guidebook's final reference to the signare—where she collects the sand from the chevalier's last steps on the island—the signare is lovelorn, tragically attached to the island, like a ghost doomed to haunt the place of its demise.

As a ghostly subject, the signare of this guidebook at once intercepts and amplifies the echo between Pruneau's description of a historical subject in eighteenth-century Saint-Louis and Deren's description of a goddess in twentieth-century Haiti. The figure here is an apparition, her visual appearance in the guidebook unmoored from its original production and designation, her textual appearance framed only in how she appeals to the senses rather than how she functions as a social being. Even Pruneau's eighteenth-century male European colonial gaze places the figures he describes within the context of social and economic life on an eighteenth-century slave entrepôt. At the same time, the echo reverberates in the guidebook's intricate detailing of the figure's elaborate ornamentation and insistent sensuality, marking her resonance with Pruneau's and Deren's subjects. And it is important to pause here to remember that an echo is not simply a repetition of a sound across time and space. As discussed above, both Pruneau's and Deren's subjects, the signares and Ezili, tell origins stories; indeed, each subject's meaning is rooted to a specific geography, a particular colonial history. Each subject can be thought of as her own utterance—the signares of eighteenth-century Senegal, Ezili arising from the needs of Haitian folk. In the guidebook, however, we have only the echo—the incomplete evidence of something else said.

That this echo manifests itself as a ghostly apparition is at once to riff on the signares as an echo of the free(d) mulatta concubine in diaspora and to suggest they are something slightly different. Both the echo and the ghost are ephemeral traces of an originally material subject: someone or something must make a sound; someone was here and now she is not. Both the echo and the ghost entice their witness to search for something not there, to make sense of something that seems to trick the senses. However, the ghost prioritizes something the echo does not: a claim for redress, for accountability. Indeed, the demand for evidence and the recognition of ghosts are mutually inextricable rituals in living

and theorizing African diaspora. Hershini Bhana Young's overview and intervention in the work of haunting are especially evocative. Examining the intersecting spectral theories of a diversity of thinkers, Young situates the invocation
of ghosts methodologically as "a new kind of scholarship that is fundamentally
concerned with redress, with honoring the cultural and spiritual memories of
colonized people" (*Haunting Capital*, 31). Most importantly, Young insists we
recognize haunting's centrality to diaspora's constitution: "To be black is to have
accrued a subjectivity haunted by the spectral traces of social, political and ideological history. . . . Race as a set of inherited embodied practices cannot fail to
discuss the ways in which gendered regimes of injury are performed and passed
down from generation to generation" (25). The signare's ghostly presence, then,
demands not only that we address the specifically gendered injury/trauma for
which she seeks redress but also that we recognize and discuss how that injury,
effaced by romantic and Orientalist fantasies of her seductiveness, may be "performed and passed down from generation to generation" *within* blackness.

To consider the signare's ghostly presence across time and space in this echo
is to resist the hyperstasis of the very representation that signals her haunting
in the first place and instead to hold deliberately to an understanding that the
repetitive and insistent fixing of the signare as seductive, agential, exotic may be
the very thing that underscores this figure's unruliness. To consider the signare
as a ghostly presence demands that we imagine her injury against the historical record and contemporary romances attached to her presence. How to do so
without understating or otherwise reducing the import of the signares' evident
economic and social power and status underscores one challenge of seriously
attending to the diverse and multiple genealogies that constitute diaspora. I suggest, however, that her ghostly presence demands that we consider the costs of
that status and power to this specifically gendered and sexualized diasporic figure. And if the signare is indeed an iteration of a transatlantic echo as much as
she is a ghostly presence in a consummately diasporic space, then it may also be
true that the dimensions and consequences of her haunting can only be understood by reading her within diaspora's relief. And here, while it is the historicity
of the signares that makes them so important to understanding their geographic
echo, it is the supernatural, palpable presence of Ezili that makes her so crucial to
understanding the signares' own haunting of diaspora. That is, because "Erzulie
continues to articulate and embody a memory of slavery, intimacy, and revenge,"
then we must consider too the full range of memories the signare, in her ghostly
presence, may embody (Dayan, "Erzulie," 11). In other words, we must attend not
only to the spectacle of the powerful, sensual, hypersexual free(d) mulatta concubine but also to how she arrived in this apparent power in the first place. To
do so would allow us not only to address the injury signaled by the ghost's presence but also to consider the contours of the memory of how intimate practices

of sexuality and domesticity and the spectacle of such practices, the visibility of these practices, may have proffered the possibility of freedom for the captive Africans who saw the signares, encountered them in these most diasporic of places, and carried with them that possibility.

The obscurity of the signares' origins, as delineated above, indicates that for at least some of the signares, their paths to social and economic prominence emerged from subject positions decidedly outside of power. Notwithstanding the signares' remarkable and specifically gendered acquisition of status and power (Knight-Baylac emphasizes that in 1749 ten of thirteen houses on Gorée belonged to "the mulatto element and more particularly nine belonged to mulâtresses" ["La vie," 402]), the consensus in the historical and popular record is that at least some signares had their roots in captivity. Such speculation ranges from matter-of-fact to fantastical accounts of how enslaved women became signares. Somewhere in the middle is the 1985 UNESCO guide's description of the circumstances that led to the signares' role and status on Gorée:

> The difficult conditions of the tropics debarred European women from Africa, where tropical diseases, against which contemporary medicine was powerless, ravaged the immigrant population. Company agents and soldiers alike were obliged to find a wife or concubine among the local women, often among those who were slaves. These so-called "native" marriages were automatically dissolved when the husband was repatriated or one of the partners died.
>
> These temporary unions produced mulattos who managed to take handsome advantage of their situation at the crossroads, as it were, of the two races. Their ease of communication with both made them natural intermediaries between the companies, on the one hand, and the traders and chiefs of the interior on the other. The mulâtresses, known as *signares*, owned many slaves and often several houses. (*Gorée*, 29)

This description is remarkable in a few ways. It reiterates the preponderance of scholarship that describes sexual unions between European men and African women as merely a matter of demographics; it also naturalizes the intermediary role played by the mixed-race progeny of these unions. Most startling, however, is the apparently seamless transition of "local women, often among those who were slaves," to the celebrated signares. Indeed, the published archive describes, often without comment, traditional practices of providing wives to strangers and how "local women provided sexual services and domestic labor to European men" (Searing, *West African Slavery*, 98). Black African women, subject to patriarchy, enslavement, and sexual commodification, become, within the historical and imaginative narratives of the signares, seductive, powerful mulattas. The trace of their subjection evaporates in contemporary representations of the "opulent signare" who stands in stark contrast to the anonymous slave. To distinguish between the before and after of anonymous black African women becoming signares is to press against the question of redress and reparation. On the one hand, the evidence of their enslaved history suggests that even for the celebrated free mulatta signares, "the erasure or disavowal of sexual violence engendered black femaleness as a condition of unredressed injury" (Hartman, "Seduction," 556). On the other hand, one must consider what such redress would look like and how it would look different from the acquisition of gold, property, slaves, social status, and finally, commemoration apparently enjoyed by the signares and their descendants.

To consider the signare's haunting means also to attend to the diversity of experiences and the multiple genealogies of diaspora that constitute a black transatlantic. What the signare's presence signifies and what the redress she demands looks like surely depend on where one is "positioned" in diaspora and blackness. Here again, Stuart Hall's conceptualization of the "politics of position" within diaspora suggests that in thinking about the signare as a ghostly figure within diaspora, we must simultaneously attend both to the specific dimensions of her presence in precise and explicitly historical moments and to her construction from the moment of her appearance in the archive through its repetitious iterations. Thus, we should understand the signares and their descendants as both distinctly situated within their specific social and political histories and cultural matrices and as uniquely positioned within a broader spiraling transatlantic black diasporic "memory, fantasy, narrative and myth" (Hall, "Cultural Identity," 226). And if, as Young insists, the ghost's ability to "disrupt our sense of the linear progressive nature of a history that passes naturally and easily from past to the present to the future" means that "the fixed and discrete quality of these time periods explodes as specters move back and forward and events that were experienced in the past are experienced again for the first time," we must also ask what the past event "experienced again for the first time" when encountering the ghostly signare may be (*Haunting Capital*, 41).

UNESCO's virtual tour of Gorée, a multimedia on-line experience, illuminates the stakes of this negotiation most vividly and disturbingly. After describing "where the young girls were packed . . . separated from the women because they were more expensive," the text, written by Boubacar Joseph Ndiaye, the "chief conservationist of the site" until his death in 2009, asserts across four pages of the virtual visit: "Some slave traders had sexual relations with the young girls and when they got pregnant, they were released in Gorée or Saint-Louis, Senegal. It was thus in the young girls' interest to give themselves to the slave traders in order to gain freedom. It was for these young girls the only way to salvation. So, the mixed-race girl in Gorée was commonly called 'Signare,' a deformation of the Portuguese noun 'Segnora.' These mixed-race persons formed the aristocracy in Gorée, like the Creoles did in the French West Indies" (*Virtual Visit*). The horror of captivity and the rape of young African girls become romantic and sacred possibility. *It was for these young girls the only way to salvation.* Against the specter of the ontologically deadlier fate of being made slave ship cargo, the history of these girls who would become signares, the founders of an aristo-cratic and politically important mixed-race society, offers a gut-wrenching and abhorrent narrative of freedom, triumph, and redemption. At the same time, the description participates in (indeed produces) a perpetually new experience of diaspora that returns to the imagined site of traumatic rupture, an encounter where past and present collide, where those made diasporic confront those lucky enough to have been left behind, to have remained at home. The description is nearly incredible in its simultaneous disavowal of a sentimental narrative of what happened to those left behind (the girls remained only because they had been raped, had become pregnant) and its assertion of a triumphant outcome through a perversion of the sacred.[40]

Against the simultaneous violence and prurient delight in Ndiaye's account, the ghostly signare's heavy, voluminous dress, stiff, erect posture, and folded hands, closed on her lap, demand an account of the costs both of her histori-cal subjection and of the contemporary elisions of the sexual violence against black women necessary to invocations of the free(d) mulatta concubine. Indeed, it is against the elision of their sexual subjection that the visual appearance of the signares becomes this ghost's most haunting feature. Against European male travelers' descriptions of free(d) mulatta concubines extravagant in their seduc-tive and sensual beauty, and against contemporary rituals of memory that sensa-tionalize the sexual violence endured in order to become signares, sits this figure, whose rigid back, solemn gaze, folded hands, and, finally, nearly completely con-cealed body belie the guidebook's deliberate and lascivious account of her body as a publicly available spectacle of sensuality and seduction. In the visual, the heaviness of the voluminous amount of cloth covering her body, the constraint of the shoes laced onto her feet, the deliberate balance required for her head-wrap, the status conveyed by her adornment, speak to a subject confronting and negotiating a relentless sexual and colonial gaze upon her female, African body.

Read against the echo between Pruneau's and Deren's descriptions of power-ful mulatta concubines lavish with riches and servants, the ghostly signare pres-ent in the narratives of contemporary guidebooks to Gorée demands that we attend to the limits of ascribing sexual agency to the free(d) mulatta concubine even as we consider what her presence offers for imagining a possibility of being otherwise proscribed by the devastation of the transatlantic trade. Her haunting presence in the echo also invites us to reexamine the echo's geographic dimen-sions, to reread other stereotypic representations of the signare in order to dis-

FIGURE 2. Édouard Nousveaux, *Un bal de signares (mulatresses) a Saint-Louis (Senegal), d'après une aquarelle inédite de Nousveaux, de 1844.* Colonel Henri Frey, *Côte Occidentale d'Afrique: Vues, scènes, croquis* (Paris, 1890), 12–13.

Lending library, Michigan State University Libraries; digitization, Wayne State University Libraries.

cern the trace of diasporic practice and rituals signaled by the echo. Indeed, if the representation in Seck's guide reiterates eighteenth- and nineteenth-century discourses of the mixed-race female body, so too does its genealogy remind us of the transatlantic circulation of these discourses and their attendant representations. As stated above, the guide's *Portrait de signare* comes from Henri Frey's 1890 *Côte Occidentale d'Afrique*; in the same work Frey proffers an 1844 illustration titled *Un bal de signares* (figure 2). The illustration depicts a multitude of signares, marked by their towering turbans, voluminous dresses, and light skin, dancing in a packed room. While the ball's attendees constitute a multicultural, multiethnic mélange of darker-skinned drummers and female attendants, the signares' partners are the clearly marked European men. Read alongside and against diaspora's relief, the illustrated signare ball appears at once familiar and haunting.

While Frey's text includes an extended description of the signare balls, which he notes were "one of the spectacles that struck us most extraordinarily" and which happened regularly "prior to the abolition of the slave trade," marking "blissful times," the visual effect of the image on its own is staggering, especially within a transatlantic context.[41] The illustration of the signare ball is striking in its apparent familiarity, reminding the viewer of the notorious "quadroon balls" of antebellum New Orleans. Free women of color famous for their proximity to whiteness, their beauty, and their extramarital sexual relationships with wealthy white Creole and American men, the quadroons frequently received great interest in nineteenth-century European and American travelers' journals. Especially noted were the quadroon balls, which purportedly functioned as sites for negotiating extralegal sexual and financial contracts between these free women of color and white men whereby the women earned property, wealth, and, most importantly, security in a racialized slave society. As Emily Clark details, the purpose and mechanics of the quadroon balls varied and shifted greatly during the antebellum period, beginning as quasi-legitimate, genteel affairs and finally, in the 1850s, existing as "portholes to a demimonde of vice" (*Strange History*, 180). Against such variances, the fascination with and mythical representation of the balls appeared and remains fixed across time and space.

That the 1966 Seck guide's *Portrait de signare* comes from an 1890 French book about Africa that implicitly references antebellum travelers' accounts of a class of women whose racialized and sexualized social subject positions and celebrity echo the signares suggests that "cyclical, spiral relationship" that VèVè Clark insists is central to reading diasporic societies and their cultural productions. One must consider, for example, that while entrenched in U.S. history and memory as a phenomenon specific to antebellum New Orleans, quadroon balls were, in fact, as Emily Clark makes clear, "a Haitian import adapted to exploit the boomtown, male-dominated market of New Orleans, perhaps promoted in the 1820s to advance the material prospects of refugee-descended women" (*Strange History*, 172). Against such historical context, Frey's depiction of a signare ball directs us to consider the simultaneity of multiple genealogies of diaspora. As well, while popular representations and scholarly analyses of the quadroon balls emphasize their function in facilitating conjugal relationships between white men and free women of color, the illustration of a signare ball in Frey's text invites us also to consider the transatlantic presence of these balls as evidence of a diasporic practice that moves *beyond* the simultaneously constrained and subversive negotiation of sexual and racial economies imposed by European colonialism and American slavery. Indeed, while descriptions of signare balls evoke representations of quadroon balls, the underlying economy of each place was distinct: whereas the quadroon balls in antebellum New Orleans appeared engineered to help free women of color acquire financial security by virtue of wealthy and free white men, the dynamics of the signare balls on Gorée and Saint-Louis underscored the dependence of European men on the business savvy of African women. As Brooks explains, "What better opportunity for newly arrived or unattached Europeans to meet potential partners, perhaps through the introduction and manipulation of signares attached to the most influential men in a trading company or military garrison who acted as matchmakers, preceptors, and confidants for their daughters, female relatives, and friends? Such matchmaking involved promising commercial opportunities, especially regarding men with privileged access to merchandise, shipping, or other resources controlled by the Europeans in the community" (*Eurafricans*, 216–17). Noting European men's dependence on signares for their own "survival and well-being," Brooks's assessment of the signare balls underscores the very distinct power relationships on Gorée and Saint-Louis within a transatlantic racial and sexual economy.

Within this context, what may be most striking in the illustration is that alongside its visual and textual resonance with American quadroon balls is that the image's representation of the music played at this ball rests in the two male African drummers, visible just left of the illustration's central focus, two signares who dance with a single male partner. Frey's accompanying textual description elaborates how the drummers and drums signal the ball's distinctively African contours:

> During this era [before the end of the slave trade] the barrel organ and its pretentious counterpart, the mechanical piano, which since then has made the delight of the ball more of a colonial functionary, were little or not at all known in Saint-Louis. One thus settled to dance there to the sound of the tom-tom, which the griots, with a lustful eye, made vibrate with fury and which was accompanied by the frenetic clapping of the young Negresses. To the sound of this infernal music, and despite torrid temperatures, often the ball continued in such spirit for ages, until the first rays of dawn whitened the horizon![42]

Frey's description of the dissonance produced by and through indigenous African instruments and musicality illustrates Sara Johnson's reminder that within the eighteenth- and nineteenth-century American slavery landscapes of black music production, "white observers . . . heard what they wanted to hear. Put another way, they did not hear what they were not trained to understand. Hence, although many chroniclers noted the musical prowess of black musicians, just as frequently they complained of 'backward,' out-of-tune, or monotonous noise" (*Fear*, 142).

At the same time, drawing from Johnson's revelatory reading of Jamaican artist Isaac Mendes Belasario's *French Set Girls* (1836), in which she documents that illustration's evidence of what she terms "transcolonial" intellectual production in its representation of African diasporic musical performance, I suggest that the presence of a specifically African musicality in *Un bal de signares* invites us to read against the stereotyping of Frey's description and instead use this presence as a point of departure for speculating how the signare ball and its echo across diaspora may be read to be as much a black diasporic practice and ritual as they are a series of sexual and financial transactions driven by the racialized economy of a slave society. The presence of drums, played by griots, accompanied by the rhythmic clapping of young black women, invites us to consider how in this space, in this place of dispossession and of becoming something else, as it did in the Americas, the performance of music and dance not only produced and sustained community but also signaled an intellectual practice wherein black diasporic subjects theorized and responded to "an intensely violent world" (Johnson, *Fear*, 123). Johnson explains: "As mnemonic devices, dance and music (both instrumental and lyrical) also created, stored, and disseminated memories of former homes with responses to new ones. This process occurred on a collective level, and performance was thus a mode for fostering participatory interactions and forging a sense of community. In addition . . . performance itself provided a kinesthetic, physic connection to spiritual forces. Such an outlet for the emotions could provide comfort in times of despair, stimulate opposition to abuse, or help process rage so that it was not directed against the self" (123). While Johnson's analysis of music and performance as a site of intellectual production focuses on enslaved black subjects in the Americas, that the spiritual uses of African diasporic music are rooted in African traditions indicates that we should also consider the signare ball to be a space in which the various performers and dancers enacted and practiced their responses to the alien and "ultimately artificial" society that "was sustained from the outside by a continuous one-way drain of men from Europe, whose function was to support and further an even larger drain of men from Africa to America" (Curtin, *Economic Change*, 120).

The signare ball especially illuminates the multiple and conflicting "politics of identity, politics of position" involved in producing and inhabiting this consummate diasporic space (Hall, "Cultural Identity," 226). The signares are at once African and something else (but definitely and decidedly not white or European). The presence of the griots drumming works doubly here: from a European perspective it marks the signare's distance from whiteness; from within diaspora it marks their connection to indigenous traditions and social mores. For example, within the caste system of Wolof culture, griots, "regarded with contempt," also "play important roles as validators of status and agents of communication between different groups," their function as musicians, praise-singers, and storytellers central to daily Wolof life (Leymarie-Ortiz, "Griots," 186, 183). The griots' presence at the signare ball thus underscores the signares' aristocratic status within an indigenous African context. As well, the presence of the "young Negresses clapping" suggests that they too were griot women, or griottes. Isabelle Leymarie-Ortiz explains that in addition to the activities undertaken by male griots, "griot women dressed hair, prepared ceremonial food and washed pots after the celebrations" (188). David Boilat, the métis son of a signare and a Frenchman whose 1853 encyclopedia of Senegal I examine in chapter 4, suggests another role played by the female component of this otherwise scorned caste. According to Boilat, "It is from the griottes that young (Wolof) girls learn these sensual postures which they know so well to feature in their dances."[43] Indeed, the bodily position and gestures of the signares in *Un bal de signares* echo those of the Wolof woman featured in another illustration from Frey, *A damalice foubine! (Danse des Ouoloves de Saint-Louis)* (To the Damalice Foubine! [Dance of the Wolofs of Saint-Louis]) (figure 3).[44] The Wolof woman dances in the center of a group of men and women marked visibly African, including women whose appearance approaches the distinctiveness of the signares, as they wear the canonical headwrap, while their skin tone, dress, and bare feet, as well as their proximity to the dance, mark their distance from the aristocratic signares, who look down on the performance from the rooftop of a nearby building, their male companion in clearly marked European clothes (Frey, *Côte Occidentale*, n.p.).

Placing *Un bal de signares* alongside *A damalice foubine!* underscores how reading the free(d) mulatta concubine through diaspora illuminates complexities of belonging in diaspora.[45] If the signares' performance at the balls was thus intricately embedded in a specific Wolof cultural and social context, then we must at least ask how the signares' apparent and perhaps deliberate incorporation of indigenous practices, movement, and rhythm might reflect a diasporic practice, a negotiation of the strange, "artificial society" that constituted the slave societies of Gorée and Saint-Louis. And if the signare balls signal the resilience of indigenous social and cultural systems and forms in the face of the assault of transatlantic slavery, then we should also consider the ball's echo across the Atlantic as evidence that the free(d) mulatta concubine's participation at these balls may have also been drawn from a diasporic repertoire of performance.

At the same time, the illustration's depiction of persistent indigenous social systems serves as an important reminder of the jagged terrain of belonging, dispossession, and freedom across the black transatlantic. The griots, the young "Negresses" clapping, and the signares whose status depended—at least in part—upon the presence of the first two all inhabited legible and familiar social categories, as well as degrees of freedom utterly unavailable to the black captives passing through the island. Indeed, as much as the ball offered a spectacle to

FIGURE 3. *A damalice foubine! (Danse des Ouoloves de Saint-Louis)*. Colonel Henri Frey, *Côte Occidentale d'Afrique: Vues, scènes, croquis* (Paris, 1890), 44–45.
General Research and Reference Division, Schomburg Center for Research in
Black Culture, New York Public Library, Astor, Lenox and Tilden Foundations.

the European male gaze, it is unlikely that the captives brought to the island for transport to the Americas would have witnessed the activities of the signare ball. And here, in this consummate diasporic place, the signares, at least, executed and enjoyed the dimensions of their social, legal, and economic freedom. Here, the signares apparently responded to the inevitability of their existence by making and inhabiting this place on their own terms.

Indeed, it may be that this moment of the free(d) mulatta concubine's iteration, this apprehension of the ghostly signare, signals an irreconcilable dissonance in the echo's reverberation. But if polyphonic rhythms are a distinct marker of African diasporic music, if, as Paul Gilroy insists, black music's "characteristic syncopations still animate the basic desires—to be free and to be oneself" (*Black Atlantic*, 76), then should we not also read the echo's dissonance as specifically and productively diasporic? I want to be careful to follow Sara

Johnson's injunction against "facile equations of black performance with resistance"; I thus again underscore the echo's evidence of the irreconcilability of difference in diaspora (Johnson, *Fear*, 123). Instead, I suggest that the dissonance in the echo is emblematic of what it means to be in diaspora and thus signals the centrality of the free(d) mulatta concubine and her always-contingent but always-possible relationship to freedom and unfreedom in theorizing diaspora. Rather than resistance, the echo's dissonance and its evidence of practice and rituals necessary to its production signal a theorization of what it means to be in this sudden, unexpected, and traumatic diaspora and the ways in which time and space collapse and explode, where for the exile returning for an account of loss and responsibility, "distress settle[s] in as present time compresse[s] to meet the past" (Ebron, *Performing*, 200). The signare's simultaneous presence as object of fantasy in European travelers' journals, as an echo in a Haitian goddess, and as a ghostly figure representing African accountability in contemporary guidebooks signals that the invocation of her presence is itself a ritual inextricable from the persistent and unending making of diaspora. If, as Avery Gordon insists, the first of "the three characteristic features of haunting" is that "the ghost imports a charged strangeness into the place or sphere it is haunting, thus unsettling the propriety and property lines that delimit a zone of activity or knowledge" (*Ghostly*, 63), then we might ask, What were the "propriety and property lines" disrupted by the signares not only for the European *but also for black and African subjects,* and how does the resonant echo of the signare in diaspora reflect both the persistent "unsettling" of these lines and the possibility suggested by the unsettling? Against the repetitive elision of the sexual violence that produced the signares' appearance in the archive in the first place, the "seething presence" that seeps through popular representations of the figure demands an accounting, a redress not yet granted. That the redress demanded by this ghost remains elusive, that the echo of the free(d) mulatta concubine spirals across time and space, suggests, too, the very limits of the possibilities for freedom offered by the presence of the "opulent signare."

CHAPTER 2

Intimate Acts

(*Once*) At the top of a flight of stairs on a landing in the Cabildo of the Louisiana State Museum hangs a portrait reminiscent of visual depictions of the signares of Senegal (figure 4). The painting features a woman seated with her head turned slightly to her left as she gazes directly at the viewer. The portrait's subject wears a black dress with a V-shaped neckline and cinched at the waist. Over her shoulders is draped a printed shawl with a rose on a pink background. Covering the woman's hair, save for a dark-brown tendril that frames her left eye, is an elaborately wrapped striped scarf, again with a rose, but on a white background. The woman's complexion is the color of cream, with a natural blush on her cheeks and lips. Her face is soft and round, her eyes wide and direct. Besides her scarf, her only adornment is a small, dangling earring. In 2005 the plaque beneath the portrait identified the subject as Marie Laveau and described her as a "legendary African American voodoo queen in New Orleans during the early nineteenth century."

(*Again*) In an 1861 French travel magazine, in an article detailing Senegal's colonial history, appear two drawings depicting the signares. The first, captioned "Signare dame de couleur, et négresses de Saint-Louis au bain de mer," presents a signare, marked clearly by her dress, who sits in the center of the scene facing the viewer, framed by three black women, all unclothed from the waist up, all looking away from the viewer. The signare's clothing is elaborate and carefully arranged, and she wears the conical headwrap that signifies her status as signare. Despite the signare's multilayered garb, which might otherwise shield her from the desiring (or scornful) gaze of what would have been a white French viewer, the sexuality of the illustration is almost overpowering. In Darcy Grimaldo Grigsby's words describing stereotypical representations of the mulatta, this signare's gaze is "demure but entreating" (*Extremities*, 260).[1] Her left breast appears to be bare and caressed by the voluptuous drape of cloth. She is surrounded by nearly naked

FIGURE 4.
Marie Laveau, by
Frank Schneider, after
a painting attributed
to George Catlin, oil
on canvas, 1912–23.
Courtesy of the Collections of
the Louisiana State Museum.

and visibly black female figures. Each of these women is distinct in shade, appearance, position, and hair. They are all touching the signare, who gazes at the viewer as if unaware of her protruding breast and the salaciousness that nearly engulfs her. The visibly black women seem similarly unaware of the viewer or their own signification, as none of them looks either at the viewer or the signare. The black woman lying at the feet of the signare has her legs crossed. She leans back and tilts back her head, closing her eyes as if in absolute rapture, even as her body's position looks awkward and uncomfortable. The woman behind the signare's left shoulder contorts her body, her torso and breasts jutting toward the signare, her head, atop a neck bulging with muscles, turned away from the viewer toward the back of the scene, her left hand on her left hip. And the woman farthest away in the frame, whose skin color nearly matches that of the signare, displays a muscular back, which faces the viewer squarely, the front of her torso completely invisible to the viewer. Both of her hands are on her hips, and two earrings dangle on each side of her neck, the latter perhaps to help mark her gender in the absence of a view of her breasts and against the muscularity of her back. Atop her head is a bundle wrapped in cloth. This image reappears in at least two contemporary works on Senegal, one scholarly (the 1998 English translation of Boubacar Barry's *Senegambia and the Atlantic Slave Trade*) and one popular (Armand Lunel's 1966 pictorial history of Senegal). In its grotesque objectification of the black women framing the signare, the image both enacts and reflects the repeated colonial violation of black women's authority over the display and use of their bodies. I have chosen not to replicate the image here.

(*Together*) This chapter begins with the assertion that between the two images travels the same echo that resonates so decidedly between witnesses' testimonial accounts of the signares of eighteenth-century Gorée and Saint-Louis and the Haitian lwa Ezili Freda. The echo may not announce itself here so clearly or resoundingly. Where Laveau is presented as a solitary figure, the signare is engulfed by the female subjects who surround her. While Laveau sits resplendently in an oil painting that hangs prominently in a state museum, the signare appears in an engraving, one of several depicting stereotypical scenes from Senegal, in a nineteenth-century French travel magazine. Viewed in isolation, the two images appear to have little in common, other than the intricate headwrap worn by each figure. However, it is precisely the headwrap worn by both women that thrusts these images into an African diasporic relationship. And as the echo between the signares and Ezili Freda disrupts a linear framework for understanding the process of diaspora, so does the near replication of the signare's headwrap in Laveau's tignon (the popular term for the headwrap worn by enslaved and free women of color in colonial and antebellum New Orleans) disquiet the discourses of memory that so often define our understandings of African diasporic histories and practices. On the one hand, as James Smalls notes, by the time both of these images appeared in the nineteenth century, the headwrap in visual representations of black people had become a signifier, at least for white audiences on both sides of the Atlantic and later for twentieth-century historians, of "African continuity in the new world" ("Slavery"). However, Helen Bradley Foster's examination of European travelers' accounts dating from the fifteenth century leads her to insist that the headwrap did not become "popular in either West Africa or the Americas until the eighteenth century, that is, until sometime after European contact" (*"New Raiments,"* 280). The evidence leads Foster to "hypothesize, therefore, that the [black] woman's headwrap comes into being sometime after the start of the European trade expansion in Africa" (281). The headwrap, then, may function less as a visual marker of cultural continuity in face of the rupture of the transatlantic slave trade and more as both witness to and evidence of the trauma produced by that trade: the rendering of persons into servile, fungible commodities.

At the same time, as Steeve Buckridge's work insists we recognize, "undoubtedly the most popular garment in this separate sphere [that of the slave community in the Americas]—the garment that represented the continuity of African heritage in dress and served as a symbol of resistance—was the African woman's headwrap" (*Language*, 86). Thus, while Buckridge explores the multiple and often subversive ways that enslaved black women in the Americas styled their headwraps, including cultural and practical uses but most importantly as a "'uniform of rebellion' signifying absolute resistance to the loss of self-definition and deculturation," he grounds his analysis in the headwrap's significance within enslaved black people's memories and reinterpretations of traditional African contexts (95). Foster's caution against reading the headwrap as a marker of African authenticity and Buckridge's evocation of the headwrap's appearance in the Americas as evidence of a persistence of African culture and traditions should be read not as mutually contradictory but rather as a productive reminder that diaspora is a process, that multiple sites and events of dispossession, resistance, and reconstitution are linked in diaspora. To recognize, then, that the headwrap thrusts both figures into a diasporic context is not to insist on a static and flat equivalence between the two but rather to speculate how the subjects signaled by each figure may have drawn from a shared repertoire of negotiation and navigation in the face of familiar and repeated affronts and violations.

Indeed, while the historical contexts that produced each figure's relationship to the headwrap are, as I explore below, distinct, what the headwrap's appearance in visual images produced by white or European men underscores is the scrutiny enslave(d) and free(d) black woman subjects endured under a white desiring gaze across the transatlantic. From travelers' journals to legal codes to newspaper accounts, the official archive obsesses over their sexual lives. In the engraving of the signare, this obsession is explicitly reflected in the image's framing of the signare with the three half-naked women: the depiction invokes what Jennifer Morgan describes as a "sexual grotesquerie" that signals "the complex interstices of desire and repulsion that shaped European men's appraisal of Amerindian and African women" (*Laboring Women*, 26). The portrait of Marie Laveau may at first appear to resist such framing in that it makes no explicit reference to the famous quadroon concubines of antebellum New Orleans.[2] However, as I examine in this chapter, popular narratives of voodoo are as immersed in pornographic accounts of the excessive sexuality of free(d) black women as are those of the signares.

For black subjects in diaspora, a central aspect of the possibility of freedom was the prospect of privacy and authority over one's own body. The headwraps as worn by Marie Laveau in the portrait and by the unnamed signare in the engraving signal an insistence on claiming such privacy and authority and thus serve as a point of departure for examining such insistence. Developing the book's argument that the free(d) mulatta concubine is central to understanding both the unfreedom and the freedom of black subjects in diaspora, this chapter turns to the problem of privacy in reading the lived experiences of free(d) women of color in slave societies. The prodigious documentation of the sexual lives of the

free(d) mulatta concubine underscores the centrality of intimate sexual negotiations in the production of African diasporic subjects and reveals the treacherous
dimensions of those negotiations.

This chapter opens with an examination of Marie Laveau as yet another
articulation in the echo between the signares and Ezili. While Marie Laveau
was a historical subject real enough to have earned a *New York Times* obituary
upon her death in 1881, her legend persists in the religious iconography of New
Orleans voodoo, where her qualities and representation often echo and mirror
those of Ezili.[3] I examine the tension between Laveau's celebrity and the mystery that surrounds her in order to consider the possibilities for privacy and intimacy for free(d) women of color in antebellum New Orleans. I am particularly
interested in two interrelated issues: (1) how the instability of and contradictions
in Laveau's archive suggest the dimensions of her negotiation of and resistance
to dominant white society's persistent violation of free(d) women of color's intimate lives, and (2) how Laveau's simultaneous occupation of two otherwise
disparate cultural narratives—those of New Orleans voodoo and the city's quadroon women—helps us imagine the centrality of said intimate, sexual lives to
the (re)production of an African diaspora across Atlantic space and time.

I then turn to the second figure that opens this chapter, "Signare dame de
couleur, et négresses de Saint-Louis au bain de mer." I analyze the phantasmal
depiction as a visceral reminder of the sexualized and racialized terror endured
by the enslaved *and* free(d) women of color in Atlantic slave entrepôts. Reading this image against eighteenth-century travelers' descriptions of the signares'
domestic spaces and religious practices, I consider how the signares' negotiations
of privacy in the face of an intrusive and desiring white heterosexual male gaze
reflected a production of knowledge derived from practices of the sacred. I argue
that the dominant archive of the signares, one that emphasizes their modesty
and femininity, at once suggests the success of their efforts to resist the violation
of their privacy at the same time that it invites a contemporary viewer to be persistent in our efforts to uncover the most intimate details of the signares' lives.

Finally, while each of the first two sections treats its subjects—Marie Laveau
and the signares, respectively—discretely, the final section considers the space
between them via an examination of Lasirèn, the mermaid/siren in Haitian vodou and also an iteration of Ezili. I examine Lasirèn as a third intervention in
reading the questions of privacy for the free(d) mulatta concubine. Looking at
the free(d) mulatta concubine through the lens of Lasirèn at once invites speculation about what captive subjects may have understood when they saw the
free(d) mulatta concubine and illuminates the violence of the archive. On the
one hand, to read this archive is to capitulate to the voyeurism that violated these
women's authority over their bodies. On the other hand, the archive's refusal of

privacy to these women produces a space to examine how these women processed and navigated that same violation. In its examination of privacy, intimacy, and unfreedom, this chapter thus invites scholars to reflect on the replication of violence and terror our own efforts to recover histories might engender. Lasirèn's archive, I contend, offers a paradigm for navigating the treacherous terrain of excavating the intimate spaces of the free(d) mulatta concubine across Atlantic slave societies.

Untouched

The portrait of Marie Laveau that hangs in the Cabildo museum is as fraught as it is authoritative in its representation of the notorious "voodoo queen" of nineteenth-century New Orleans. Its presence in an official state museum and the identification of its subject by name convey an authority and legitimacy to both the painting and Laveau's historical significance. However, key details of both the portrait and its subject disquiet such signification. First, despite the proliferation of visual representations of Marie Laveau, whether she ever sat for a portrait during her lifetime is, at the very least, debatable. Much of what we think we know about Laveau comes from secondhand sources. She was made famous through the late nineteenth-century writings of George Washington Cable, immortalized through Robert Tallant's freewheeling biography of her, as well as his history of voodoo, and rendered iconic through a diverse and perpetual commodification and marketing of both her likeness and the Afro-diasporic religious practice of voodoo in New Orleans. Carolyn Morrow Long's careful excavation of Laveau's life and biography offers an informative chronology of the development of the voodoo queen's legend. As Long explains, "Throughout most of the twentieth century, an astonishing number of academics accepted the Laveau Legend without question, quoting the usual sources—particularly Robert Tallant's sensationalized rendition of the Louisiana Writers' Project [the Louisiana division of the Federal Writers' Project] interviews from *Voodoo in New Orleans*—and even incorporating 'information' gleaned from the works of fiction" that feature or otherwise include Laveau (*New Orleans*, xxxv). Regarding the authenticity of the portrait hanging in the Cabildo, Long notes, "When Louisiana Writers' Project interviewees were asked by fieldworkers if the portrait resembled the Marie Laveau they remembered, they uniformly agreed that it did not" (57). (Long provides a concise history of the painting's history and appearance in the Cabildo.) Indeed, the consistency of the ex-slaves' assessment of the portrait's authenticity is striking, given that the very question of Laveau's physical appearance is up for grabs. Martha Ward thus observes, "Marie Laveau's color—people said—was red, yellow, brown, black, golden, rosy brick, peach, banana, apricot, light, bright, fair, and high. Her color, the so-called social fact around which cultural life in New Orleans revolved, depended on who was looking at her" (*Voodoo Queen*, 9). Furthermore, the original painting is attributed to George Catlin, well known for his portraits of Native Americans. While Catlin did visit New Orleans frequently, and Long posits that he "may have been intrigued by New Orleans' famous free women of color," he "is not known to have depicted people of African-European heritage" (*New Orleans*, 57). Finally, the original painting's whereabouts are unknown; the painting that hangs in the museum today is a copy produced by Frank Scheider, an artist employed by the Louisiana State Museum. Lost to the archive, then, is the evidentiary trail of both the circumstances of the portrait's painting and the certainty of its subject.

Of course, given the rumors and legends that surround Marie Laveau, the possibility that the portrait may not actually represent her is not surprising. As the above quote from Ward suggests, everything that might be known about Laveau—from the national and racial origins of her parents and husbands, to the number of her children, to the color of her skin, to the fact of her profession—is subject to contestation. Popular and historical accounts variously describe Marie Laveau as a free woman of color, a quadroon, a French-speaking Creole, the daughter of a Saint-Domingue refugee, the widow of a free man of color, the beneficiary of a wealthy white man's favor, a voodoo queen, a yellow fever nurse, a hairdresser who traveled between and into the homes of both French and Anglo wealthy white women, and so on. And while her death in 1881 was marked by obituaries in the *New York Times* and in several of New Orleans's daily newspapers, the diverse tones of these obituaries underscore the instability of her archive. As Long describes, "Reporters for the *Picayune*, the *City Item*, and the *States* treated Marie Laveau as the cherished relic of a more romantic past, portraying her as a traditional herbal healer and a Christian woman of unfailing charity" (*New Orleans*, xxiii). In contrast, the *New Orleans Democrat* described Laveau "as the leader of 'that curious sect of superstitious darkies who combined the hard traditions of African legends with the fetish worship of our creole negroes'" (xxv; Long quotes from the *New Orleans Democrat*'s June 17, 1881, obituary of Laveau, "Marie Lavaux—Death of the Queen of the Voudous," 8).

Thus, while Laveau is most famous as a voodoo queen, and while she occupied the legal status of free woman of color in antebellum New Orleans's tertiary racial system, even for her most intrepid and diligent biographers, Marie Laveau "remains untouched and unknown, secure in her enduring aura of mystery" (Long, *New Orleans*, 211).[4] The portrait, with its mysterious and unverifiable trail, its existence affirmed only in its replica, may itself be the "ultimate privacy shield."[5] The contradictions within and across sources are bewildering. My intention here, then, is not to offer an authentic portrait of Laveau in the face of the apparent unreliability of the most popular and familiar visual representation of her. At least three contemporary, full-length, scholarly biographies of Laveau offer compelling examinations of the myths and legends that surround her celebrity in order to access the "historical Marie Laveau," a woman who indeed left a trail of "sacramental, conveyance, notary, court, police, census, and city directory records" as evidence of her presence in New Orleans history (Fandrich, *Mysterious*, 180). Rather, I want to engage her resistance to the archive's authority and certitude against the discourses of recalcitrant black bodies and hypersexual quadroon women that otherwise frame her celebrity.

It is in this context that we might consider how Laveau's tignon signals her simultaneous occupation and thus the intersection of what might at first appear to be two distinct objects of analysis and their associated archives: that of free women of color and that of voodoo. That is, in historical and popular representations of both free women of color and voodoo in New Orleans, descriptions of the headwraps worn by black and mixed-race, free(d) and enslaved women abound. However, while the religious practice of voodoo and the class of quadroon women involved in extramarital contractual sexual relationships with wealthy white men are both emblematic of New Orleans's extraordinary place in American imagination, they each would appear to occupy a discrete space in the official archive and popular histories of the circum-Atlantic city (see Roach, *Cities of the Dead*). Thus, many contemporary scholarly and popular accounts of free people of color focus primarily on the relationship between this intermediary racial group and its access to white racial, political, social, or economic privilege in colonial and antebellum New Orleans.[6] Overwhelmingly, histories of free people of color in New Orleans ground themselves in textual and official archival evidence that documents this group's relationship to property, the law, and the Catholic Church.

Voodoo operates outside this archive. That is not to say that written accounts of voodoo in New Orleans do not exist. For example, travelers' journals recount "eyewitness" reports of "sacred" rituals, typically centering on enslaved or freed Africans and dances in the public space of Congo Square.[7] However, as Stephan Palmié argues regarding the historiography of voodoo, the veracity of these textual accounts—particularly the travelers' accounts—is not supported by their facts. Palmié's archaeology of late nineteenth-century canonical accounts of voodoo in New Orleans, including those by Henry Castellanos, George Washington Cable, and Hélène d'Aquin Allain, demonstrates that these "eyewitness" reports reiterate and recast an eighteenth-century account of a vodou ceremony in Saint-Domingue whose authenticity Palmié also questions ("Conventionalization," 315–44).[8] Rather than offering evidence of the practice of voodoo, the archival record often displays representations of voodoo as a spectacle charged with savage sexuality and recalcitrant, visibly black bodies.

I suggest that the disjuncture between archival representations of free people of color and voodoo is in fact reflected in and mediated through the body of the quadroon in nineteenth-century New Orleans. As Monique Guillory notes, the story of the quadroon balls and plaçage is one charged with spectacle, fantasy, and the fantastic. Specifically addressing the history of the quadroon balls, Guillory writes:

> Given the substantial social forces at work in the occasion of a quadroon ball, these dances became mythic long before they became historic. By their very nature, these mix-raced, sexually loaded venues hardly typified the social conventions of the slave-holding South. But while they may not have been exemplary of mainstream tastes for leisure and entertainment, the quadroon balls evolved precisely in the ruptures of rigid, binary social systems like slavery and black/white racial taxonomies. Such circumstances preserve the quadroon balls in the realm of myth which Claude Lévi-Strauss described as "no logic, no continuity." ("Some Enchanted Evening," 20)

Furthermore, a key aspect of the myths surrounding free women of color was an assertion of their extraordinary agency. For example, contemporary descriptions of New Orleans's quadroons as a distinct subgroup of free women of color who engaged in long-term sexual and extralegal domestic relationships with white men persistently insist on the women's seductive power. Likewise, what pervades reports of voodoo practices in New Orleans specifically and the Americas more broadly is the question of voodoo practitioners' spectacular agency. Nineteenth-century accounts purporting to describe clandestine voodoo practices in New Orleans often cast the religion in disparaging and even mocking terms. As Marcus Christian has observed, "It is noteworthy that the frequent charges of voodooism against the Negroes were made during periods of turbulence and stress."[9] The heightened attention to voodoo reflected not an increase in the practice of the African-diasporic religious tradition but rather a rise in historically specific "fears of white New Orleanians," first of the possibility of slave insurrections in the antebellum period and then of the threat of black political power in the early days of Reconstruction (Long, *New Orleans*, 103). Further, as Long contends, of special concern to authorities was that these meetings included an otherwise proscribed mix of racial and legal subjects—"slaves, free people of color, and whites" (103). In nineteenth-century New Orleans, then, both voodoo and the quadroons (as a distinct subgroup of free women of color) occupied a fantastic space of impossibility, the erotic, and unexpected power in the white imaginary.

It should not be surprising, then, that a free woman of color whose biography includes various assertions of her or her mother's purported relationships with white men should stand as the iconic voodoo queen of New Orleans. Indeed, as I explore below, these two archives—the official and the popular—converged in a flurry of newspaper reports in 1850 documenting police raids on voodoo ceremonies presided over by free women of color. As well, Marie Laveau's distinctive headwrap—as crucial to her legend as the signares' headwraps are to their celebrity—is rooted in a specific event in New Orleans's colonial history, a sumptuary law issued under Spanish rule directed at free women of color and most popularly known as the "tignon law." The 1850s newspaper reports and the "tignon law" have received considerable scholarly attention, with a specific focus on one or the other, mostly depending if the work examines voodoo in New Orleans or the history of free women of color. Reading them together, however, helps us understand not only how the two separate archives of free women of color and voodoo in fact overlap and intersect but, more importantly, how such intersections help us recognize more fully the centrality of intimate practices of femininity and motherhood both to free women of color's strategies of resistance and to the reproduction of African diasporic cultures and identities.

Furthermore, while Marie Laveau's headwrap places her in a broadly African diasporic context, her location in New Orleans's history and memory, a place as iconic and consummately diasporic as Gorée and Haiti, allows us to probe the specificity of the free(d) mulatta concubine's relationship to the headwrap as one overlapping with, yet distinct from, that of enslaved black women. As Gwendolyn Midlo Hall writes, "Retrieved from the swamps" and founded by the French in 1718, colonial New Orleans emerged as "an extremely fluid society where a social hierarchy was ill defined and hard to enforce" (*Africans*, 120, 128). For a variety of quantifiable and less-than-quantifiable reasons, including race and gender demographics, the treachery of the place's landscape and climate, the economic and political instability of the region, and the fact and mystery of sexual desire, interracial sexual unions proliferated, as "the practice of white settlers taking slave women and free women of color as cohabitants continued unabated throughout the early decades of the colony" (Gould, "'Chaos,'" 235).[10] With the arrival of the Spanish and thus Spanish colonial law in 1768, free women of color involved in interracial unions confronted a set of conflicting legal edicts regarding the security of their own and their children's liberty. Whereas the French Code Noir limited "slaves' access to freedom [and] placed restrictions on their ability to receive property," Spanish law was more generous (235). Thus Kimberly Hanger explains: "[Spanish colonial law] promoted the integrity and importance of the family as a corporate body by upholding partible inheritance, whereby each child, whether male or female, received a part of his or her parents' estates and could not be disinherited. This legislation applied to all women and children—white and nonwhite, slave and free, wealthy and poor" ("Coping," 220–21). At the same time, Jennifer Spear reminds us that although many relationships between "Euro-Louisianan men and women of African an-cestry ... were publicly acknowledged," given that "all racially exogamous rela-tionships were extramarital, women of color involved in them lacked legal claims to the community property that was formed on marriage under both French and Spanish law" (*Race*, 142–43, 149). Furthermore, colonial authorities were alarmed by these interracial relationships. Thus, Virginia Gould explains that in response to an "edict issued in 1776 [by] Charles III of Spain" that demanded that the colonial governor of Louisiana "establish public order and proper standards of morality," with specific reference to a "large class of 'mulattos'" and particularly "'mulatto' women who were 'given over to vice,'" the Spanish "implemented spe-cific restrictions against interracial unions in the Black Code of 1777" ("'Chaos,'" 235–36).

As Hanger, Gould, Hall, and Spear make clear, the contradictions in French and Spanish colonial policies reveal two interconnected issues: first, the multi-dimensional ways in which "such liaisons threatened the social order" (Gould, "'Chaos,'" 236), and second, the "uphill battle" (Hanger, "Coping," 219) enslaved and free(d) women of color fought to achieve and maintain security and liberty for themselves and, significantly, their children. Indeed, by all accounts, and the fluidity and instability of colonial New Orleans's social order notwithstanding, the day-to-day existence of free black women was precarious. As Hanger de-scribes, "For most libre women work was a necessity, not an option; many a free black woman appealed to the mercy of the court as a '*pobre muger*' whose family depended on her *jornales* (daily wages) to survive" (219).

And yet, against this precarious liberty and security, free women of color also presented, or at least appeared to present, themselves in public as elegant and refined feminine subjects worthy of the dominant society's attention and admi-ration. Perhaps the most-cited evidence of such public displays of near-white femininity is Spanish colonial governor Esteban Miró's 1786 "*bando de buen gobi-erno*, or proclamation of good government" (Gould, "'Chaos,'" 237). Miró's edict made plain that his "foremost concern was the behavior and appearance of the region's free women of color" (237). Gould summarizes the ban and its intent thus: "Recognizing that free women of color threatened the social stability of the region, Miró ordered them to abandon the licentious ways from which they subsisted and to go back to work with the understanding that he would be sus-picious of their indecent conduct. The extravagant luxury of their dress, which was already excessive, he warned, would compel him to investigate the mores of those who persisted in such display.... Finally, he prohibited them from wear-ing feathers or jewels in their hair. Instead, they were to cover their hair with handkerchiefs as was formerly the custom" (237). Across the Francophone and Hispanophone Americas, Miró's edict was not unique. And just as the mulatta "courtesans" of colonial Saint-Domingue responded to sumptuary laws forbidding them to wear shoes by "appear[ing] in sandals, with diamonds on the toes of their feet," so did free women of color appear to embrace the tignon, with its "bright reds, blues and yellows," wearing in public a "brilliant silk handkerchief, artfully knotted and perhaps enhanced with a jewel."[11]

The historical event of the "tignon law" and the response of the city's free women of color are usually read as revelatory moments exemplifying the audacious agency of the city's free women of color in their dress and public displays of wealth and luxury. Scholars have also examined how the tignon bando and sumptuary laws across the Americas like it were not so much about the ostentatious vanity of free women of color but rather about the problem of maintaining the racial economy of slavery despite the persistent sexual disruptions of that economy and their consequent human evidence in the city's population. I extend such analyses by considering how the sumptuary laws both reflected and enacted violation of free women of color's intimate lives.

Sumptuary laws specifically directed at free women of color and explicitly loaded with moral condemnation at once ascribed agency and authority to the women in their intimate lives and rendered it impossible for the women to define the public dimensions of such intimate practices. To speak of intimacy here is to speak not only of the sexual activity of free women of color but also of the intimacy of family and friendship in a slave society and the maintenance of its integrity. The colonial authorities' investment in the intimate lives of its subjects is one well examined; as Ann Laura Stoler explains, "The notion of the 'intimate' is a descriptive marker of the familiar and the essential *and* of relations grounded in sex.... It is 'sexual relations' and 'familiarity' taken as an 'indirect sign' of what is racially 'innermost' that locates intimacy so strategically in imperial politics and why colonial administrations worried over its consequence and course" (*Carnal Knowledge*, 9). However, I am less concerned with the colonial authority's investment in intimacy and more interested in how free(d) black women may have inhabited and navigated the surveillance of their most intimate practices and how they may have enacted notions of intimacy outside those centered on sexual relationships. To think about intimacy here, then, is again to think about all that might produce pleasure outside the purview of the dominant society: the rituals of femininity, the comfort of friendship, the nurturing of family. That is, if freedom in a slave society means, at least in part, to have authority over one's body and one's relationships, then Miró's bando reveals certain limits of that authority for free(d) women of African descent in a racialized slave society, because the "tignon law" was not only about how the women appeared in public but also about how they navigated their sexual lives, how they imagined, produced, and presented their persons, and how they imagined and managed their familial relationships. Miró's bando was not about ending interracial relationships but rather about attempting to circumscribe the women's enjoyment of any and all of their relationships. Of course, it is treacherous to imagine such enjoyment or even employ the vocabulary of enjoyment when speculating about how free(d) women of color experienced their sexual lives in an economy so overdetermined by racialized and sexual violence. I suggest, however, that the forms of resistance employed by free(d) women of color against sumptuary laws—the women's simultaneous adherence to the letter of the laws and their spectacular transgression of the intent of these laws—offer "public transcripts" of their pleasure—one of the most intimate of feelings—at, if not in, resisting Miró's bando.[12]

Stephanie Camp's work on enslaved women's use of dress in the U.S. South helps us understand the site of pleasure not to be in the sexual relationship itself but in the resistance to public efforts to shame and humiliate free women of color: "As much as [enslaved] women's bodies were sources of suffering and sites of planter domination, women also worked hard to make their bodies spaces of personal expressions, pleasure, and resistance. . . . When they adorned their bodies in fancy dress, rather than in the degrading rough and plain clothing, rags, or livery that slaveholders dressed them in, they challenged the axiomatic (doxic) quality of their enslaved status" ("Pleasures," 561). Buckridge's examination of the uses of dress in the Caribbean also emphasizes the same "pleasures of resistance" enacted by enslaved women, here emphasizing the "Creole" style of dress found in the Caribbean, accomplished via the "merging of European and African characteristics" (*Language*, 93). Arguing that it was "subversive by nature," Buckridge asserts, "Creole dress was fundamentally radical because it defied easy categorization. In essence, it visually and symbolically challenged the colonial regime's apparent deep-seated desire to divide the colonial world into clear-cut opposites of black and white, or European and African" (93; see also Johnson, *Fear*, chap. 4).

While the uses of dress as a site and means of resistance by enslaved black and mulatta women and free(d) women of color are subjects well traversed by the scholarship, what is missing is a consideration of what such dress might reveal about the relationships between enslaved and free(d) women of color as they shared and reproduced a repertoire and rituals of adornment and toilette that marked their status and belonging in diasporic communities. That is, while free women of color in fact undertook and displayed rituals of femininity that resisted the racist "ungendering" of black female subjects, they may have done so by demanding the labor and cultural knowledge of unfree black women.[13] Can we imagine the complexity of sentiment as free women of color, in the privacy of their domestic lives, combed and arranged their hair and, with the help and skill of enslaved black women, carefully and skillfully wrapped, knotted, and sometimes decorated their tignons? And if we recognize the often-sacred aspects of West African traditions of hair care and styling, as well as the persistent motif of elaborate attention to hair and toilette in the free(d) mulatta concubine's echo across diaspora in the signares and Ezili Freda, then we must also consider how this intimate practice may have also served as a site of the reproduction of diaspora.[14] At the same time, that such rituals may have entailed the unfree labor of enslaved black women who served free women of color should inform our reading of the limits and possibilities for black femininity as a site of resistance in slave societies. Thus, in the case of colonial New Orleans, that free women of color appeared, at least in a public way, to at once embrace and resist the tignon law is important because these women's actions articulated a performance of femininity inextricable from their specifically gendered, racialized experience as women of African descent in a slave society.

Miró's bando also attempted to revise and elide the intimate familial dynamics of interracial households. The historical record makes plain that in colonial and antebellum New Orleans, free women of color in extramarital sexual relationships with white Creole men labored persistently to ensure their security and liberty and that of their children. The specificity of New Orleans as a place, and specifically the sedimentary nature of its colonial history, framed their efforts. As Spear explains, while the 1724 French Code Noir made allowances for slave manumissions with the exception of "slave consorts and children," "more than half of the slaves whom owners tried to free were women, who they sought either to manumit alone or with their children, or were children" (*Race*, 85). Spanish colonial rule introduced *coartación*, which "allowed slaves to be freed at their own initiative, even if they did not have their owners' consent, although the latter received some form of compensation for their loss of property" (109). Regarding free women of color, Kimberly Hanger explains: "Free black women fought daily oppression and sought to assert their identity, in part by striving to attain what was important to them: freedom for themselves, friends, and relatives; stable, long-lasting unions that produced children and cemented kin networks; prosperity for themselves and future generations; and respect as hardworking, religious members of the community" ("Coping," 219). Finally, Judith Schafer documents the legal efforts of free(d) women of color in antebellum New Orleans to purchase or otherwise assure the freedom of their children (*Becoming Free*). The persistence of this strategy into the antebellum period underscores the perpetual possibility of freedom against the simultaneously perpetual threat and reality of never achieving that freedom.

Thus, on the one hand, we can imagine how free women of color navigated their households as mothers and domestic partners in terms that recognize their will and self-determination to do so. Jennifer Spear also offers a powerful example of how a free woman of color whose white father had helped her purchase her freedom resisted assumptions about the intimate lives of free women of color when she insisted in her manumission petition, "I have not earned my freedom on my back" (*Race*, 153). On the other hand, the documentary trail of free women of color who regularly had to petition for their own or their children's freedom should give us pause. While the example Spear offers in her insistence that "violence frequently imbued these relationships" involves an enslaved mulatta mistress, we must remember that free women of color stood at the intersection of two social categories—black and woman—that enjoyed little public protection from patriarchal control and violence (153). Official declarations that free women of color in interracial relationships were no more than prostitutes who lived in "idleness" and were given to "carnal pleasures" not only erase the roles these women played as mothers and domestic partners but also elide the very likely probability that these women, female and black in a heteropatriarchal slave society, endured domestic violence.

Finally, while the ban was largely symbolic and with the transfer of New Orleans to U.S. control no longer a legal mandate in the antebellum city, Carolyn Long notes that "many Afro-Creole women" continued to wear "the traditional Madras head wrap" well into the nineteenth century (*New Orleans*, 21). The tignon, then, emerges not only as a symbol and site of resistance to white colonial intrusion upon and violation of the intimate lives of free women of color. Its persistence in antebellum New Orleans, well beyond the dictates of a colonial edict directing free women of color to wear it as a badge of their connection to slavery, suggests that it constituted a cultural practice as well, one suggesting a reproduction of diaspora and the complex intimacies such reproduction demands. That the tignon as worn by free women of color worked as a visual reminder (to whom?) of their connection to slavery underscores the complexity of diaspora and its intimacies. First, free women of color across Atlantic slave societies held other black women as slaves. While the more comforting narratives assert that slaves held by free people of color were sometimes blood or fictive kin and were held as slaves for legally expedient reasons only, to depend on such framing to tell the whole story would be to enact a different kind of violence to the histories of those held in bondage. Second, certainly not all free women of color wore the tignon, especially in the antebellum period. We may also imagine that those who wore the tignon did not necessarily wear it every day. We might then question when and why a free(d) woman of color would wear her head covered in a madras scarf, especially in the antebellum period, long after the bando's terms had expired.[15] Indeed, the ex-slaves interviewed for the Louisiana Writers' Project did not in fact uniformly agree on whether Marie Laveau wore the tignon for which she was so famous. One informant, Mrs. Marie Dede, for example, asserted, "She did not wear nothing on her head or nothing around her waist like the hoodo [sic] people do today."[16] Such caveats to reading the tignon direct us to consider the unevenness of diaspora's production and reproduction in public and intimate spaces.

It is perhaps most useful here, then, to remember that the tignon's very practical function, to cover the hair completely, suggests the tignon's discursive function as well, to render the black female subject mysterious, exotic, and unknowable. Griselda Pollock's analysis of Édouard Manet's depiction of Laure, the "African-Caribbean-French" woman in his iconic painting *Olympia*, is instructive. Assessing the portrayal of the woman's headwrap, Pollock explains: "The headwrap is richly coloured, but not excessively. . . . The bandana is a highly specific signifier precisely in the combination of its being there atop the head of a black woman clothed in European cast-offs and its understated facticity. More insistently painted, it would have become too powerful a sign of the exotic. It could have *Orientalised* the painting" (*Differencing*, 285). In contrast to that in Manet's painting, the tignon in the portrait of Marie Laveau is towering, vivid, and intricately wrapped, reflecting the artist's fascination with Laveau's otherness. And yet, while both the tignon and its signification may have been imposed on free women of color, that free women of color continued to wear it into the antebellum period, that they exercised authority in how it was worn, that they drew from an African diasporic repertoire of dress and "coding" shared by enslaved women invite a reading that moves beyond the objectifying and desiring gaze of a white patriarchal and colonizing gaze.[17] Read in conjunction with free women of color's prominent roles in the New Orleans–specific African-diasporic religious practice of voodoo, these women's ownership of the tignon articulates a deliberate protection of their intimate lives, an insistence on the unknowability of their interiority.

Testimony

Beginning in the 1850s and reaching a peak just after the end of the Civil War, New Orleans witnessed a series of newspaper reports documenting voodoo ceremonies in the city both in public homes and then in hard-to-reach public spaces. As noted above, the increased attention of white residents of New Orleans to voodoo activities in the antebellum period reflected their fear of slave insurrections and abolitionist fever. According to Long, the most frequent "charge under which Voudou devotees were arrested" was "unlawful assembly" (*New Orleans*, 103). Intersecting this threat of interracial cooperation was the apparent domination (both in numbers and in leadership) of free women of color in these arrests and their subsequent reports. Thus, if the threat of slave insurrection and abolitionist fervor were not enough, the fabled hypersexuality of free women of color meant that white New Orleans also had to contend with "voodoo ceremonies as sites of potential interracial sexuality" (Thompson, *Exiles*, 107).

Reports of voodoo activities in antebellum New Orleans thus suggest the centrality of free women of color to perceived and actual threats to legal and social order in an Anglo-Americanized city intent on holding fast to a binary racialized economy of slavery and freedom.[18] Underexamined, however, is what these reports of voodoo activities might suggest about free women of color's intimate lives and efforts to protect such intimacies.[19] And it is important to pause here to remember that the majority of New Orleans's free women of color were not actively leading voodoo ceremonies, nor were they involved in interracial sexual relationships. Indeed, the spectacle of free women of color leading clandestine voodoo ceremonies stands in apparent opposition to a "politics of respectability" employed by a vast number of New Orleans's free women of color. In their examination of "Afro-Catholicism" in colonial and antebellum New Orleans, for example, Emily Clark and Virginia Gould document "a general process by which thousands of women of African descent in New Orleans became Catholic and eventually employed their religious affiliation to transform themselves from nearly powerless objects of coercion into powerful agents" ("Feminine Face," 412). Further, as Emily Clark insists, "marriage, not concubinage, was the tradition New Orleans free people of color established and perpetuated" (*Strange History*, 96). Most poignant is Clark's reminder that the quadroon in New Orleans "was, as well, a wife and mother who watched her husband's militia unit march off to the Battle of New Orleans and stood in the sanctuary to see her daughter marry the boy from around the corner" (197). And yet the specter of voodoo is there: the fact of the arrests and, more importantly, the women's responses to these arrests suggest a fissure, a space to imagine the possibilities free women of color may have considered in assessing their options for authority and self-determination.

Indeed, the flurry of arrests of free women of color practicing voodoo is telling in what those arrests reveal about the surveillance of this group in antebellum New Orleans. Criminal and civil records and newspaper reports reflect the focused surveillance by police of two neighborhoods populated by free people of color: Faubourg Marigny and Faubourg Tremé. That Faubourg Marigny was also the preferred place for quadroon *placées* (those free women of color involved in plaçage, "placed" as the mistresses of wealthy white men) to live deserves particular attention. Thus, according to Carolyn Long, "During the summer of 1850 the Third Municipality Guards, charged with policing the Faubourg Marigny ... regularly raided Voudou ceremonies and arrested the participants for unlawful assembly" (*New Orleans*, 103). A particularly "spectacular incident" of 1850 was reported in the July 31 edition of the *Daily Picayune*: the arrest of "Betsey Toledano and her Voodoo sisters" at a house on Conti Street, located in Faubourg Tremé (Fandrich, *Mysterious*, 141, 140). According to the *Daily Picayune*, "The officers stated they had often noticed slaves entering the house and had heard singing. Yesterday evening, hearing the singing and knowing that a number of persons were inside, they broke into the building" (140). The surveillance endured by free women of color came not only from authorities but also from free men of color. For example, Marcus Christian recounts the 1851 arrest of a free woman of color named Keen: "Keen and several slaves had been spied upon by R. Thompson, another free man of color, who reported the incident to the police of the First Municipality, claiming that he had seen voodoos singing and dancing around Keen. Moreover, he had seen other performances of this type on various occasions at the same address and claimed that Keen had intimidated and attempted to frighten him, by throwing a charmed bag or 'wanga' into his yard to condition him against reporting the orgies to authorities" ("Voodooism," 13). Free women of color's intersectionality becomes clear; apparently threatening to both civil authorities and free men of color was the potential for free women of color to assert authority over their own intimate lives.

Described as both a "free colored woman" and a "négresse" in contemporaneous and historical accounts, Betsey Toledano was neither a quadroon nor likely a placée. However, that she readily acknowledged and even asserted her role in presiding over voodoo rituals that allowed as participants only women—free(d), enslaved, and white—underscores not only the possibilities these spaces offered for free(d) women's bodily authority but also the centrality of intimate spaces to the production of diasporic subjects in slave societies. At the same time, the *Daily Picayune*'s account of her trial both underscored the limits of privacy and security for free and enslaved black women and complicated the racialized power relationships when it noted the names and owners of "two slaves arrested with her" and left unnamed a "white man [who] was found in the house, but escaped" ("More of the Voudous," July 31, 1851, quoted in Fandrich, *Mysterious*, 140–41).

Arrested at least twice during the summer of 1850, Toledano asserted a defense of both her religious tradition and her role in leading rituals that reverberates across the echo of the free(d) mulatta concubine in diaspora. Brought to court the morning following her arrest and that of "her followers ... at her home on Bienville Street in Vieux Carré," Toledano was "called up as the chief vaness of the society, as she called it" ("More of the Voudous," quoted in Fandrich, *Mysterious*, 140). Rather than "attempt to deny the accusation," she insisted that "Voudouism was an African religion with its signs and symbols, that she had been educated in its precepts and mysteries by her grandmother, who came over from Africa, and that she never thought there was anything wrong with it"

("More of the Voudous," quoted in Fandrich, *Mysterious*, 140). Furthermore, she "acknowledged that she frequently had meetings of women only, at her house, to go through certain feminine mysteries, sing, etc." (140).

As Ina Fandrich notes, "What we learn from the courageous Betsey Toledano is that free women of color who engaged in these 'African sisterhoods' were keenly aware of their constitutional rights" (*Mysterious*, 142). Indeed, Toledano was not the only free woman of color to resist authorities' violations of her rights and privacy. On July 14, 1850, a group of women sued the Third Municipality Guards in response to a police raid on a voodoo ceremony. As Long describes, the women "claimed they had been illegally arrested while in the performance of religious ceremonies . . . and subject to assault, batteries, and general ill-treatment" (105). And Marie Laveau herself, "the head of the Voudou women" (105), sued to have a statue allegedly stolen by one of the officers during the raid on Betsey Toledano's home returned to her.[20] Carolyn Long and Martha Ward both quote the *Daily True Delta*'s description of the crowd attending the hearing, which included "Africa's daughters of every age, of every shape and every . . . color, from a bright yellow hue to sooty black" ("The Virgin of the Voudous," August 10, 1850, 2, quoted in Long, *New Orleans*, 106; see also Ward, *Voodoo Queen*, 134). At stake was a statue described in the *Daily True Delta* as "a quaintly carved figure representing something between a centaur and an Egyptian mummy" (Long, *New Orleans*, 106). The public resistance on the part of free women of color to violations of their intimate lives was indeed remarkable.

Of course, how to read the testimony of Toledano and the other free women of color arrested again underscores the frustration of the archive. That Toledano's testimony was recorded and reported in the newspaper at the time of her trial lends some credibility to its accuracy.[21] At the same time, the reporter's evident bias against Toledano means too that parts of the account may be exaggerated and even outright lies. Thus, Fandrich reminds us regarding the *Daily True Delta*'s account of Toledano's assertion of the roots of her practice, which specifies the roots to be "Congo," "it is also possible that this expression (Congo) does not stem from Toledano herself; it could have been inserted by the journalist" ("Defiant African Sisterhoods," 195). Rather than use the unverifiable account to attempt to trace the specific ethnic and cultural roots of the items described in the report, Fandrich instead focuses on the verifiable aspect of the incident, the interracial composition of the women arrested. Indeed, perhaps recognizing the limits of white newspapers' reports of the testimony of free women of color, Fandrich and Long each investigates the voodoo arrests to a specific end: Fandrich argues that the arrests signal an interracial sisterhood inherently subversive to the racial economy of New Orleans, and Long uses her careful delineation of the court cases primarily to document voodoo's evolution as an African-diasporic religious practice comprised of a "unique North American blend of African and European religious and magical traditions" specific to New Orleans (*New Orleans*, 118).

Building on their analyses, what compels me here is how Betsey Toledano's resistance turned on a (re)production of diaspora and imaginative articulations of Africa and how we might use the official record's own limitations against itself in order to see her resistance. Thus, we might read the report's inability to accurately represent voodoo's specific ethnic and cultural roots not only as evidence of the reporters' fantasy but also of the reporters' illiteracy regarding the signs and symbols offered as evidence. I contend that Toledano's insistence that "Voudouism was an African religion with its signs and symbols, that she had been educated in its precepts and mysteries by her grandmother, who came over from Africa," enacts a subversive paradigm for reading and producing knowledge. That is, public accounts of voodoo consistently depicted the religion as unintelligible, orgiastic savagery. Betsey Toledano's testimony offers a counternarrative that positions her religious practice as one that demands literacy; her statements about the "signs and symbols" also foreground the deliberate (re)production of that knowledge across African diasporic space and time. Furthermore, Toledano's articulation of the foundational role her grandmother played and her assertion of her resolve that the meetings included only women in order to "go through certain feminine mysteries" produce a complex revision and subversion of ideologies of femininity and womanhood. Against dominant ideologies of womanhood that presume whiteness and a purity predicated on protection from male desire, Toledano asserts a womanhood grounded in visible blackness and dependent on the memory of slavery and enslavement—in the unprotected body of her grandmother "who came from Africa."

While Toledano makes voodoo a legible and coherent religious practice, she also insists on its unknowability. Thus, although she forthrightly explains the uses of some of the items seized by police in the raid on her house, she steadfastly refuses to divulge all of the "mysteries" of her religious practice. The public account of Toledano's necklace is particularly intriguing. The *Daily Picayune* describes how Toledano "showed a necklace which she wore, of beautiful sea shells, of different and brilliant colors and of a small size, which her grand-mother had given her many years ago, and which gave her great power over rain, she being able thereby to bring down a shower whenever she pleased." The *Daily Picayune* reports that a male bystander called out, goading Toledano "to use her power, to sprinkle and cool the crowded room" ("More of the Voudous," in Fandrich, *Mysterious*, 141). Despite the crowd's jeering, Toledano's only response was a "scornful toss of the head and curl of the lip" (141). That the voodoo priestess did not use the necklace to produce rain on the spot might certainly be read as evidence of voodoo's ineffectiveness or inability to produce material results.

But what if we read Toledano's silence on the terms her own testimony has articulated? Reading her delineation of how she acquired her knowledge against her insistence that the secrets she held were intended only for women reveals that Toledano asserted not only her authority to explain her religious tradition but also her right to keep its most intimate aspects private, out of the purview of a dominant patriarchal society. What if we read her silence in the face of the nonevent of the rain as a refusal to explain more than she has already offered? What if, with the understanding that Toledano is indeed charged to protect the intimate practices of voodoo, we can imagine that the story Toledano offers regarding the necklace's value is not the true story at all? What if this is another enactment of black women's dissemblance in order to protect another truth? Contextualizing her analysis of black women in the late nineteenth- and early twentieth-century midwestern United States within a longer history of black women's experiences in the antebellum period, Darlene Clark Hine theorizes: "Rape and the threat of rape influenced the development of a culture of dissemblance among Black women.... [T]he behavior and attitudes of Black women ... created the appearance of openness and disclosure but actually shielded the truth of their inner lives and selves from their oppressors" ("Rape," 912). The necklace's connection to her grandmother could mean that the true story was that the sentiment Toledano attached to the necklace was too intimate a feeling to convey in a public space. In the space of her defiantly silent response to the male bystander's mocking question, Toledano held her tongue, refusing to be inscribed into the official record. Instead, she inserted a material artifact into the archive, an object that at once represents the terms of her presence in the archive and refuses to tell a story without her.

Police had arrested Toledano before, about one month prior to the testimony above. On June 27, 1850, police interrupted a gathering of "about a hundred women." Of these, "two white women, fifteen free women of color [including Toledano], and one slave were apprehended" (Long, *New Orleans*, 103). The consistent presence of white women at these voodoo ceremonies further underscores how these activities in private and hard-to-reach public places enacted spaces of resistance vis-à-vis an oppressive patriarchal order. The presence of enslaved women is, however, more challenging. It is not always clear from newspaper reports and contemporary histories whether the enslaved women present at the various ceremonies were in attendance with their slaveholders (who could have been white or free people of color) or had somehow arrived independently of them. As noted above, the July 31 *Picayune* report of Toledano's arrest states that two slaves were arrested and names their owners, neither of whom appears to have been arrested. And again, the presence of the white man who eluded arrest suggests the limits of privacy and autonomy within even purportedly free domestic spaces. As cited above, Toledano and the other women arrested on June 27 filed suit against the authorities, asserting that they had been illegally arrested for the "performance of religious ceremonies" and endured "assault, batteries, and general ill-treatment." Most importantly, the women insisted that "but one slave girl was present, who accompanied her mistress, and because she could not pay the fine imposed on her, was corporally and wrongfully punished."[22] While Fandrich reads the presence of enslaved women to signal the egalitarian ethos of the religious practice, stating that the women "were particularly concerned about the treatment of the sole enslaved sister of the group who had been cruelly singled out for more severe punishment," impossible to retrieve from the archive was whether the unnamed girl wanted to attend (Fandrich, "Defiant African Sisterhoods," 192). Nor can we know whether, once in attendance, she was coerced into participating or did so of her own accord. I am pressing against the specific context of the June 27 arrest, for we know surely that enslaved black people across the Americas practiced African-derived religions and enacted resistance from and within these practices. The women's inclusion of her rights and injuries in the lawsuit is there. However, in both cases, the voices of the enslaved girls and women present at these ceremonies appear to elude the dominant archive. While free(d) women of color may have produced spaces of possibility for imagining or practicing freedom, the inaccessible presence of the enslaved women underscores the limits of or constraints upon such imagination.

As Long explains, notably absent from the voodoo arrests was the legendary Marie Laveau, despite being described in a July 1850 *Picayune* report as "head of the Voudou women" (*New Orleans*, 105). Long argues that Laveau's freedom from persecution alongside the public recognition of her status "seems to indicate, that although Betsey Toledano acted as both scapegoat and spokeswoman, Marie Laveau was actually the reigning queen" (106). Implied is that Laveau's freedom from prosecution derived at least in part from her status as voodoo queen. I would like to press on the question of Laveau's apparent ability to avoid arrest and suggest that such liberty may be further theorized through the racial economy of the free(d) mulatta concubine. To do so may at first seem counterintuitive: while Laveau was a free woman of color, popular and academic narratives of her sexual relationships do not foreground the economies of quadroon balls and plaçage that otherwise serve as the dominant paradigm for popular and academic representations of New Orleans's famous free(d) quadroon mistresses of white men. However, as Long demonstrates, Christophe Glapion, the man with whom Laveau entered into a domestic partnership following the disappearance of her legal husband, was, contrary to popular contemporary narratives that name him a free man of color, "the legitimate son of white parents and descendant of an aristocratic French family" (51).[23] At the same time, while the legend of Marie Laveau casts her as the daughter of a white man and a quadroon placée, Long offers evidence that Laveau's father was in fact a "prosperous free man of color who traded in real estate and slaves and owned several businesses" and was likely the son of a white man (23). Thus, while Laveau herself is not remembered as a New Orleans quadroon in all the mythic understandings of the term, she is nonetheless inextricable from the economies of race, sex, freedom, and slavery that produce the free(d) mulatta concubine across the Atlantic. Reading her as an iteration of the echo can thus help us better understand how black subjects *imagined* the limits and possibilities for freedom within the space of New Orleans.

While the historical record is less decisive and even contrary, the popular archive persistently describes Laveau as mulatta and/or quadroon. In a lay history on women in New Orleans, drawing heavily from Robert Tallant's 1946 sensationalistic work, *Voodoo in New Orleans*, Mary Gehman writes, "Marie Laveau and her daughter were said to look remarkably alike, with regal bearing, black curly hair, golden skin, and a penetrating look in their eyes. Both were quadroons and worked as hairdressers for a trade" (*Women*, 28). While Gehman offers a stable description of Laveau's racial position, anthropologist Martha Ward follows her own reminder to the reader of the unreliability of the dominant archive when it comes to Laveau's appearance, quoted above, almost immediately with a note that "in 1842, an English visitor noticed dark, liquid eyes, coral lips, pearly teeth, and 'long raven locks of soft and glossy hair'" (*Voodoo Queen*, 9–10, quoting Buckingham, *The Slave States*, 36). Ward's slippage, effortlessly moving from rumors of Laveau's appearance to quoting an English visitor's impressions of the city's famous quadroons as if he is describing Laveau, affirms Carolyn Long's point that in New Orleans "almost every nineteenth-century portrait of a woman of color is said to represent the Voudou Queen" (*New Orleans*, 57).

Placing the mystery of Laveau's appearance within the context of the free(d) mulatta concubine reveals that at stake in the emphasis on Marie Laveau's appearance is the question of how one remembers and represents freedom and agency within a racialized slave society. Laveau's appearance also begs the question of whose truths the published archive values and allows. That is, as all three of the contemporary scholarly biographies of Laveau concur, while the archive bears evidence of the mundane details of Laveau's life—her birth certificate, baptismal and court records, property deeds—what the archive reveals about her connection to voodoo are stories so full of exaggeration and misrepresentation that the truth of her spiritual role in an African-diasporic religious practice and the community that practiced it will likely never be known. The accounts that are closest to eyewitness testimony come in the form of the WPA narratives of ex-slaves, collected more than fifty years after the appearance of her obituary by white and black writers in the Louisiana Writers' Project. African American writer Marcus Christian, head of the Dillard Project, or, more colloquially, the "Colored Project" of the LWP, his own labor, knowledge, and unpublished manuscript on the history of black Louisiana marginalized in popular and academic histories, offers the ex-slaves' testimonies as corrective evidence against the myths surrounding Laveau. Christian explains, "Various elderly Negroes maintain that Marie Lavaud [*sic*] was not a mulatto but a 'brown-skinned' woman. They declare emphatically that she was not a very light woman, in spite of all printed statements to the contrary" ("Voodooism," 39).

While Christian indicates "brown-skinned" to be a direct quote, his project is to correct the record rather than offer close readings of how the declarations come to be offered in the first place. I want to build and press upon his intervention further by turning to the transcript cited by Christian and assert that attending to the transcriptions not only places evidence into the record but reveals the very stakes of interrogating the events in the first place. One of the ex-slave informants cited by Christian is Creole-speaking seventy-two-year-old Oscar Felix, interviewed in 1940. Having acknowledged that he practices voodoo, and in response to his interviewer (the transcript records only the informant's answers, not the questions), Felix states: "You want to know about Marie Laveau? Why, yes, I know her ever since I was old enough to remember. I used to sing in the ceremonies when I was a boy. . . . She was a good-looking brown-skinned woman, tall and like a queen." Then, following a blank space on the page indicating a pause in Felix's testimonial account, the transcript continues: "Oh yes, I am positive she was brown-skinned. . . . She was nice, friendly, but a little cold. But she was a good person if you knew her well enough!"[24] Important are Mr. Felix's repetition of the phrase "brown-skinned," his subsequent descriptions of her as "nice" and a "good person," and his admonishment "if you knew her well enough!" Mr. Felix offers the description, and then, as one can infer from the structure of his response, the interviewer questions him regarding Laveau's appearance: "Oh yes, I am positive she was brown-skinned." In this moment, Felix makes clear what freedom and power looked like to a child just out of slavery who would have seen the elderly but apparently still formidable free woman of color in the early years of emancipation.

This moment offers a counternarrative to the master discourse regarding Laveau's meaning for imagining freedom in antebellum New Orleans. Why does the interviewer seek to verify Mr. Felix's initial statement regarding Laveau's skin color? What is at stake in imagining her brown skinned rather than mulatta or quadroon? I contend that representations of Marie Laveau as a mulatta, as light skinned, enable a kind of spectacular black agency while they simultaneously disable any way of imagining freedom for visibly black bodies. For many reasons—some outside our ability to discern, some perhaps not so—Mr. Felix insists on his particular memory of what Laveau looked like. Through his description of Laveau as not only "brown-skinned" but also "nice, friendly, but a little cold," Mr. Felix's responses to his interviewer reclaim Laveau and insert her into a story of the everyday, in which black people daily encountered and endured power, subjection, and freedom as a complex set of negotiations rather than in spectacular displays of savagery and sexuality. Indeed, Mr. Felix's comments remind us of the importance of color and visibility in remembering, representing and imagining freedom.

Terror

If the security and privacy of free women of color in antebellum New Orleans were precarious, that of the signares in eighteenth-century Gorée and Saint-Louis would appear at first to be exceptionally assured. After all, the signares played essential roles in the physical and economic well-being of the European men they married. As part of the habitant class, and indeed the dominant members of that class for a good part of the eighteenth century, the signares functioned as crucial trade intermediaries rather than as buffer zone between a minority white slaveholding class and a majority black enslaved population, as did free people of color in the Americas. Both historical sources and the contemporary histories of the signares emphasize the women's status and security. As Hilary Jones explains, "Signares occupied a position of high social standing. ... Signares played an essential role in establishing the systems and structures needed to facilitate trade and reproduce colonial society" (*Métis*, 38–39).

Against the evidence of the signares' standing and power, the travel magazine's depiction of the signare and her attendants that opens this chapter startles. It is important to take into account that the 1861 publication date of the magazine and illustration is well after the height of the signares' power. As George Brooks explains, "Signares, long respected as wives and partners in commerce, came by the 1870s to be regarded as courtesans, or worse, by some Frenchmen newly arrived in Senegal with little appreciation of what signareship had represented in past times" ("Artists' Depictions," 82). As a consequence, "French artists' representations of signares ... were highly flattering and continued to be so until the 1870s" (82). The depiction at hand, then, perhaps reflects a transition in French perceptions of the signares: the signare's posture and clothing appear to continue what Brooks calls "'classic' signare portraiture": she is "dignified, serious, graceful, sedate, demure, and passive" (83). At the same time, the signare is nearly engulfed by the sexuality of the African women who surround her; their sexuality disrupts the signare's attempt to present herself as a modest example of femininity. While Mark Hinchman offers a more nuanced reading of depictions of signares, arguing that "even 'respectable' images could be embedded in an erotic discourse," the overt sexualization and racialization of the signare are distinctively palpable here ("African Rococo," 152).

The presence of the women both emphasizes and disrupts the iconography of the mulatta in the colonial imagination. Marcus Wood's examination of Francesco Bartolozzi's 1796 engraving *Joanna*, which depicts Captain John Stedman's enslaved mulatta mistress, and his analysis of how that portrait, in which "Joanna is respectably clothed except for one nude breast, shown standing out firmly with erected nipple," is instructive (*Slavery*, 128–29). Wood asserts that the image is pornographic not only because of the "voyeuristic and erotic elements of the presentation of Joanna" but also because "Joanna as a sexual object exists outside Stedman's power to protect her. She can be sold and used at any point" (129–30). The travel magazine's presentation of the signare mimics Bartolozzi's stylization of the mulatta: like Joanna, the signare here "exists on the sexual and race borderline between black and white, wanton and demure, civilized and barbarian. As a result she enjoys a fetishized and idealized status, and her 15-year-old breast is its visual core" (129). And the lascivious depiction of the black women surrounding the signare emphasizes her availability; though free, she inhabits the same visual register of the three women who, presumably, could be "sold and used at any point." Indeed, it is their presence that compels the viewer to do a double-take, to peer closely at her left breast in a futile effort to discern whether it is indeed bare. And finally, there is the space between the signare and her attendants and what that space between might tell us about the signares' experiences of a racially and geographically specific womanhood in the century before the appearance of this image.

I contend that the visual demands that we confront the precariousness of the signare's liberty by attending to the specter of terror that surrounds her. It is there, palpable, if we see the women that surround her, the captive subjects who are not allowed even a pretense of modesty. It bears repetition that scholarly and popular historiographies of the signares narrate a linear progression from the signares' roots as African women, whether free or captive, to their entrance, deliberately or by force, into the sexual relationships that secured their status as signares. In these narratives, the signares' cultural hybridity and mélange notwithstanding, their roles (always sexual), first as intermediaries, then as extralegal wives (concubines) and commercial agents, and finally as elite women in "demographically mature" Saint-Louis and Gorée, acquire a predictability, consistency, and stability that assert an inevitability to their hypervisible presence in the islands' material and imaginative spaces and a transparent stability of their agency and power within the protocolonial slave societies.

Still, there is a tension. The record cracks. The presence of the black women, their reminder of the cyclical relationship between slavery and freedom so inextricable from the islands' liminal, diasporic geography, belies the coherency of such narratives. Indeed, James Searing insists that we understand, against their political and economic power, the precariousness of freedom for the islands' habitants: "The *habitants* could easily fall victim to the trade system they served. . . . During the British occupation [of Gorée from 1779 to 1784] a free Muslim *habitant* from Saint Louis, who was employed by the British as a courier, was kidnapped while delivering dispatches to the Gambia and sold to a French slaver in spite of the fact that 'he was a freeman . . . spoke the French language fluently, and had dispatches in his pocket to a French governor'" (citing *House of Commons Sessional Papers*, LXXIII, 6, in *West African Slavery*, 115). After almost two weeks and forceful negotiations, the habitant was finally returned to the British commander of Gorée, "but in such a condition as would have forced compassion from a Savage" (115). According to Searing, it was this precariousness of the habitants' freedom that led them to develop and assert a "political and military autonomy" in "reaction to their daily experience of the brutality of the slave trade, aggravated by European rivalries on the coast" (115). As I examine in chapter 3, the male habitants used their access to spheres of publicly recognized power—including holding public office, participating in military operations, and publishing petitions to the French general assembly—as means for negotiating their autonomy. Significantly, the male habitants of the island came to hold such power because the relationships between the signares and French administrators and soldiers produced a male class of mulattos who, as they came of age within these patriarchal slave societies, gradually became "political spokesmen and heads of households" by the late eighteenth century (113). In contrast to the male habitants, the signares, by virtue of their gender within a heteropatriarchal-dominated society and despite the resultant power accorded them, engaged in a more private set of negotiations for their autonomy, especially as their dominance declined over the course of the eighteenth century.

And here let me be clear. I am considering what happens *within diaspora*, how the subjects represented in the image's figures might subvert or otherwise avert the heteropatriarchal gaze that otherwise defines what and whom we see in the image generally and in the signares specifically. What I am interested in is how we might think through questions of self-possession for the subject marked African, female, and black or mulatta outside of male claims to her body and its signification. And neither am I interested in fantasy: I am not invested in delineating an intraracial sisterhood that trivializes differences in captive status. Rather, I am interested in reading these figures as social subjects who encountered the discursive and material spaces of Gorée and Saint-Louis as African women. These subjects moved through and inhabited overlapping intimate spaces.

Thus, to consider the intimate negotiations of desire and sexuality is not only to consider heterosexual acts between African black and mulatta women and European men as sexual transactions that mark commercial and cultural struggles and exchanges between African and European merchants and politicians; it is to consider such intimate acts made public to be constitutive of a gendered diasporic experience. (And here again is the violence of the archive: How do we center the signare in an analysis of this particular image without further disappearing the black persons transformed to pornographic objects framing her?) Even the most celebratory accounts of the signares indicate that their status and power was fluid and even relative. Brooks tells us that protocolonial defenses of the extralegal marriages à la mode du pays between Frenchmen and indigenous women on the islands "invoked Christian precepts, arguing that Eurafrican women and girls would be saved from living in sin, since circumstances made Eurafricans dependent on whites for their livelihoods" (*Eurafricans*, 211). He thus surmises: "That Eurafrican females were alleged to be dependent suggests that they—and their mothers—were held apart by Wolof society" (211). The signares' apparent simultaneous power and vulnerability raise important questions. How do gender and sex shape our own understanding of what it means to have power in a slave society, to negotiate one's social identity and one's own safety? How did indigenous structures of gender shape the women's ability to make choices about their sexual partners within their own communities? Was it possible for a woman to refuse a relationship with a white male stranger? What would such refusal look like? What conditions might have enticed or coerced her into such a relationship? How would she have understood the relationship? Once established in such relationships, did women have recourse to protection from their indigenous ethnic group should they suffer abuse at the hands of the European men? Would the women have experienced and theorized such abuse differently depending on the race and nation of the abusive man? As middlewomen, did the signares negotiate on their own behalf or on that of their indigenous communities?

We need also consider, here and again, the significance of these acts happening in the geographically and imaginatively liminal spaces of Gorée and Saint-Louis. It is also important to remember that while the islands' liminality rendered them open to possibility and resistance for subjects who inhabited them, neither Saint-Louis nor Gorée was a safe place for subjects marked African, male or female. Indeed, looking backward from the present, the amputation of that possibility for power and agency for subjects produced by and marked African, black, and mulatto/a in an Atlantic trade triangle seems inevitable. However, as Barbara Myerhoff reminds us regarding liminality, "Underlying all these traits [of liminal subjects] are lurking sacrality and power that accompany movement toward the borders of the uncharted and unpredictable" ("Rites," 117). What we need to hold in mind, then, is that none of this was inevitable. While it is evident from popular and historical accounts that the signares eventually established a unique ethnic group on the islands, the habitants, the question of how the women imagined themselves and what resources or repertoires they drew from in negotiating their new positions demands our attention.

The abundant descriptions of the signares in eighteenth- and nineteenth-century travel narratives make clear that they were under constant observation, indeed surveillance, from white European males invested in guiding their respective national and company policies vis-à-vis the relationships of administrators, soldiers, and employees with these women. Of course, given the heterosexual and patriarchal paradigm central to the colonizing enterprise, such attention to the island's women should not surprise us. As Jennifer Morgan notes, citing Stephen Greenblatt in examining the Spanish colonial project in the Americas, "The female 'go-between' was crucial in encounter narratives. This woman figured as a pliable emissary who could be returned to her people as a sign of Spanish generosity.... Indeed, her ability to receive European goods—to be made familiar through European intervention—served as evidence of her own people's savagery, disorder, and distance from civility" ("'Some,'" 172). Indeed, the nomenclature of the signares precludes their full immersion into white womanhood. Archival and contemporary sources repeatedly remark the etymology of the term to be derived from the Portuguese *senhora*, thus marking the women as Portuguese. Within the historical context of seventeenth- and eighteenth-century Africa and French and British travelers' accounts of the people they encountered, "Portuguese" was a marker for blackness and African. For example, Richard Jobson's 1623 account of travel along the river Gambia describes the inhabitants:

> And these are, as they call themselves, *Portingales*, and some of them seeme the same; others of them are *Molatoes*, between blacke and white, but the most part as blacke as the naturall inhabitants: they are scattered, some two or three dwellers in a place, and are all married, or rather keepe with them the countrey black women, of whom they beget children, howbeit they have amongst them, neither Church, nor Frier, nor any other religious order. It does manifestly appeare, that they are such, as have been banished, or fled away, from forth either of *Portingall*, or the Iles belonging unto that government.... The conditions

they live subject unto, under the blacke kings, makes it appeare, they have little comfort in any Christian countrey, or else themselves are very careless. (*Golden Trade*, 35–37)

Jobson's description makes clear the distance between "Portuguese" in an African context and whiteness. Those who call themselves Portuguese are indistinguishable from the "natural inhabitants" of Africa; for Jobson, their distance from whiteness is marked by their skin tone and the absence of an identifiable (from a European perspective) "religious order." It is not clear from the historical record whether the women named themselves "signares" or whether Europeans assigned the name to them (Brooks, *Eurafricans*, 215). And while, as Brooks notes, one high-ranking French official "observed that 'signare' was applied to all Eurafrican women, but only to those African women who were free and rich," this official's framing of the nomenclature opens with the African women: "All the free and rich African women, and all the mulâtresses, call themselves Signares, and the custom of taking this title is general enough in all of West Africa . . . dating from the arrival of the Portuguese in Africa."[25] Thus, the term marked the women, regardless of how much their skin tone ranged from "a complexion the color of cream to that of coffee touched with milk," to be as "blacke as the naturall inhabitants." And whether or not the sources use the specific term *signare*, European travelers' descriptions of the women inhabitants of Saint-Louis and Gorée in terms of their complexions, dress, and how "strongly attached" they are to the white men consistently remind the reader that no matter how closely the signares may have approached white womanhood, at the end of the day, they were sexual objects reduced to their use-value in a heteropatriarchal transatlantic slave economy.

Through these same sources, however, seeps the "seething presence" of the signares' experiences of this surveillance. Reading against the grain of archival sources opens a space suggestive of the signares' subjectivity.[26] For example, the Reverend John Lindsay, after detailing the women's chastity and beauty, warns:

But with these good qualities in the southern ladies, I must not omit another, tho' I shall leave it to yourself in what catologue to place it,—whether in the noble or ignoble column.—As we in England have a weapon, conveniently laying by the fire-side,—vulgarly stil'd the woman's weapon; so have they here, but of a nature far more tremendous. There are few women who have not in their houses, ready hanging on a nail, the saw of a sword-fish, with which in occasions of quarrel they tear and mangle each other in a manner most dreadful. (*Voyage*, 79–80)

No matter how "wonderfully tractable, remarkably polite both in conversation and manners, and in the point of keeping themselves neat and clean . . . far surpass[ing] the Europeans in every respect," the women of Gorée are, at the end of it all—literally so, as Lindsay's commentary on the violent nature of the women closes the chapter—savages (77). Lindsay offers no speculation as to why the women "tear and mangle each other in a manner most dreadful." He is confident his reader will not question the "why"; after all, the women are women, and they are not white. As women, as not white, in 1758, reason and rationality were not accessible to the signares. Just as the nomenclature of the signares marks their blackness, so too do travelers' asides and caveats remind their readers and us that these subjects are always framed through a classifying lens that reads the women as first and foremost African.[27] Lindsay's description thus depicts an unreasoned, savage competition amongst the women.

In the same breath, however, Lindsay's description reveals the extent of the surveillance to which the signares were subjected and in that revelation inadvertently offers evidence of how the women may have negotiated that surveillance. That Lindsay, a British chaplain traveling with a military squadron, can reveal what is "hanging on a nail" inside any woman's house indicates the limits of privacy for the signares. Likewise, Pruneau's details of the signares' intimate preparations in their toilette before venturing in public, discussed in chapter 1, reveal even the domestic space to be yet another place where the signares found themselves on display, subject to the prying, desiring eyes of stranger European visitors. Rather than reading along with an archive that naturalizes the visual and textual spectacle of African subjects reduced to being black bodies on perpetual display, reading against the grain of the archival evidence means to cast a skeptical eye upon the reasons offered by the archive for understanding what European travelers saw. Reading against the grain, that Lindsay ends his chapter detailing the "ladies" of the island with this stunning revelation haunts the reader searching for an account of how these "ladies" inhabited, experienced, and understood the status of signareship.

Lindsay's seemingly throwaway observation of the weapon every signare keeps, ready at hand in her home, forcefully reminds us that the signares were black women who lived their lives on two island slave entrepôts. Indeed, the signares' sexual and racial identities placed them within the same visual taxonomy as the captive African women who would have lived on the islands as household slaves held by the signares or would have been forcefully moved through the island as cargo, and who most certainly would have suffered the racial and sexual violence endemic to the transatlantic slave trade. As Euro-African mixed-race concubines to European men, the signares were subjects not only marked but indeed constituted by the transatlantic trade. And here again, to insist on the persistence and centrality of sexual violence in constituting a black Atlantic female subject across captivity and freedom is not to flatten or trivialize the differences that matter between those girls and women made commodity and cargo and those made intermediary businesswomen. Indeed, what I am working through here is precisely that difference and how both captive and free(d) subjects may have imagined that difference and the possibilities for moving across it. At the same time, to only understand that difference as a given, as an inevitability, is to miss something crucial: that the acquisition of that status afforded the signares depended not only on the signares' desire to be free but also on their desire not to be unfree. In order to understand the process of diaspora, we must understand its incoherency, its nonlinearity, that these two things are true at the same time: the signares' hypervisibility very likely ensured a particular kind of safety and security at the very same time it signaled their very vulnerability.

Reading their apparent seamless transition from enslaved, captive subjects to highly visible and highly desirable "ladies" demands we keep in mind Saidiya Hartman's observation, in the context of U.S. slavery, that "it is not simply fortuitous that gender emerges in relation to violence; that is, gender is constituted in terms of negligible and unredressed injury and the propensity for violence" ("Seduction," 554). Because what we are left with, in the "tearing and mangling," at the end of a chapter describing their beauty, chastity, and utility to European men on the island, African diasporic female subjects marked by privilege, visibility, and power across the archive, are "hieroglyphics of the flesh" (Spillers, "'Mama's Baby,'" 67). In Hortense Spillers's formulation, "If we think of the 'flesh' as a primary narrative, then we mean its seared, divided, ripped-apartness, riveted to the ship's hole, fallen, or 'escaped' overboard" (67). Of course, Spillers is speaking about the effects of theft, captivity, and enslavement on the "ungendering" of the black female subject. Indeed, the most useful analyses of black women's subjectivities examine the "layers of attenuated meanings, made an excess in time, over time, assigned by a particular historical order" that captivity, theft, enslavement, and their constitutive rapes and other brutalities have imposed on possibilities for living and experiencing black womanhood in the Americas (65). "Ready hanging on a nail, the saw of a sword-fish," coupled with the specter of the signares' mangled and torn flesh, underscores the precariousness of the signares' free status and the inextricability of their subject formation from that of the captive black female subject bound for slavery in the Americas.

In her consideration of the "ungendering" of the captive black female subject, Spillers "suggest[s] that 'gendering' takes place within the confines of the domestic, an essential metaphor that then spreads its tentacles for male and female subject over a wider group of human and social purposes" ("'Mama's Baby,'" 72). Within the contexts of Saint-Louis and Gorée, the domestic space defined the near incorporation of the signares into European notions of womanhood. As early as 1685, the Senegal Company director on Saint-Louis, Michel Jajolet de La Courbe, "reported that each company employee kept a female servant to do his wash" (Searing, *West African Slavery*, 98).[28] By the mid-eighteenth century, such "female servants" had emerged in travelers' journals as "ladies" and "women" as they achieved the status of wives or mistresses of European officers, soldiers, and administrators. However, such status remained inextricable from the domestic services they provided their European male "husbands." Thus, immediately preceding his description of the women's violent savagery, Lindsay described the benefits of having African women serve as sexual companions to white men temporarily stationed at Gorée, noting:

> If we consider the good of the public, our mixing with the natives settles their affections on the most lasting foundations: and if we consider the benefits accruing to those in particular whom we have sent to the continent, it must have still a greater weight. A few women amongst so many men, find it almost impossible to continue chaste, especially in the army; but on the contrary contract distempers, which, with the other drudgeries camp-women are subject to, as washing, ironing, and cooking, in so scorching a climate, hurries them to their graves, dragging even many of their male companions with them. . . . Whereas, on the other hand, the natives have a thousand times their chastity, and by being in their natural climate, are capable of being of much greater use in a family. (*Voyage*, 78)

The signares, then, were valued by Europeans both because they explicitly and directly kept European men temporarily stationed on the islands alive and comfortable and because they indirectly protected the chastity and lives of white European women, as the signares precluded the need for and thus the consequences of having "camp women" on the islands.[29] Lindsay's comments underscore that, despite repeated emphases on the signares' beauty and sensuality, at stake was European survival, itself dependent upon African women's work in the domestic sphere. As cooks, housekeepers, and nurses, the signares offered the stranger European men, who had brought themselves to a hostile landscape and climate, the comfort of health, nourishment, and intimate relationships.

At the same time, Lindsay's closing note on "the saw of a sword-fish" and its putative use signifies that this same domestic sphere was, for the signares, treacherous. Lindsay's description, coupled with his decision to end a chapter in which he has portrayed the "native women" of the island as chaste and even "desireable" with such a vivid picture of these same women's reversion to savagery, reminds us that the signares' gendered status as virtuous ladies was never a foregone conclusion but rather one that had to be constantly and forcefully negotiated and protected by the women themselves (*Voyage*, 78). Furthermore, Lindsay's preceding discussion of the women's chastity inadvertently suggests that the signares endured constant challenges and threats to their sexual autonomy even as these threats were cloaked in the language of desire and admiration. Lindsay admonishes: "But tho' I talk in this free manner of those females, a European will find himself prodigiously disappointed, if he shall fancy he has nothing to do but to take himself a seat and sit down: I believe, that although there are prostitutes amongst them, yet while many may confess they have been rebuff'd with disdain, few of the English as yet, with any share of truth, can boast of having obtain'd illicit favors" (79). Read against the grain, Lindsay's caveat reveals a place where, despite all contrary signals from the women, who have "a thousand times" the "chastity" of European camp women, white European men, assuredly soldiers, officers, and company officials, would likely presume, upon first arrival on the islands, these women to be wanton and thus available for the taking. Lindsay's assertion of the women's sexual agency absolutely depends upon the fact of their constant subjection to unwanted sexual advances from stranger European men. Read thusly, Lindsay's description demands that we imagine what it would have meant to be free women on these islands, separated from one's family and community, facing a constant influx of European men who most surely arrived with the expectations of sexually licentious African women. Here again, the geography matters: Gorée and Saint-Louis were island entrepôts that frequently changed hands between the British and the French and thus witnessed continuous arrivals and departures of administrators, officers, and soldiers. In addition, as Searing notes, "The dangerous [disease] environment contributed to the development of a merchant community which focused on quick profits for individual merchants, followed by a return to the metropole or some healthier French colony" (*West African Slavery*, 97). With a constant influx of European men desiring both sexual intercourse and domestic services, and with their own economic and social reasons for entering into such unions, the islands' women had to be available and indispensable to these men while constantly protecting themselves from unwanted sexual advances. Read against Lindsay's efforts to ungender the women by ending his chapter with a note on their savagery within a domestic sphere, "the saw of a sword-fish" hanging in the women's homes signals the violence that permeated the signares' private lives.

Lindsay's accusation that the women of Gorée used "the saw of a sword-fish" to "tear and mangle each other in a manner most dreadful" should thus give us considerable pause: we are supposed to believe that the biggest physical threats on a racialized slave entrepôt facing the "native women" were "occasions of quarrel" with other black and mulatta women. Again, Lindsay does not make explicit any causes for "occasions of quarrel" that would lead to such brutal violence amongst the women on Gorée. For Lindsay and his readers, that the women are native would be a self-evident explanation for their savagery.[30] But given the precariousness of the signares' freedom as outlined above, compounded by the specificity of their gendered and sexualized subject positions within these slave societies and their subjection to constant observation and scrutiny by stranger European men, the assertion that the women inflicted violence upon each other is unsettling, to say the least. At the same time, the illustration depicting the signare and her attendants at the beach underscores what from the perspective of diaspora is another obscenity: a signare's modicum of privacy is predicated upon the pornographic display of the women she holds as slaves. Thus, rather than romanticize an imagined racial and gendered sisterhood among the women with an outright dismissal of Lindsay's claims, it may be worthwhile to consider how the conditions of living as black and mixed-race women famous for their beauty, sexuality, and wealth may have shaped relationships among the signares.

I suggest such a consideration not because of a presumption of or a desire for the validity of Lindsay's assertion; indeed, the rhetorical work of Lindsay's narrative precludes a presumption of an objective, neutral perspective on his part. However, just as Pruneau's description of the exquisite signares echoes in Deren's descriptions of the beautiful, ephemeral mulatta goddess Ezili Freda, so does the very different spectacle of black and mixed-race women who "tear and mangle each other in a manner most dreadful" echo both in another quality of Ezili Freda and in the characteristics of her sister, the battle-scarred Ezili Dantò, whose tongue was cut "by her own people, people fighting on the same side, people who could not trust her to guard their secrets" (Brown, *Mama Lola*, 229). Perhaps most urgently, as the object of Ezili Freda's jealous rage for bearing the child of Ogou, Ezili Dantò "still carries the mark of Maitress Erzulie's sword on her cheek" (Brown, "Olina," 11). Ezili Freda's jealousy extends to any woman who might desire her divine and mortal husbands. Zora Neale Hurston describes Ezili Freda's absolute possession of the men who marry and serve her, explaining: "To women and their desires, she is all but maliciously cruel, for not only does she choose and set aside for herself, young and handsome men and thus bar them from marriage, she frequently chooses married men and thrusts herself between the woman and her happiness" (*Folklore*, 384–87). Furthermore, should any woman dare to interfere in the devotion of Ezili Freda's serviteurs, "no woman could escape the vengeance of the enraged Erzulie" (387).

And here is what it means to read the echo from within diaspora. Lindsay's desire and inability to categorize the presence and uses of "the saw of a sword-fish" as either "noble or ignoble" underscore his outsider status. Because what is at stake within diaspora is not whether the women are "noble or ignoble," not whether their "chastity" or "savagery" exceeds that of English women. If we understand the literal tearing of the signares' flesh to echo in the cut-off tongue and scarred cheek of Ezili Dantò, then we understand that what is at stake are the very possibilities and limits of being free in diaspora. What is at stake is how to forge and maintain the bonds of kinship and community within a freedom born of violence and seduction. In their examination of women's roles in vodou, Claudine Michel, Patrick Bellegarde-Smith, and Marlène Racine-Toussaint begin by quoting a "well-known song sung in ceremonies in honor of Dantò" ("From the Horses' Mouths," 70). The singer pleads with Dantò to save her children from drowning. The authors argue that the song "reveals a free flow between 'me' and 'us,' between the singular and the collective. One seldom notices the change if one ever did. 'If you see *me* fall in the waters, [it means we are drowning]'" (70, square brackets in the original). While describing Dantò's "maternal love," including the fact that she takes care not only of her own children but also of the children "of her sister Ezili Freda, who pretends not to have any," the authors here do not mention the rivalry between the two (70). However, it is precisely the juxtapositions between care and peril that strike me here: in Freda's violent rivalry with Dantò against her entrusting of the care of her children to the mother she mutilated, and in the need for Dantò's serviteurs to plead for her to rescue them from drowning. From here, within diaspora, that the signares may have indeed "mangled" each other in a fierce rivalry means that these things are all true at once: they were privileged, they enjoyed a degree of safety unavailable to captive black women, and what protection that privilege may have offered was so important that they guarded it fiercely even as they may have loved and cared for one another, and even the protection of privilege and status was not guaranteed. And finally, it matters too that Dantò is a Petwo-Kongo spirit, that in the words of her devotee and spiritual husband, Georges, she is from "l'Afrique Ginen" (the Haitian Creole term for West Africa or West African origins), that while her speech may be unintelligible without translation, she "talks in some African dialect" (René and Houlberg, "My Double," 39, 291). Here again, the echo refuses a coherent story of origins.

Under the Waters

Here again, the echo spirals; here again, the volume of the echo is such that it demands attention. Here again, a haunting: a possibility that the signares did indeed "tear and mangle each other in a manner most dreadful." For the intersection of seductive powers and potential for violence echoes not only in Ezili Freda and Ezili Dantò but yet again in a third iteration of Ezili, Lasirèn, the mermaid. This haunting refuses a facile story of power and resistance, community and affinity. It demands an accounting of the costs of that community. I suggest that listening to Ezili's iterations in Ezili Dantò and Lasirèn begins an accounting as it enables a shift not only from how one reads the archive but from where one in fact sees an archive. Indeed, thus far I have considered the view from a white patriarchal gaze and consequent experiences of that surveillance by free women of color in Atlantic slave-port societies. What the archive does not tell, of course, is how free(d) and enslaved Africans saw and viewed the women the official record presents as free, seductive, and in control of their bodies. This is the question that the official record neither asks nor attempts to consider.

While the resonance between visual and written representations of the quadroons of antebellum New Orleans, the signares of Saint-Louis and Gorée, and Ezili Freda and Ezili Dantò signal a diasporic geography that subverts the official geography of the transatlantic slave trade, it is ironically the official history of the Middle Passage that draws one to Ezili's third iteration, Lasirèn, described briefly in chapter 1 and elaborated below. To see Lasirèn here is to again turn back to another African diasporic water spirit, Mami Wata, in order to contemplate the question of what enslaved black subjects saw passing through these ports. While most studies of Ezili's various manifestations focus on what she embodies as a postcontact manifestation of the Haitian female subject, and while the goddess's immediate signification as a reflection of the lived experience of Haitian women cannot be overemphasized, so the meaning of her taking her devotees beneath the sea cannot be left underexamined.

Indeed, within the context of the slave trade, Lasirèn's danger exceeds what might otherwise be her classical mythic function as a generic siren. Deren informs her reader that the racially illegible Lasirèn "is said to steal children and take them to the bottom of the sea or of a stream, but is also known to bring them up" (*Divine Horsemen*, 308n78). As Brown explains, "People are captured by Lasyrenn and pulled under the water, down to Ginen. . . . A person, usually a woman, disappears for a time—three days, three months, three years. When she returns, she is a changed person. *Her skin has become fairer, her hair longer and straighter.* Most important, she has gained sacred knowledge. Immediately after her return, she is disoriented, *does not talk, and does not remember what happened to her*" (224, emphasis added). And Marilyn Houlberg explains, "Lasirèn has the ability to bring riches and romance, but she can also be violent, and even has the power to lure mortals to a watery death" ("Sirens," 32). At once black and white, at once seductive and dangerous, Lasirèn's pull upon her subjects into the sea and back to Africa invokes a reversal, an undoing of the Middle Passage.

First, perhaps even more than that of Ezili Freda and Ezili Dantò, Lasirèn's racial identity is fluid and often inscrutable; this goddess's inscrutability within an African diasporic religious practice reflects and enacts the resistance to an intrusive, violating, white male heterosexual gaze evident, as the first two sections of the chapter insist, in both mundane and sacred activities of the signares

in eighteenth-century Gorée and Saint-Louis and of the quadroons of antebellum New Orleans. While the desirability of the free(d) mulatta concubine
depends on the near-whiteness of her skin, Lasirèn's inscrutability, in conjunction with the white mulatta Ezili Freda and the black Ezili Dantò, from both
of whom she is inextricable, suggests an insistence on the part of the captive
witness to connect the goddess's seductive powers to something "black, black."
At the same time, read against the signares especially, the transformation of the
captive subject from black to "fair" with "longer, straighter hair" who has "gained
sacred knowledge" may suggest not a valorization of white skin but rather an assessment of how subjects linked to blackness are able to preserve their liberty in
the slave societies.

Second, as noted in chapter 1, Lasirèn echoes Mami Wata, a West African
water goddess who, "like the Haitian mermaid . . . brings wealth and love as
long as 'contracts' with her are not broken. Both spirits are associated with foreign contact, times of rapid change, and new technologies" (Houlberg, "Sirens,"
33). Indeed, Mami Wata, a diasporic goddess whose pervasive presence across
West Africa belies her "origins[, which] lie 'overseas,'" resonates here especially
(Drewal, "Introduction," 23). As Henry Drewal explains, "Of special note, she
can bring good fortune in the form of money, and as a 'capitalist' par excellence,
her power increased between the fifteenth and the twentieth centuries, the era
of growing international trade between Africa and the rest of the world" (23).
Again, what if we imagine Lasirèn to constitute an archive of what captive subjects passing through slave ports like Gorée and Saint-Louis may have understood when they saw free(d) black and mulatta women who profited from their
sexual connections with foreign white men? And what might the echo of Lasirèn in Mami Wata suggest about the nonlinearity of temporality and geography in how one imagines freedom in an African diaspora?

Finally, Mami Wata "also represents danger, for a liaison with Mami Wata
often requires substantial sacrifice, such as the life of a family member or celi-
bacy in the realm of mortals" (Drewal, "Introduction," 25). Lasirèn's connection
to Mami Wata and the specificity of the commercial dimensions of this connection help us consider the possibilities for and stakes of reading the free(d)
mulatta concubine as a diasporic subject. The geography of the free(d) mulatta
concubine is what matters here. While interracial sex was more mundane and
pervasive than official histories would want us to believe, the fact that the most
iconic of free(d) mulatta concubines inhabited consummately diasporic ports,
drew their wealth and importance from their proximity to water and waterways,
is no small detail. Against the histories of celebrated or at least notorious free(d)
mulatta concubines in slave entrepôts, how do we understand the worship of
goddesses who draw their wealth and importance from the commerce enabled

by their proximity to water? How do we understand such worship against the threat of violence the presence of each signals to her devotees? And if Lasirèn reflects or enacts a memory of what enslaved subjects saw, understood, and remembered when catching a glimpse of the signares, if Lasirèn is part of an archive that resists knowing, what does it mean to explain this subaltern, resistant, and even subversive archive in terms anyone can understand?

To attempt resolution here would, as VèVè Clark insists, "undermine the principles of revision" enacted and demanded by the theory and practice of "marasa consciousness" that propels my exploration of the echo's spiral ("Developing," 57). Following Clark's beguiling and generative "final comment: to defamiliarize our tidy, binary constructs is in *marasa* practice to divine" (57), I offer instead a pause to contemplate the water's edge. There is a song for Lasirèn cited in several places and offered here as transcribed and translated by Karen McCarthy Brown:

> Lasyrenn, Labalenn,
> Chapo'm tonbe nan lanmè
> M'ap fè karès ak Lasyrenn,
> Chapo'm tonbe nan lanmè
> M'ap fè dodo ak Lasytrenn,
> Chapo'm tonbe nan lanmé.
> The mermaid, the whale,
> My hat falls into the sea.
> I caress the mermaid,
> My hat falls into the sea.
> I lie down with the mermaid,
> My hat falls into the sea. (*Mama Lola*, 222–23)

The song is sung by Lasirèn's serviteurs who seek either wealth, "a deeper and truer picture of self," or simply comfort (Brown, *Mama Lola*, 223). As Gerdès Fleurant explains, however, it is "usually a man" who is lured by Lasirèn's promises of riches, and it is this man who "may soon follow" his hat into the sea, drowning ("Vodun," xxiii–xxiv). Against this song, within the echo's spiral, what if we consider the portrait of the signares at the beach? What if we imagine the subject whose gaze she draws, helped by the overwhelming fantasy of hypersexual black womanhood that surrounds her? What if here we imagine the person who loses his hat to be that white male European whose desire for African, black, and mulatto women was inextricable from his desire for wealth and power? What if it is about the possibility that he must be careful—not because of a colonial concern for morality and the integrity of the white family and white property but because of a desire from within diaspora, from within blackness, to imagine something besides, other than, the dichotomous ways we read the free(d) mulatta concubine, that she was either happy to sleep her way to freedom or that she experienced every moment as rape. How do we talk about this possibility without disavowing both the injury of rape and the myriad sexual and racial violences that attended the utter imbalance of power between Europe and Africa, black and white, captive and free, male and female? Here, to ask these questions is to press upon the tension between what was desired and what happened, and what could happen. Here, to ask these questions is to suggest that what is important about Marie Laveau, the signares, what is important about the free(d) mulatta concubine within diaspora is not whether they held power but the possibility that their power could have been even greater.

CHAPTER 3

Authority, Kinship,
and Possession

Two intersecting and insistent silences run through academic and popular representations of the free(d) mulatta concubine across the black Atlantic: the invisibility of free(d) men of color who historically shared these women's racial and class positions, and the absence of first-person narrative accounts from the free women of color identified in primary and secondary documents as lovers and mistresses of white European and American men.[1] Within the framework of a black Atlantic triangle, these silences are startling, especially when one considers that they are not archival, that both groups in fact produced documentation of their presence. Across French Atlantic colonial spaces, free men of color played active and visible roles politically, materially, creatively, and socially and left behind an evidentiary trail of written documents attesting to their historical impact.[2] As well, within a U.S. African American context, free(d) black women produced a literary archive that testifies to the particularly gendered precariousness of their lives within racialized slave societies. Furthermore, in contrast to their portrayal in popular and academic representations as historical subjects, free(d) women of color who found themselves sexually attached to white men were as surely attached familially to free(d) men of color and to a wider black free(d) and enslaved cultural and social milieu.

This chapter begins with the contention that together, the erasures of free(d) men's and women's perspectives in the published archive of the free(d) mulatta concubine produce a hypervisible figure whose apparent familiarity and recognizability in turn enact a domino-like chain of silences and erasures of free(d) and enslaved black subjects. In this chapter I focus on two specific consequences. First, within the heterosexual and patriarchal economy of racialized slavery and its legacy, the invisibility of free(d) men of color from the published record of the free(d) mulatta concubine implies a relinquishment of black and mulatto male claims to her possession. Second, the apparent absence of first-person narrative accounts by subjects identified as free(d) mulatta concubines circumscribes our understanding of how these women imagined their own social identities, possibilities for freedom and mobility, and control over their sexual bodies in slave societies across Atlantic places. The effect of this double-pronged erasure is ironic: the free(d) mulatta concubine, an arguably quintessential African diasporic subject, appears in the popular archive as a solitary, spectral figure, fully possessed by white men and absolutely detached from any recognizable black kinship community.[3]

Indeed, to frame and read the free(d) mulatta concubine as such—free, near-white, licentious, and attached to white men—suggests that the question of her possession and belonging were settled long ago. The popular narrative of the near-white woman of African descent who achieves freedom, or at least the appearance of freedom, through her sexual desirability and availability to white men does reflect at least one material dimension of the sexual and racial economies of slavery and colonization. However, this narrative has acquired a hyper-visibility that distorts a comprehensive understanding of the dynamic interplay between kinship, race, sex, desire, and violence in the making of such freedom. And that such a narrative requires silence on the part of free(d) men and women of color paradoxically signals that the question of the possession of the free(d) mulatta concubine is very much unsettled. Furthermore, that the erasure of authoritative free men of color and the nonacknowledgment of the silence of the free(d) mulatta concubine continue to happen in popular and academic narratives produced well after the time of the transatlantic slave trade and American slavery suggests that the stakes of possession exceed that time as well.

While the causes of the silence may seem self-evident in their reflection of a dominant white patriarchal racial and sexual order, it is the question of how claims to possession of the free(d) mulatta concubine in diaspora exceed the mundane that concerns me here. Within a heteropatriarchal paradigm, that the free(d) mulatta's sexualized person becomes a site of contestation for masculine claims to authority seems obvious (see especially Garraway, *Libertine Colony*; and Morgan, "'Some'"). As I contend in this chapter, however, contestations over possession of the free(d) mulatta concubine in diaspora exceed the mundane in part because of where they happen. That is, if the celebrated free(d) mulatta concubine inhabits places that are materially diasporic in their location and function, as surely were Gorée, Saint-Domingue, and New Orleans, where the interdependent meanings of freedom and race are at their most tenuous, then the struggle for her possession marks a struggle not only for claims to masculine power within a colonial or national heteropatriarchal framework but also, and more importantly, for control over the very meaning and nature of freedom within these places where racialization, captivity, and dispossession happen.

Furthermore, I am compelled by how these struggles ~~~~
the racial legibility of the free(d) mulatta concubine in ~~~~
enter into and negotiate racialized, diasporic identities. As previous chapters explore, across the black Atlantic enslaved and free(d) women of African descent
thrust into sexualized relationships with white men came from a variety of social
positions, including captivity, and inhabited a range of skin tones and racialized
identities. And yet, over and over, the archive produced by white European and
American men writes these women as almost exclusively mulatta and always
powerfully seductive. Thus, claims to possession of the free(d) mulatta concubine
turn not only on who claims to possess her within heteropatriarchal and racialized discursive spaces but also on the question of her very appearance in history
and memory. Furthermore, the hypervisibility of the free(d) mulatta concubine
renders the treachery of these spaces for any woman of African descent, notwithstanding where she falls on a skin-color spectrum, invisible. The revision of
the sexual economy of slavery to a story that focuses on a suddenly appearing
mulatta absent any apparent connection to a social community outside her white
male sexual partner erases the origins of these economies in forced and coercive
sexual relations between stranger white men and black African women.

However, I am not interested in correcting the historical record. That is, I
am not so much interested in recovering the voice or presence of free(d) men
of color in order to affirm their claims to heteropatriarchal possession of free(d)
women of color. Nor am I invested in proving what the signares of Senegal, the
quadroons of New Orleans, or the mulatta women of colonial Saint-Domingue
looked like. And certainly, I do not seek to offer a silenced voice of a free(d)
mulatta concubine as any kind of authentic representation or redemption. What
I am interested in is this: How does the archive of the free(d) mulatta concubine
produce absences, and how might reading through these absences demand that
we understand the experience of diaspora, so often cast as a collective experience, to be also the most intimate, private, and individual of practices? Thus, it is
those spaces between—between white and black masculine claims to the free(d)
mulatta concubine, between historical subjectivity and imaginative objectification—that most interest me here.

This chapter thus begins with the intersecting erasures of the perspectives of
free(d) men of color and free(d) mulatta wives and mistresses of white men as
a point of departure for considering the sexual and racial economies of blackness in diaspora as a set of domestic, intimate negotiations. I argue that free(d)
women *and* men of color resisted white male claims to possession of the free(d)
mulatta concubine and that they did so explicitly from within and through diaspora. Accordingly, I assemble this chapter's objects of analysis first to assert and
then to read against competing male claims to possession of the free(d) mulatta

concubine. I open with an examination of a 1789 work, Dominique Harcourt Lamiral's *L'Affrique et le peuple affriquain*. Opening the work is a forty-page *cahier des doléances* (list of grievances) composed by the male habitants of Saint-Louis; it was presented to the French Estates-General by Lamiral, a French commercial agent. In this cahier, the black and mulatto habitants protest the unfair trade relationships enforced by the Senegal Company and assert their rights as men made French by virtue of their blood-kinship to France via the signares. Attached to the petition is Lamiral's nearly four-hundred-page appendix, in which he purports to "paint truthfully and frankly the mores" of the people of Senegal and offers, according to George E. Brooks, one of the earliest-known visual depictions of the signares ("Artists' Depictions," 82).[4] Examining the tension between the claims to authority and agency in the petition and Lamiral's accompanying and undermining appendix, I establish the centrality of the signares and by extension the free(d) mulatta concubine in the legibility and recognition of the habitants' authority. Again engaging Clark's theory of marasa consciousness, I consider how the visual image in Lamiral's text disrupts a facile reading of binary claims to possession of the mulatta by tracing the image's (re)iteration in an 1806 English edition of a French text by a former French trading company official stationed in Senegal in 1785–86, Jean Baptiste Léonard Durand's *A Voyage to Senegal*.

Finally, against these readings, I turn to a two-page letter written from the island of Gorée on July 6, 1737. The letter's author signs herself, "A—— Gusban, Negresse [*sic*]."[5] I argue that this letter's appearance is at once utterly disruptive of the discursive history of the signares and barely legible outside the paradigm of the free(d) mulatta concubine in diaspora. As with the habitants' cahier des doléances, at stake in Gusban's letter is her unfair treatment at the hands of the current French trading company. Addressing her letter to company officials in France, Gusban writes on behalf of her ten-year-old daughter, who should receive an inheritance from the trading company that formerly employed her deceased father. As I examine below, the contents of her letter and the place and date from which it was written strongly suggest that she was a signare and that her daughter's father was white. Her signature as "Negresse" thus invites us to consider how women otherwise almost unanimously represented in contemporaneous and contemporary accounts as free(d) mulatta concubines may have discursively and imaginatively resisted such labeling. And more importantly, Gusban's assertion of her role as a mother writing in order to defend her young daughter's rights enacts a paradigm that resituates questions of privacy and freedom in diaspora from focusing on the sexuality of the free(d) mulatta concubine's body to centering on the intimacy of her capacity to protect her own daughter.[6]

These documents, read together, thus reveal the centrality of kinship in black diasporic claims to authority and autonomy. Furthermore, central to the documents' assertions of kinship are claims to discursive and bodily possession of the free(d) mulatta concubine. And while the appearances of these documents are inextricable from the material histories of eighteenth-century Saint-Louis and Gorée, the stakes of possession, gender, kinship, and authority echo across diasporic time and space, most resonantly in Ezili Dantò. In this chapter, Ezili Dantò is a fleeting but significant presence, appearing briefly to illuminate how claims to possession of the free(d) mulatta concubine turn not only on who claims to possess her within heteropatriarchal discursive spaces but also on the question of her very appearance in history and memory. Thus, at stake in this chapter is not only how the archive and its selective publication shape our ability to see and recognize self-possession in Atlantic spaces as diasporic acts but also how practices of self-possession may limit as much as open possibilities for family, kinship, and freedom across a black Atlantic.

Methodologically, I center my reading here specifically on objects from Gorée and Saint-Louis for the following reasons. First, to be in diaspora is to be in two contradictory places at once: where one is, dispossessed, and where one wants to be, a place of belonging. There is in diaspora an unavoidable (although not necessarily undesirable) tension between the specificity of one's location—be it geographic, racial, gendered, sexual, and so on—and the appeal of a cohesive, coherent collectivity across time and space.[7] The signares, as "African" mulattas inextricable from and materially grounded in the consummate diasporic spaces of Gorée and Saint-Louis, offer a unique opportunity to explore the paradox articulated by Dionne Brand in *A Map to the Door of No Return*, that the site of dispossession is also the imagined place of belonging. Gusban's letter and the habitants' petition invite us to examine a different nuance of this paradox. Unlike black and African subjects in the Americas, the signares appear to have stayed in place. Thus, on the one hand and in contrast to the limits imposed by law, demography, location, and political will in the slave societies of the Americas, the habitants—the free men of color on Gorée and Saint-Louis—are able to rise to a degree of political and economic power because of their geographic location and their kinship with the signares. On the other hand is Gusban's letter, which details the insecurity of her and her daughter's claims to property ownership and thus to freedom even in this place of imagined belonging, even as the presence of women like Gusban is what facilitates the political and economic power of the habitants.

The second rationale for this chapter's focus on eighteenth-century objects from Gorée and Saint-Louis arises from the problem of temporality in theorizing African diasporic identities. As recent scholarship in the field insists, conceptualizing diaspora invokes anachronistic paradigms that distort our understandings of how and when subjects become black and/or diasporic. Building on this theoretical framework, I contend that the signares' archive itself implores a nonchronological ordering and reading. As noted in previous chapters, many of the most widely circulated visual representations of the signares originate in a book published well after the decline of the signares' economic and social prominence, Colonel Henri Frey's 1890 *Côte Occidentale d'Afrique: Vues, scènes, croquis*. In inescapable ways, we can only imagine and see the signares of eighteenth-century Senegal through a lens saturated with late nineteenth-century circum-Atlantic discourses of race, sex and sexuality, power, and colonial and imperial geographies. Here then, focusing on the signares enables a reading of claims to possession of the free(d) mulatta concubine that attends to a most constitutive symptom of diaspora: the palpable, disorienting, and decidedly nonlinear experience of experiencing one's present, past, and future simultaneously.

Assertion

In 1789 the black and mulatto habitants of Saint-Louis submitted their cahier des doléances to the French Estates-General via Dominique Harcourt Lamiral, a French commercial agent. Entitled "Très humbles doléances et remonstrances des habitans du Sénégal aux citoyens français tenant les États-Généraux" (Truly humble complaints and remonstrances of the habitants of Sénégal to the French citizens of the Estates-General), the petition calls for an end to the trade monopoly of the Senegal Company in the region. Within a circum-Atlantic and diasporic context, the political atmosphere in which the petition appeared was remarkable. The Société des amis noirs, the first French abolitionist organization, had been formed just one year prior to the petition's publication. And of course, 1789 marked a year of upheaval for all of France, including the reinstatement of the Estates-General, political concessions from the king, the storming of the Bastille, and the publication of the Declaration of the Rights of Men. Cahiers de doléances flowed from nearly every sector of French society. That same year Vincent Ogé, a free mulatto from Saint-Domingue, traveled to Paris to "press mulatto claims for full civil and political rights" (Hunt, *French Revolution*, 105). And just two years later, enslaved and free blacks and mulattos in Saint-Domingue would commence their own revolution.

Preceding the habitants' forceful and detailed petition is Lamiral's brief foreword; his appendix to the petition, which runs just over 350 pages, follows. Together, the foreword, petition, and appendix compose Lamiral's *L'Affrique et le peuple affriquain*, published in November 1789. Reading the habitants' petition against Lamiral's accompanying text lays bare competing claims to possession of the free(d) mulatta concubine as they emerge contemporaneously and simultaneously into the archive. As I have argued, representations of the free(d) mulatta concubine travel across the black Atlantic's material and imaginative spaces in circuitous ways that belie a linear production of diaspora. At the same time, we cannot understand the free(d) mulatta concubine's diasporic significance without attending to the geographic and temporal specificity of her manifestations. Thus, reading the habitants' petition, we must consider how, as described by Searing, during the second half of the eighteenth century Saint-Louis and Gorée witnessed an increase and consolidation of the habitants' trading power as "the *habitants* became nearly obligatory intermediaries in the trade between the islands and the mainland. European merchants increasingly remained confined to the coastal islands and relied on the *habitants* to deliver export commodities to them" (*West African Slavery*, 107). Whereas the signares in their interdependent roles as businesswomen and sexual partners initially established their economic power on the islands, by 1789 the male habitants had supplanted the signares as heads of household on both islands, thus achieving "demographic maturity," and they had "[come] of age politically and economically" (113, 114). The historical record therefore indicates that within an Atlantic slave economy, these two island entrepôts, in large part due to their diasporic geography, were places where black and mulatto men and women had the best chance of achieving self-possession. Reading the habitants' petition against Lamiral's accompanying text offers a lens through which we may discern the shape, dimension, potential, and limits of that possibility.

Within this context, the habitants' appeal is full of pathos in its deliberate rhetoric of rights, liberty, nation, and masculinity. The petition opens with a plea that the members of the Estates-General listen to the complaint and act in order "to assure forever the liberty and happiness" of the habitants. The petitioners ask the assembly to entreat the king to listen "to the timid and plaintive voice of the unhappy inhabitants of Sénégal, *who are bent under the intolerable yoke of the horrible despotism of a privileged company.*" Protesting the granting of exclusive rights to the gum and slave trade in the region to the French Senegal Company, the petition details the integral role the habitants play in France's economic and military control in the region: "Whether black or mulatto, we are all French, since it is the blood of Frenchmen that runs through our veins or those of our nephews."[8] The habitants assert not only their right to trade in the region but also their right to be recognized as French subjects.

Indeed, the petition included in Lamiral's work was but one of a series of protests conveyed by the habitants of Saint-Louis and Gorée during the second half of the eighteenth century as they worked to establish their political and economic authority with respect to European trade power in the region.[9] As

Searing insists, the habitants consistently "defined themselves in their protest as slave traders and slave owners, and portrayed themselves as essential links in France's African commerce" (*West African Slavery*, 112).[10] This record of the habitants' protests and petitions is compelling in that it simultaneously reflects the group's awareness of and insistence on their essential role in France's political and economic position in the region, while, by virtue of the need to protest in the first place, it also underscores the vulnerable position of this group within the geographically intermediary slave-trading spaces of Saint-Louis and Gorée, as discussed in chapter 2. Again, it is important here that two things are simultaneously true: the habitants were, from the French point of view, a force to be reckoned with, a group that was "described as being capable of mobilizing 1,000 slaves," including the highly skilled *laptots* (slave sailor-soldiers), and the habitants were nonwhite men subject to the brutal terms of a racialized slave society.

Read within this context, the habitants' insistence that "whether black or mulatto, we are all French, since it is the blood of Frenchmen that runs through our veins or the veins of our nephews" suggests a complex interplay of race, freedom, gender, desire, and kinship in making their social, political, and economic authority visible to a French supervisory gaze. Their self-conscious reference to their racialized status recognizes the tenuousness of their claim to French citizenship and by extension to French masculinity. At the same time, the allusive reference to the signares through the invocation of the "blood of Frenchmen" is subversive. As emphasized in the historical scholarship, officials in France early on excoriated the roles signares played on Gorée and Saint-Louis; contemporaneous records called the signares prostitutes and deplored the immoral influence the women exerted over European men.[11] The official position against the signares notwithstanding, by the time of the habitants' petition, the system of the signares had produced not only an accumulation of property and wealth but also a stable population of predominantly mulatto families on both islands, with the male habitants having supplanted the signares as heads of households. According to Searing, "The growing political consciousness of the *habitants* encouraged the existing mulatto families to try and maintain a privileged relationship with the French merchants, including supplying them with local wives" (*West African Slavery*, 113). Thus, when the habitants remind the Estates-General that "the blood of Frenchmen runs through our veins or those of our nephews," they cast their claim to a public recognition of their status as Frenchmen through an indirect reference to sex, intimacy, and possession. Their rhetoric here is subversive because it casts the European male possession of the free(d) mulatta concubine not as evidence of conquest or domination of the subordinate male habitants but instead as a strategic maneuver to engender a recognition of the rights of the habitants—"black or mulatto"—to French citizenship.[12]

At the same time, the habitants' allusion to the sexual relationships between French men and the signares as a means toward claiming the men's rights to trade ironically foregrounds their rootedness in African trade and kinship relationships. As noted earlier, histories of the signares frame their emergence within a larger geohistorical context by citing a common West African practice providing women as slaves, concubines, or wives to esteemed male visitors (see especially Brooks, *Landlords*, 121–41). In contrast to such narratives that place control in the hands of indigenous African communities, academic and popular representations of interracial sex and cohabitation between European men and colonized and enslaved women on both sides of the Atlantic focus most often on unequal gender demographics and domination of colonized and enslaved male subjects.[13] At stake between these two frameworks is the possession and status of the women as sexual commodities. By alluding to the signares via an invocation of kinship and community, the habitants' petition thus implicitly asserts a patriarchal control over the women that draws on West African practices of "landlords and strangers." In a deft rhetorical move, the habitants' acknowledgment of the sexual relationships between the signares and French men in order to assert the habitants' blood ties to France depends upon and enacts black and mulatto male possession of the women against the claims of French men.

It is important here to insist that a foregrounding of the habitants' rootedness in African practices of trade and kinship is ironic because the cahier has the explicit goal of attaining for the petitioners the rights of legitimate subjects under a French authority. They must thus make themselves visible, recognizable, and legible within a sign system produced and maintained by a French supervisory gaze. The tension produced through their explicit assertions of their racialized identities, their subversive claims to French nationality, and their implicit reference to indigenous African practices of trade and kinship is productive because it suggests how subjects marked African, black, and mulatto might theorize resistance against the "binary nightmare" of slavery and colonization and how central articulations of place, space, and location are to imagining the possibilities of such resistance (Clark, "Developing," 45).[14]

Indeed, this tension is crystallized in the habitants' complaint later in the petition that "the Company wishes to reduce us to such a state of misery that we will be forced to sell our slaves [into the transatlantic market], when we can no longer feed them. The Company is wrong to form such a project, because many of our slaves are slaves in name only, whom we regard as our brothers and children."[15] The habitants frame their relationship to slavery and the captives they hold as qualitatively different from the European transatlantic economy of racialized chattel slavery. Remarkable is the assertion of the familial status of their slaves, especially if we consider the habitants' racialized vulnerability to the

Atlantic slave trade. That is, in order to insist on an authority over their economic status and commercial practices, the habitants foreground an indigenous understanding of the social and cultural economy of slavery. As Philip Curtin explains, the habitants' resistance to French attempts to "force Goréens to sell 'excess' domestic slaves for service in the Americas" arose from the habitants' grounding in "Wolof law and custom, which prohibited the sale of domestic slaves without cause and judicial condemnation" (*Economic Change*, 116). To thus resist a European economy of slavery means to underscore the habitants' racialized identities as African, black, and decidedly not white. They enact this rhetorical move from a place subject to the violent insecurity of European rivalries and where the mechanics and logistics of the transatlantic slave trade both produce and depend upon fixed economies of race and slavery. The habitants' liberty and autonomy are precarious, subject to the protection of the occupying European power.

Read within its specific geographic context, then, the habitants' assertions of kinship, patriarchy, and racialization are suggestive of the men's awareness of and resistance to the transatlantic economy, which would otherwise foreclose European recognition of their masculinity and humanity. Their assertions suggest that they, too, inhabited a liminality specific to the island's diasporic geography and function within the transatlantic slave economy. That is, if liminality, as articulated in Victor Turner's foundational work, is that space of fantastic possibility enacted through ritual before the liminal subject is reabsorbed into an existing, stable social order, then the habitants' petition reveals a self-aware assessment of the possibilities for their incorporation into that social order and the stakes of revising the terms of that order.

And here, the arbitrariness and unevenness of diaspora's production demands attention. For captives brought to the entrepôts, the islands' liminality was as stark as it was traumatic. Thus, drawing from Orlando Patterson's seminal work in *Slavery and Social Death*, which argues that "in many slaveholding societies the social death of the slave functioned precisely to empower him to navigate, in his liminality, through betwixt-and-between places where full members of society could not," Stephanie Smallwood contends that for "saltwater slaves," those captives bound for the Americas, "the social death was something more, something horrifyingly different" (*Saltwater*, 60, 61). As Smallwood insists, "Those who left on the slavers were neither venerated, like the deceased, nor suspended in balance between marginalization and integration, like local slaves, but rather assigned to an interminable purgatory" (61). For captives bound for the Americas, the liminality of the slave entrepôt and its attendant possibilities for reinvention were fleeting and devastating, as "the special violence of commodification produced not only social death, but more ominous still a kind of total annihilation of the human subject" (61).

In contrast to the "total annihilation" faced by captive Africans thrust into the Middle Passage, the habitants entered into a liminality full of promise and possibility once grounded in the island's unique geography. Because Gorée and Saint-Louis were uninhabited, indeed apparently not useful to local African communities before the incursion of European traders, their geographies are fundamentally different from other slave ports along the mainland coast of West Africa. Thus, for example, while the signares as "merchants, interpreters, and intermediaries" had precedent and predecessors on the mainland, their roles on Gorée and Saint-Louis were not subject to being "replaced by [local African] royal officials, usually slaves, who filled the roles once held by the Afro-Portuguese" (Searing, *West African Slavery*, 100). The signares on Saint-Louis and Gorée achieved an economic and social prominence and stability and gave birth to a powerful slaveholding merchant class that, unlike the Afro-Portuguese of the mainland, did not reassimilate into local populations and instead maintained an identity distinct from local African populations. As Searing notes, however, the habitants' negotiation of their status on the islands was deliberate and often in contention vis-à-vis the occupying European powers. As the habitants' petition reveals and Lamiral's undermining appendix confirms, the black and mulatto men of Senegal had to articulate consistently and repeatedly their importance to the French by rendering themselves legible as French subjects.

What I am underscoring here is that Gorée and Saint-Louis offered free black diasporic subjects unique opportunities to revise their social position and status vis-à-vis the emerging social order of the transatlantic power matrix. While captive Africans bound for the Americas had no choice in how they fit into that new social order, the free African diasporic subject was faced with inventing a social identity that was at once legitimate and authoritative in the new social order. In this petition, the habitants, rather than simply idealizing and aspiring to mimic French ideas of masculinity and rights, seek to make themselves legible neither as French nor as African subjects but as something else.[16] While they insist that they are French, the habitants assert a social and cultural autonomy through their articulation of kinship in terms of race (black and mulatto), familial patriarchal positions (an allusive reference to the signares), and self-defined social relationships with their slaves. Through such revisions of nation, race, and kinship, the habitants deliberately articulate a third space, that liminal space of possibility, one more liberating for the black diasporic subject, a space that reinvents the social order that otherwise prevails in the Atlantic economy. And most importantly here, for the black and mulatto habitants, possession of the free mulatta concubine is an integral component of their claim to self-possession vis-à-vis the French governing political and economic discursive structures.

Perhaps ironically, then, it is precisely the habitants' resistance to incorporation into existing social structures that makes them, including the signares, less recognizable as black diasporic subjects. That is, the petitioners' rhetorical negotiations of race, nation, rights, and kinship, coupled with their historical roles as merchants, slaveholders, heads of household, and civic leaders on eighteenth-century Gorée and Saint-Louis, raise questions about which subjects we see when we imagine and examine collective identity in the African diaspora. As J. Lorand Matory notes, a significant and influential body of scholarship on African diasporic cultures in the Americas has, for good reason, given "priority to the 'slave sector' as the baseline of African American culture and the source of enduring 'collective memory'" (*Black Atlantic Religion*, 13). Thus, the diasporic subjects we see when considering the black Atlantic are those enslaved and their descendants in the Americas. The habitants' petition, in its claim to possession of the signares—free(d) mulatta concubines—insists, however, that we examine how we account for those other subjects marked and produced by the transatlantic slave trade and slavery. When it comes to those other subjects produced by the Atlantic trade—Euro-African middlemen and free black and mulatto slaveholders—historical and popular narratives strive to reconcile their presence within available binaries of African and European, black and white, slave and free (e.g., the popular and romantic sentiment that most free people of color and free blacks in the United States who held slaves actually held family members in order to protect and support them). And in the case of Saint-Domingue, many of the free mulatto class of slaveholders attempted to align themselves with the white, propertied elite class. The habitants' deployment of kinship and slavery, however, resists a reduction of free people's interests to only either the enslaved black community or the free white slaveholding class. Furthermore, unlike New Orleans's free men of color, who, in a geographic socio-historical context that precluded simultaneous black and white male possession of the free(d) mulatta concubine, decried the practice of quadroon balls and plaçage, the male and female free(d) inhabitants of eighteenth-century Gorée and Saint-Louis appear to have exercised authority in and through the sexual and familial relationships between the signares and European men.[17] And while the habitants affect a framework of kinship regarding the domestic slaves they held, it must be stressed that, more than likely, such captives were not, in fact, blood relations.[18] Thus, the habitants' social relationship to the "slave sector" was neither familial nor purely mercantile. Furthermore, it is absolutely not trivial that the habitants themselves were vulnerable to becoming captives in the trade.

Is it then possible or reasonable to assert that even as they asserted French belonging, the habitants created, articulated, and maintained a specifically African diasporic identity as a form of resistance and subversion? Do the habitants' repeated petitions to protect their right to hold and trade slaves along with other commodities suggest that to be in diaspora is not always to long for a return to before the rupture or to desire assimilation but perhaps to exploit that rupture in order to access an otherwise unavailable agency and authority?[19] Can freedom in diaspora be imagined or produced without recourse to the unfreedom of another group? And what does that mean when unfreedom and blackness are nearly inextricable from one another? The deployment of kinship in the habitants' petition suggests the limits of racial solidarity even as it embraced the dangers of thinking of the liberating potential of diaspora in racial terms. But, then, what are the other terms in which we can imagine a coherent and useful African diaspora?

By itself, then, the petition is a productive literary document that suggests how free black and mulatto subjects imagined their possibilities for authority and power in an island slave entrepôt. At stake for the habitants are their visibility and legitimacy as subjects entitled to the right to hold and sell captive Africans. Within an African diasporic context, the petition at once resonates with and challenges how we imagine relationships between free people of color and the "slave sector" across Atlantic spaces. And the petitioners' passing, allusive, yet deliberate reference to the signares, coupled with their assertion of their right to hold and sell captive Africans, suggests that for them, the liminal geography of Saint-Louis enabled an assertion of identity and authority that resisted the "binary nightmare" and violence of a racialized slave society.

Derision

Whereas the petition asserts the crucial political and economic roles the male habitants play in France's commercial interests in the region, Lamiral's appendix opens with a one-paragraph description of the men and then proceeds with a detailed three-page account of the women of the island. Throughout the appendix, Lamiral's descriptions of the women generally and of the signares especially serve to repeatedly undercut the habitants' claims to authority, rationality, and thus French masculinity. In many ways, Lamiral's descriptions of the island's population are not unique and in fact reiterate stock tropes of indigenous Africans found across eighteenth-century travelers' narratives. For example, he simultaneously expresses sexual desire for the island's women even as he delineates their distance from legitimate femininity. The women are "full of grace and sweetness" but also "go naked to the waist" and are "hardworking, untiring" in performing domestic labor. Lamiral also affects a mocking tone when describing the religious practices of the islands' inhabitants, describing how they "profess to be Catholic, albeit with a peculiar mixture of Mohammedism and idolatry" and "speak much more of providence than reason."[20]

However, while Lamiral's text appears to say nothing particularly new when read against other travelers' narratives, the specific context of his appendix suggests the stakes of his work to exceed the mundane. He is writing directly against an explicit, forceful, and immediate claim to agency, authority, and, above all else, recognition by free men of color submitted on the eve of the French Revolution. Indeed, while this petition is not the first to be put forth by the habitants of Saint-Louis and Gorée, that it is framed as a cahier de doléances and addressed to the Estates-General signifies the habitants' participation in building the revolutionary climate of the Atlantic world. Furthermore, while the Bastille would be stormed that same year, more pertinent here are the competing and yet paradoxically resonant transatlantic movements pressing for the abolition of slavery, on the one hand, and the assertion of civil and political rights for free men of color, on the other. Lamiral states in his prefatory remarks that part of his project is to contest the rhetoric and agenda of the Société des amis noirs, a French abolitionist organization. It is not enough for Lamiral to reiterate how heathen and savage black African people are in contradistinction to Christian and civilized Europeans. Instead, he must contend with the ramifications of "nearly all the whites living in Senegal who associated with Negresses, had children with them, who then married without regard to color, mixed the races, and formed an unusual space that constitutes the population of the island of Saint-Louis." In his note appending the habitants' claim of French fidelity, which rests in the "French blood" that "runs through [their] veins," Lamiral insists: "They are inviolably attached to the French, but I believe that this attachment holds more to the prejudices of birth, the habits of childhood, than to any rational sentiment and any political view."[21] The specter of free men of color who, though not white, assert a claim to French subjecthood and its attendant rights and privileges threatens the existing European heteropatriarchal social order. Lamiral's appendix thus endeavors to integrate this "unusual space" into a recognizable and thus nonthreatening narrative of race, nation, and kinship.

Lamiral devotes a considerable amount of space in his appendix to enumerating just how not-French are the signares. Most importantly, Lamiral introduces the signares in the appendix's first explanatory note, attached to the title of the petition. Extending just over thirty pages, this first endnote is remarkable in its structure, which appears deliberately to confuse Lamiral's descriptions of the islands' inhabitants, which include "about three hundred free habitants, black or mulatto, and around five or six thousand slaves, or foreigners of the various nations that neighbor the country."[22] Thus, his description of the islands' women flows nearly unremarked from a description of "une vieille Mulatresse Chrétienne" (an elderly Christian Mulatta) (42) to general descriptions of "the women of this country" to the signares and back again to the women in Senegal. This slippage makes it difficult to discern when Lamiral is speaking specifically about the signares, when he is speaking about the free black and mulatto women, and when he is speaking of enslaved women.

Invoking rote and often paradoxical stereotypes of African women, Lamiral's initial description suggests desire and admiration, as he exclaims: "Upon seeing the women of this country, one cannot but regret infinitely that they are not white. They are, moreover, full of grace and sweetness, their voice expresses a seductive sweetness, their songs exude sensual pleasure." Lamiral expresses desire for and thus a claim upon the women's sexuality even as he places them outside the bounds of legitimate femininity. He then, as cited above, details precisely how different Senegalese women are from French women. And where the women of this country do share characteristics of French women, Lamiral casts their version in disparaging terms. For example, as with other eighteenth-century accounts, Lamiral extensively details the signares' unique mode of dress (and here he marks the women as explicitly signares but introduces them within the same paragraph that details how Senegalese women go "naked to the waist"). In the signares' apparent love of jewelry and finery, however, Lamiral finds the signares "as capricious and as fickle as our elegant women."[23] For Lamiral, the main problem with Senegalese women, including the signares, is that they are completely given over to sentiment, and thus their expressions of femininity are excessive.

At the same time, while Lamiral seeks to disparage the women and by extension the children they bear—the boys who will become the men who petition the Estates-General—when read against the habitants' assertion of kinship and authority, Lamiral's assertions reveal the signares' role as mothers to be formidable. After describing the island's women as exceptionally fertile, Lamiral explains how the women indulge their children:

> They love them tenderly, refusing them nothing, and although slaves for the most part, their children enjoy the most unlimited freedom, until they are old enough to carry weapons, or to work in the fields. It is for this reason that they become so proud, so vigorous, and they acquire a bold and easy gait. They speak more of good luck than reason because they are, almost since infancy, treated

as men, and they have not been humiliated by reprimands nor intimidated by the cane of a schoolmaster. They know neither the arts nor the sciences, but by twelve years old they know very well the history of their country, thus their interests in the civics and politics of the society where they live.[24]

Lamiral's statement thus suggests a worldview of the signares that produces a mothering practice that showers their children with affection, provides their children's every need, and, most subversively, imparts a geographical—political, social, and cultural—knowledge of the place they inhabit.

This revelation notwithstanding, Lamiral's slippage appears strategic. The paragraph containing this passage immediately follows two paragraphs that explicitly describe the signares and begins with the words, "In Senegal the women are like everywhere."[25] In his opening description of the island's population, Lamiral also makes a clear distinction between the island's free and captive inhabitants. And yet here we are told that the children and the women "are slaves" without a clear explanation of what he means. Because the signares impart a "history of their country" and an emphasis on "the civics and politics of the society where they live," their indulgence of their children is, in fact, a deliberate socialization and politicization of a society that at once undergirds and stands apart from French rule and power on the island. That some of the male children grow up to carry weapons signals that they will become laptots, the sailor-soldiers who "were usually domestic slaves owned by the well-to-do of Saint Louis" but who could also be "any African who worked with the Europeans, whether as sailor, soldier, clerk or administrator" (Curtin, *Economic Change*, 114). In this slippage, Lamiral attempts to undercut the habitants' claims to a political and propertied manhood by making ambiguous their status as free men and by infantilizing their understanding of nation and history by locating it within the indulgence of their mothers. Read against the grain, however, emerge mothers who subversively enact the mutually constitutive relationship between intimate and public spheres to produce children acutely attentive to the "civics and politics of the society where they live."

This politicization of the signares' mothering practices becomes even more compelling against Lamiral's description of the sexual violence endured by the young captive girls who, according to Lamiral, eventually become signares. In his annotation that describes the mechanics of the slave trade within Africa, Lamiral describes how the Moors, in their slave raids of black African villages, "take many more children than women and men as they are the easiest to capture."[26] From these, according to Lamiral,

> The whites choose the prettiest and most sprightly as domestic servants. There are few whites who don't have one of these young girls as housekeepers, of

whom become the great signares. But it is necessary that they take these girls when they are quite young, if they want to obtain that flower [deflower] to which we prejudicially attach such great value; indeed, it is rare that these young women, once they've passed through the hands of the Moors, reach us with their virginity intact. They [the Moors] defile the girls' innocence with their impure kisses, and extract tears, groaning grief, and the suffering from these trembling victims who know not how to move their souls from these twofold monsters of nature.[27]

Between Lamiral's apparent outrage at the monstrous violence inflicted by the Moors and his prurient attention to the girls' degradation, it becomes clear that what is at stake here for Lamiral is not so much the sexual violence endured by the captive young girls as their consequent value for white male claims to possession. But given Lamiral's description of the signares' mothering practices and the habitants' insistence on familial and specifically brotherly relationships with the signares ("our nephews"), that the signares are "young girls" whose virginity is a prize to European men suggests we consider the sanctity of family as a protective space for African women thrust into diaspora. To be clear, I am not suggesting that being ensconced in a family unit would shield girls and women from sexual violence, especially given the family's centrality to maintaining the patriarchal domination of the society and state. What I am suggesting is that what is important to consider is how the legitimacy of the family unit and the domestic sphere may have offered some space for free Senegalese mothers to enact a measure of authority over at least the nonsexual intimate relations occurring in that space. Lamiral's text forces us to examine how the hypervisibility of the free(d) mulatta concubine as a powerfully seductive figure not only erases the sexualized violence endured by black and mulatta women in slave and colonized spaces but also, in its isolation of the figure, obfuscates the act of mothering by women represented as free(d) mulatta concubines as a resistant and redemptive practice against the traumatic disruption of diaspora.

At the same time, while Lamiral glosses over the sexual violence the women experience at the hands of European men, he expresses shock at a particular violence endured by the signares. Noting that the girls so chosen by the European men "soon feel proud of this distinction," Lamiral states: "I have, however, seen whites who have the baseness and the abomination to sell and to send to America slaves who have shared their bed. This atrocity has always revolted me. Never have I been able to support the idea that there are men so inhumane as to place into chains a woman whom they had desired and from whom they had obtained favors."[28] While Lamiral explicitly expresses disgust toward the white men who would sell women who have shared the men's beds, his description of the young girls sold and raped by Moors and bought and held in bondage as sexual servants by white men effectively erases the presence (or perhaps alerts his reader to the material absence) of a protective male figure for the signares. That is, against the black and mulatto male habitants' claims to the rights and authority of French manhood, an authority they derive from their blood kinship to the signares, presses Lamiral's narrative of how these women purportedly claimed by the habitants are in fact subjected to repeated sexual violence and trauma by European men. The habitants cannot protect the women they claim as mothers and sisters.

Seeing and Knowing

Lamiral's written text, then, articulates a discursive tension in reading the male habitants' subject position: Lamiral must acknowledge and mark their presence in order to dismiss the legitimacy of their claims. It is within this context that Lamiral's inclusion of one of the earliest known illustrations depicting a signare is so compelling (figure 5). Whereas his written text describes the male habitants' inadequate masculinity both directly and indirectly, the visual image decisively erases the male habitants' presence. At the same time, the image does not portray a French male figure as the surrogate patriarchal authority; to do so would risk the viewer seeing French masculinity as inhabiting the same field of meaning and signification as the African "types" portrayed. Consequently, the visual image thrusts the viewer beyond the binary male claims to possession of the signare as free(d) mulatta concubine otherwise demarcated by the habitants' petition and Lamiral's appendix. I contend that because it enters a visual field, the image's signification escapes Lamiral's authority and instead opens itself to a countertextual reading of the signare's discursive and material possession.

Given the dichotomous tension between the claims in the habitants' cahier and those in Lamiral's appendix, it would be tempting to assert a reading of the image that reconciles this binary opposition by asserting that it—the image—either substantiates one claim over the other or suggests some sort of conciliatory middle ground between the two claims. Indeed, such reconciliation could at least agree that the signare is an object to possess and that possession of her defines a particular heterosexual patriarchal authority over a place and the commercial transactions that define that place. The habitants' allusive yet possessive reference to the signares, their assertion of authority and protection over their families and slaves, and Lamiral's persistent focus in the appendix on the signares' sexual bodies work together to foreclose a reading of the image outside of one that would reproduce a desiring male heterosexual gaze.[29]

However, it is precisely in its visuality, its possibility of suggesting a "direct tes-

FIGURE 5. *1. Negresse esclave, 2. Signare de L'Isle St. Louis, 3. Marabou ou Preire du Pays, 4. Negre arme en Guerre.* Dominique Harcourt Lamiral, *L'Affrique et le peuple affriquain considérés sous tous leurs rapports avec notre commerce & nos colonies* (Paris: Dessenne, 1789).

Manuscripts, Archives and Rare Books Division, Schomburg Center for Research in Black Culture, New York Public Library, Astor, Lenox and Tilden Foundations.

timony about the world which surrounded other people at other times" (Berger, *Ways*, 10) that the illustration in Lamiral's text moves beyond a documentation of opposing claims to possession of the signare and into "another realm of discourse" (Clark, "Developing," 44) so central to African diasporic epistemologies. My reading of the image here thus explores how this image enables our reading of such "another realm of discourse." The image's content invites us to imagine the multiple, spiraling diasporic perspectives it represents and to trace the consequent knowledge production of these perspectives in the consummate diasporic spaces of Gorée and Saint-Louis. Furthermore, central to reading this illustration is understanding how the image repeats, with a difference (or is itself an altered copy) at least once across time and thus across space, as it appears in Jean Baptiste Léonard Durand's *Voyage to Senegal*, published in London in 1806 (figure 6). And though Durand is Lamiral's contemporary, and they may well have overlapped in their visits to Senegal, the different dates of publication of their respective books surely mark historical changes of epic proportions in the Atlantic world. And within a broader diasporic perspective, both images have since been digitized and are freely available online, thus spiraling their repetition across time and space. Furthermore, the composition of the image in Lamiral's text (and echoed in Durand's), specifically its representation of a signare, a lap-tot, a marabout (Muslim holy man or teacher), and a female slave, appears to be a stock composition in late eighteenth-century illustrations of Saint-Louis and Gorée. Indeed, the repetition (with a difference) of the image across texts, across time, and across space disrupts the binary opposition in Lamiral's *L'Affrique et le peuple affriquain* by literally rupturing the written text. And it is in this rupture that the urgency of seeing the free(d) mulatta concubine as a mother and sister in diaspora emerges in full relief.

The illustration I examine here is not the only visual image in Lamiral's text. The book's frontispiece offers the caption "Les habitans du Sénégal présentant leur doléances à la France" (The habitants of Senegal present their complaints to France). In that plate, a decidedly European-looking figure is kneeling while appearing to submit a document to Lady France. Behind the kneeling figure stands a tall man marked by darker skin and dressed in clothing (shorts fashioned from a piece of cloth, a nearly bare chest, and bare feet) that signals his distance from European civility. While the caption may appear straightforward, the kneeling male figure's European features and dress, coupled with Lamiral's claim that he has been asked by the habitants to submit their grievances, makes the subjects' national and racial statuses more ambivalent. In addition, the presence of the clearly marked African male figure, who echoes visually in the illustration I examine below as the laptot undercuts the legitimacy of the habitants' civility. Indeed, of the numerous visual images in Lamiral's text, which include depictions of Moorish royalty and a slave raid, none offers a representation of the habitants, whose appeal for recognition constitutes the raison d'être of the French commercial agent's book.

While the plate that opens Lamiral's work may be ambivalent in its depiction of the habitants, figure 5 is decisive in its disappearance of the black and mulatto men from the landscape of that "unusual space" of Saint-Louis. The illustration depicts four adults and one child. From left to right are a "negresse [*sic*] esclave" (female slave), a "Signare de l'Isle de St. Louis" (signare of Saint-Louis), a small child (unmarked in the image), a "marabou ou prête du pays" (marabout or country priest), and a "Negre [*sic*] armé en Guerre" (Negro armed for war). Except for the small child, each figure is enumerated and labeled in the caption below the illustration. The figures appear to stand in a clearing, framed by a stock African landscape: a tall round hut with a conical thatched roof to the left, tall palm fronds to the right, and smaller huts in the distant middle background.

To the farthest left, numbered "1" in Lamiral's caption, is the black female slave. Her body faces the viewer squarely, with her feet turned slightly toward the signare. From the waist up, the woman's body is bare, save for a strand of beads encircling her neck and crossing her torso under each breast. The viewer can discern that her lower body is covered by a square of cloth wrapped around her waist, although most of it is obscured by the signare's voluminous cloak. The woman's feet are bare. She holds a parasol above the signare's head.

The signare is positioned second from left and numbered "2" in the caption. As historian George E. Brooks observes, the signare leans slightly forward in an "energetic and forceful stance" ("Artists' Depictions," 82). Unlike that of the female slave, the signare's body is fully and voluminously clothed. A simple turban covers her head, and she wears a long, loose-fitting gown. In contrast to a centuries-long persistent emphasis in the written archive of the signares on their abundant ornamental adornment and excessive vanity, this woman wears only a simple necklace. Her right arm extends down and slightly away from her body and partially covers the face of a small black child, who stands between the signare and the marabout. The signare's left hand extends toward the marabout.

The marabout's body faces the signare, and he is leaning slightly toward her. He, in similar fashion to the signare, is dressed in a long, loose robe; he carries a small bag slung across his shoulder. While the signare wears closed shoes, the marabout wears open sandals. His right arm, farthest from the viewer, is draped behind and around the signare's shoulder, and his left hand holds her outstretched, open left hand at her wrist. His left foot is slightly extended as if he is taking a step toward the signare. His gaze appears to be slightly directed above her head, perhaps at her parasol.

The fourth adult figure in the picture, standing to the far right, is a laptot. Standing taller than the other figures, this man wears clothing akin to a pair of shorts with a rolled waistband. His chest is bare. His right arm holds a long object, likely a musket, over his right shoulder, while his left arm holds a long spear upright. Like those of the enslaved woman, the soldier's eyes appear to be fixed on the signare. The soldier is standing distinctly apart from the rest of the group.

Finally, a naked child, the only figure neither enumerated nor textually identified in the illustration and with coloring similar to the soldier, stands in the triangular space between the signare and marabout, the child's head reaching their waistlines. The child is the only figure that faces the viewer squarely, although his face and right hand are partially obscured by the signare's right hand, while his left hand disappears behind the marabout's front leg.

The illustration offers a representation of the resident population of late eighteenth-century Gorée. According to a census taken by the French, the "population of Saint Louis ... numbered 3,018 in 1779: 206 *habitants*, men and women, 177 children, 1,858 slaves, who belonged to the *habitants*, and 777 free persons without slaves" (Searing, *West African Slavery*, 115–16).[30] The importance of the laptots to the habitants' freedom bears underscoring. Subject and loyal to the habitants' command, they "bore arms to protect the river convoys from attack and to protect French merchants when they left the ships to negotiate and trade on the mainland" (123). The habitants could offer or withhold the service of the laptots to European interests. Furthermore, black male subjects could rise through the "ranks of ordinary laptots" and acquire both freedom and military leadership positions (125; see also Curtin, *Economic Change*, 114). Finally, the marabout reflects the dominance of Islam in the lower Senegal valley.

Missing from the image is a depiction of the male habitants, the very subjects whose agency prompted the submission of the cahier. The visual absence of the men reiterates and magnifies Lamiral's discursive dismissal of the political significance of the black and mulatto petitioners. Whereas the habitants' claims to a kinship possession of the signares and thus French subjectivity allude to and depend upon the signares' sexual relationships with white men, Lamiral's visual depiction disappears both the familial and sexual relationships that would support the habitants' claims to authority. The signare here is framed by neither French nor habitant men. Instead, the signare's primary relationship in the illustration is to the marabout, a symbol of the third patriarchal authority in French-African commercial relationships. Furthermore, she is framed and thus ensconced in an unambiguously African place by the female slave, the African "armed for war," and the thatched-roofed hut and tropical landscape. The habitants, French by blood or kinship, African by culture and place, are completely absent.

Not only are the habitants erased from the visual field in Lamiral's plate, but here the signare, whose hypervisibility otherwise pervades academic and popular histories of Saint-Louis and Gorée, appears to occupy a more nuanced social position. Her lighter skin marks her singularity in the illustration. And while her turban and robes mark her distance from modes of Frenchwomen's dress, that she alone wears closed-toe shoes and requires the sun-shielding parasol held by the female slave suggests her particular discomfort in the African setting. Indeed, save for the child, each of the figures, unambiguously marked African, appears to offer the signare a specific form of protection: The black female slave protects her mistress from the sun; the position of the marabout's arms indicates comfort or support, and his authority suggests this support to be both spiritual and cultural; the laptot suggests physical protection from more hostile elements even as he underscores the insecurity of the place the subjects represented by these figures inhabit. At the same time, while the signare thus appears to inspire a focused, gendered protection, her modesty, a key aspect of her legible femininity, is undermined by the female slave's nakedness. Furthermore, the signare appears left of center in the plate and is neither the largest nor the most visible figure. Instead, the marabout occupies the plate's center, and his and the signare's bodies lean toward each other as if forming two equal sides of an isosceles triangle. Their physical proximity to one another suggests that their interdependent relationship is the central focus of the illustration.

Visually, the pairing of the signare and marabout is striking not only in its displacement of both male habitants and Frenchmen but also because of the presence of a child. As Brooks notes, rarely do images of the signares depict children of the women's socioracial class position ("Artists' Depictions," 86). Given Lamiral's contempt for the signares' mothering practices and the habitants' assertion of their patriarchal authority over the signares, the absence of references to children from the visual archive of the signares ironically underscores the stakes of mothering for these diasporic subjects.[31] That this child is not obviously of the signare's socioracial class position seems to underscore the visual rarity of representations of the signares as mothers. However, the positioning of this child, who stands enclosed by the signare and marabout and whose arms touch both adults, suggests we read the trio as a family. Here, then, while the habitants assert that the "blood of Frenchmen runs through [their] veins" and the signare's markings suggest her own connection to this French blood, her pairing with the marabout and the suggestion of a dark-skinned offspring convey an inevitably ever-widening, rather than narrowing, gap between the habitants and French subjectivity. The illustration thus endeavors to support Lamiral's dedication to undermining the authority and legitimacy of the habitants' claims to French masculinity by underscoring the absurdity that these women could raise legitimate French citizens.

Like the image in Lamiral, the one in Durand's work presents enumerated figures, and its caption offers precisely the same titles as those of Lamiral (figure 6). However, while Durand's enumeration remains the same (first the black female slave, then the signare, etc.), he presents the figures in reverse left-to-right order. Furthermore, Durand's image removes the child from between the signare and marabout and places the child on the back of a fifth figure not present in Lamiral's image, a second female slave. And whereas the muscular body and face

FIGURE 6. *1 and 2. Female Slaves. 3. Lady of the Isle of St. Louis.*
4. Priest of the Country. 5. An Armed Negro. Jean Baptiste Léonard
Durand, *A Voyage to Senegal; or, Historical, philosophical, and political*
memoirs relative to the discoveries, establishments and commerce of Europeans
in the Atlantic Ocean, from Cape Blanco to the river of Sierra Leone
(London: Richard Phillips, 1806).

Manuscripts, Archives and Rare Books Division, Schomburg Center for Research in
Black Culture, New York Public Library, Astor, Lenox and Tilden Foundations.

of the laptot in Lamiral's text is turned toward the viewer almost squarely, in
Durand's image we see his back and the profile of his face. Likewise, in contrast to Lamiral's version, wherein the female slave's arm is cut off by the image's
frame and she appears as mere ornament to the signare, in Durand's image we
see the full length of her left arm. Still holding the parasol above the signare's
head, the enslaved woman is as clearly detailed as the other figures.

Finally, the differences in the presentations of the marabout and signare are
particularly striking. In Durand's image, the marabout's occupation of center
stage is more forceful and decisive. Not only is he in the middle of the frame and
of the five figures, but he also has one hand raised as if in gesture, in contrast to
the marabout in Lamiral's image, who holds the signare with both arms. And
while the marabout in Durand's image does grasp the signare's hand, as he does
in Lamiral's, in Durand's image the marabout holds the signare's hand from underneath, thus appearing to have a firmer grip on her than does the marabout
in Lamiral's text, whose hand appears to rest almost gently on the signare's arm.

And finally, of course, is the dramatic difference in the signare's skin coloring. Whereas the signare in Lamiral's image is decidedly lighter than the other figures, in Durand's text her skin coloring is rendered as dark as everyone else's, including the female slaves.

As stated above, the differences between the images are neither trivial nor incidental. Even without knowing which of the images may be the original, the respective publication dates make the differences suggestive of the dramatic changes in the Atlantic world between 1789 and 1806. Briefly, the differences in the images are perhaps most reflective of changing French attitudes toward free people of color and their concomitant changing status vis-à-vis a French colonizing gaze. Thus, for example, the signare's darker skin marks her as more decidedly African and even further from French femininity. The displacement of the child may reflect the intractability of African subjectivity. However, what concerns me here is what the image might suggest to us in terms of reading Saint-Louis as a diasporic space. It is the similarities, the resonance between the images that again opens a possibility for imagining the practice and possibilities of diaspora both for the historically specific context of the signares and, for the reasons outlined above, for subjects across the time-space matrix of the black Atlantic.

Indeed, the content of both images invites us to imagine a perspective beyond that of both the habitants, "black and mulatto," and of Lamiral, a French commercial agent. In both images, the signare and marabout occupy center stage, and all the other figures appear to gaze at the couple. The focus in each figure's eye is remarkably intense, especially given the generic characterization and accompanying stock African landscape. Thus, each figure in the image sees. As Berger asserts, "It is seeing which establishes our place in the surrounding world" (*Ways*, 7). However, as he also insists, "The relation between what we see and what we know is never settled.... The knowledge, the explanation never quite fits the sight" (7). Berger's evocative meditation suggests several considerations in assessing the images' disruptive significations. Starting from the center and reading out, for example, what do the marabout and signare see when looking at each other? Does he see in her a kindred spirit and African subject whose syncretic subjectivity is as much connected to the Atlantic trade as his? Does she see in him a religious teacher, a confidant, a connection to Islam? Does she see in him a connection to an identity outside or before her status as a signare? Is he there to offer spiritual support or to help her sustain her piety? Does she see him as a connection to Islam or to a more traditional African religious practice? What is most important to them about the particularly Wolof practice of Islam they may share? If the black female slave protects the signare from the sun, while the laptot protects her from physical threat, what protection might the marabout offer?

And if the signare and marabout together form the central focus of this image, what are the other figures seeing as they gaze at the couple? After all, both the signare and the marabout are free subjects in the island slave entrepôt of Saint-Louis. While neither image describes the soldier as a slave, the historical record indicates that the ranks of the laptots were made of slaves and former slaves. As well, the only other female subjects in either image are clearly marked by their slave status. At the same time, historical records corroborate and elaborate the habitants' claims that their slaves were like family members. Contemporary observers noted the differences between the urban slave societies of Saint-Louis and Gorée and those in the Americas. Searing describes how the Frenchman Saugnier offered in his late eighteenth-century narrative "a warning to any slave trader foolish enough to confuse the slaves of the *habitants* with slaves in transit" (*West African Slavery*, 127).[32] According to Searing, Saugnier writes that such a trader "would run the greatest risk, nor could he escape being stabbed or poisoned but by miracle: at best he would be sure to lose his merchandise, and to be reduced to slavery among the negroes or the Moors" (127). Likewise, Curtin cites an incident during which an "effort to force [habitants to sell their domestic slaves into the Atlantic trade] almost led to a bloody insurrection, and the plan had to be dropped" (*Economic Change*, 116).[33] As noted above, the laptots had considerable status and social mobility on the islands. Also, according to Searing, "women slaves sometimes were able to profit from their position as pileuses [women who prepare millet by pounding it] by trading processed grain. This could lead to a gradual movement into the merchant class and slave ownership" (*West African Slavery*, 127). And yet, due to the precariousness of this "unusual space," any one of the figures was subject to the possibility of being cast into the Atlantic trade. Thus, Searing argues, "whatever the social sanctions against the sale of [household] slaves, the threat of sale to the slave merchants was undoubtedly the greatest incentive to accepting the status of a slave in the islands" (128).

The social and kinship relationships suggested in these images thus articulate the particular liminality of Saint-Louis. Given the context of living in a place that comes into being because of the Atlantic trade, the instability of each figure's freedom is perhaps at its most visceral and urgent. What, then, for example, does the laptot see while he gazes upon the marabout and the signare? Does he see two people who, by virtue of their religious training and sexuality, respectively, have avenues to freedom outside his reach? Does he see two people whose freedom is protected, and thus guaranteed, only by his service as a soldier? Does he wonder if the signare's loyalties lie with the marabout, the black and mulatto habitants, or the French man who shares her bed? Does he desire to possess the signare? Does he equate possession of the signare with social status or power?

And the black female slave—what does she see as she stands in the hot sun, naked from the waist up, holding an ornamental parasol above the signare's head, her primary purpose to serve as a concrete display of her mistress's wealth? Does she envy the signare's social and economic status and privilege? Does she see the signare buy gris-gris from the marabout and wonder how the signare's patronage of this religious man might factor into her liberty? Does she see in the signare the possibility of her own freedom? And if she sees such possibility, what are the extent and limits of that possibility? Does she know the signare only as a signare, or does she remember when she was merely a free black or mulatto woman, unattached to a Frenchman? Or perhaps she remembers the signare when she was unfree? And if male slaves were able to sit at the same table as their masters and talk as equals, did the same rules apply to the female slaves and the signares? Can we imagine the signare and the female slave talking about what it means to (be forced to) trade sex for liberty and wealth? And if they do have these conversations, what is spoken and left unspoken? Do they acknowledge in a shared space the sexual violence in both "free" and captive spaces? Or does the female slave see in the signare simply another agent in her own subjection? And finally, is the specter of social annihilation that Smallwood argues haunts the slave entrepôt so threatening that both women's subjection to sexual violence and sexual commodification is mundane?

To raise these questions is not to presume to understand how a subject made African, female, black or mulatta, captive or free(d), and living in an eighteenth-century island slave society would have felt or inhabited her experience. To imagine how she may have experienced a place that sanctioned the sexual commodification of and assault against bodies so marked is to enact its own kind of violence. Rather, to raise these questions is to think through the dimensions of the possibilities for freedom that the intersecting economic and social systems that governed Gorée and Saint-Louis may have opened to these subjects. To raise these questions is to consider how the multiple social identities inhabited by the figures marked "Signare de l'Isle de St. Louis" and "negresse esclave" at once intersect and collide. Thus, on the one hand, the visual image marks the signare and the black slave as two distinct figures, the distinction most stark in their dramatically different states of (un)dress. On the other hand, in their presentation of a social space marked by physical proximity and knowing gazes, the images together render visible and coherent the interconnectedness between the signare and the black slave, an interconnectedness otherwise masked and erased in the archive by the hypervisibility of the signares as free and powerful mulatta concubines. The visual image as it appears in Lamiral's work thus ruptures the written text's binary claims to possession of the signare by opening a space to think through multiple claims to knowledge and thus possession of the signare's experience on these islands.

And it is here where the (re)iteration of the image in Lamiral's and Durand's texts becomes as confounding as it is generative. The image simultaneously occupies different and specific historical contexts. The repetition of the image and the unknowing of its original appearance foreclose diachronic and linear comparative analyses of the two variations. As I assert above, within its narrow textually specific historical context, the image in Lamiral's text opens itself to an analysis that resists centering the perspective of a (white) patriarchal male gaze. And yet, as soon as one sees the iteration in Durand's work, it becomes impossible not to consider one image without thinking about the other. The relationship between the two becomes not dialectical but spiraling. On the one hand, the juxtaposition of the two near-mirror images and the consequent disruption of a binary such juxtaposition enacts resonate diasporically in the vèvè of Haitian vodou, those ritual signs used to signal the crossroads between the material and the divine, and specifically the sign of the marasa trois, which, as VèVè Clark explains, "assume[s] uniformity at the horizontal and vertical crossroads thereby insuring a stable field of interaction with the *lwa*; improvisations on the grounded form, left and right, top and bottom encourage originality" ("Developing," 44). On the other hand, the visual images are most certainly produced by a male French artist. Thus forced to consider the two together, we must also confront the knowledge that diaspora, or, more precisely, an African diaspora, is produced by this white patriarchal gaze and must also be navigated and negotiated under this gaze. The images' possibilities for discerning the multiple various and even subversive perspectives of the figures portrayed run headlong into the understanding that the African diasporic subject can only imagine herself through this panoptic gaze; she can only imagine, can only experience, displacement and dispossession.[34]

Thus, to read the visual images, and specifically the knowing looks between the figures represented, in order to consider the dimensions of and the possibilities for freedom for subjects displaced and dispossessed is to confront the possibility that one can only be as free as the dominant authority allows. Following Joan Scott's work in "The Evidence of Experience," one can experience only as much freedom as the possibilities of that experience are defined by the social order one inhabits. And yet the image suggests multiple perspectives and thus multiple sites of knowledge production; it reminds us that authority must be constantly affirmed and negotiated. And I must be clear here that I am speaking about the resident populations of Saint-Louis and Gorée and not about the Atlantic slaves whose fate was "social annihilation." And I also must be clear here that to say authority must constantly be affirmed and negotiated is to assert neither unfettered agency nor culpability to the dominated diasporic subject. Rather, I am interested in the imagined possibilities that inhabiting a liminal place opens for captive or otherwise bounded subjects, especially those marked African and female.

Négresse

And then there is this. On July 6, 1737, a woman signing herself A——— Gusban penned a letter to the Senegal Company. Writing from Gorée, Gusban asserts that she is "taking the liberty of representing the rights of [her] daughter, Anne Gusban," whose father has died. This letter, succinct in its content but breathtaking in its appearance in the archival repository, describes how Anne, the daughter, inherited all of her father's property, including three "captives," and conveys the mother's disbelief that the company's director in Gorée has decided to seize the slaves as the company's property. The letter is signed, "Your most humble and most obedient servant, A——— Gusban, Negress."[35]

By itself, Gusban's letter stands out in a colonial archive overwhelmingly produced by male subjects connected to the Senegambian-Atlantic trade. The official record of the islands' histories emphasizes economic relationships between groups of people: French administrators, indigenous African political and religious leaders, merchants and traders, the habitants, and of course the notorious mulatta signares. And yet, despite the signares' apparent social power, demonstrated material wealth, and decided celebrity, their voices appear to be absent from the popular archive even as this same archive obsesses over their presence and appearance. Again, across academic and popular histories that focus on eighteenth-century life in Gorée and Saint-Louis, what receives little discernible remark is that our understandings of these African and Euro-African women's subjectivities rely almost entirely upon the writings of colonizing European and colonized African men.

Against this grain, Gusban's letter reminds us that the signares also imagined and represented themselves. Although it appears an anomaly in the French colonial archive, especially within the context of a historiography that persistently privileges a heterosexual male gaze in reading and writing the signares, the letter's very appearance and contents demand that we understand that Gusban very likely was drawing from and helping to reproduce a repertoire, a repeated and communicated practice, of black and mulatta African women's written appeals for accountability and justice. And here again, evidence seeps into the record. In his assertion that in eighteenth-century Senegal, "assimilation meant that some Senegalese consciously accepted standards and values derived from their European rulers, and in return claimed the rights which they believed such acceptance should bring," John Hargreaves quotes a part of one signare's testimony in a 1776 complaint brought by the male and female habitants of Saint-Louis against the British governor Charles O'Hara. Hargreaves explains: "It was alleged that O'Hara had sold free Africans into slavery, had confiscated houses for the use of colleagues and concubines, and generally used arbitrary proceedings and abusive language. To the latter, one formidable *signaree* [*sic*] had retorted that 'tho her skin was black, her heart was white and her blood as good as his': it is evident that an element of racial consciousness already reinforced this determination to defend the rights of the community" ("Assimilation," 182). Hargreaves's decision to cite a woman speaking in an essay (in 1965 no less) that focuses on the political dimensions of race, culture, and nation in the eighteenth century is remarkable in itself; while the scholarship on the signares foregrounds their significance to trade in Senegal, most cast the women's political significance to lie mainly in their production of sons and thus their establishment of habitant society.[36] In addition, the fact that the document cited by Hargreaves is located in the *British* colonial archives underscores the unfixedness of the signares' geography: though the historical subjects are anchored in a specific place and location, the production of their archive happens synchronously across time and place, language and nation.

Gusban identifies herself neither as a signare nor as a mulatta. However, her letter's content, date, and place of origin suggest that she functioned within the same sexual, racial, and commercial economies as the women who would come to be called signares. Indeed, in 1737 Gusban would have inhabited a place whose interracial sexual economy was already well established and whose mixed-race elite class, "dominated by the signares," held social and economic prominence (Searing, *West African Slavery*, 95). Thus, by itself, the letter suggests a glimpse into the interiority of a subject marked African, female, and black or mulatta as she navigated the liminal place of Gorée. When read against the habitants' petition, Lamiral's appendix, and the (re)iterated visual images that appear in Lamiral's and Durand's works, Gusban's letter acquires a haunting signification across black Atlantic time and space. The letter illuminates not only the precariousness of security for African women, black or mulatta, in the eighteenth-century island slave entrepôt; when read against these texts, it also begs us to consider the very terms of belonging and being in diaspora.

Indeed, while the date, location, and contents of Gusban's letter suggest her context within the economy of the signares, they also disturb popular and academic understandings of what held value in that economy. For example, that the company has threatened to take her daughter's slaves is startling given that by the time Gusban writes, it was a commonly accepted practice for the mixed-raced children of Europeans to inherit the property of their fathers.[37] And more urgently, that Gusban signs herself or is signed as "Negresse" invites a consideration of the valuation of the honorific signare in 1737 Gorée. The distinction between signing herself or being signed as "Negresse" is, of course, not trivial. If Gusban self-identified as "Negresse," then we should wonder whether she identified primarily as a black woman without a specific ethnicity or if she used the term strategically. That is, was she fully immersed in the eighteenth-century slave entrepôt's social and racial milieu, no longer with a familial or affectionate connection to any mainland ethnic community? Or was something to be gained by identifying herself primarily as a subject produced by the European trade with and of Africans? Likewise, was "Negresse" a description of both phenotype and racial status, or was she indeed a mulatta who found it more prudent to identify as a black woman within a geographically specific sexual-racial classification system? On the other hand, if she dictated the letter to someone, who was that someone, and did they inform her that she would be signed as "Negresse"? If so, what were this person's motives? Did signing her as "Negresse" undermine or substantiate the claims in the letter?

The testimony of the signare quoted by Hargreaves above is as beguiling as it is illuminating. That is, as Hargreaves contends, the quote suggests an "element of racial consciousness" in which the signare seeks to make visible a racial whiteness, that is, a claim to rights and property based on her nearness to whiteness, against the evidence apparently and otherwise offered by her "black" skin. Her skin's blackness appears to have little to do with how she imagines herself culturally or racially. At the same time, in the scrap of evidence offered by Hargreaves, "tho her skin was black," the qualifier "tho" operates in tension with the unequivocal acknowledgment of blackness. The blackness persists and insists on some kind of recognition. Who demands the recognition remains elusive, as the third-person pronouns suggest that the evidence is a transcription of the woman's assertion rather than words directly written or dictated by her. And finally, the two scraps—Gusban's letter and this unnamed négresse's testimony—are separated not only by nearly forty years but also by place, language, and respective European governing authority. In particular, the significant differences between the uses of "négresse" in French and "black woman" in English underscore the added problem of language and translation in a consideration of how black and mixed-race African women navigated the discursive and material terrain of these diasporic, liminal places.

Furthermore, not only does Gusban sign herself or is signed as "Negresse," but in detailing the "captives" held by her daughter, she counts "an old woman, a young Rapace, and a Negress about 17 years old."[38] Momentarily setting aside the young *rapace*, the discursive interchangeability of Gusban, whose age we do not know, her daughter, the old woman, and the young girl falls into sharp relief, even if we read the letter in isolation, against the (re)iteration of visual representations of the eighteenth-century signares. The inventory provided in the list, juxtaposed with Gusban's own position as mother and négresse, offers a striking reminder of the precariousness of liberty for a free, propertied, female African diasporic subject in this eighteenth-century transatlantic entrepôt. Gusban lists two subjects whose racial and gender markings mirror hers and her daughter's. For Gusban, her daughter's survival is dependent upon the captivity of bodies that may look very much like her own. The letter lists this inventory as a matter of fact, and perhaps if Gusban had signed herself "signare" or "mulâtresse," we could not have imagined that she engendered any connection between her and her daughter's status and that of the two female captives. But Gusban signs herself or is signed as "Negresse." And while Gusban does not give her own age, we know that she is a mother writing on behalf of her daughter; this dyad echoes in "an old woman" and a "Negresse, about 17 years old." The letter lays bare the fungibility of not only the enslaved body (following Saidiya Hartman [*Scenes*, 21]) but also the racially marked woman, free *and* enslaved, within the raced and gendered economy of the transatlantic trade in humans. That is, the repetition of "Negresse," the insistence on Gusban's signature within a racial and sexual economy already represented by (if not dominated by) the mulatta signares, suggests that *someone*, whether the letter's scribe is Gusban or another person, but that someone on Gorée notes that the visual markings of enslaved women on the island link them to the island's free women. To assert this fungibility is to tread carefully, given that Gusban marks the relationship unequivocally: these two women are her captives. That Gusban is free and propertied matters. So, too, does it matter that without the possession of one (or two, in this case) body that looks like her, Gusban's daughter would not survive. Within this diasporic place, the liberty of one, according to this letter, is dependent upon the captivity and enslavement of the other.

It is Gusban's writing of the young captive girl's racial identity that is important. That is, the girl's racial identity stands apart from Gusban's notation: in any case, the young captive girl would be black and African, and within indigenous and likely Wolof systems of slavery asserted by the habitants, Gusban, her daughter, and the captives would not be inherently fungible merely on the basis of their shared racial status. And as we have seen, the habitants fought to keep their domestic economy of slavery separate and distinct from the transatlantic trade. Thus, it is the writing of "Negresse" that thrusts the particular racial and sexual economy of slavery here into a transatlantic framework and both reflects and produces the racialized vulnerability of Gusban and her daughter. The mutual permeability of these two otherwise distinct economies of slavery—the domestic one, based on indigenous notions of ethnicity, group, and belonging, and the transatlantic one, based on imposed racial categories of race—is further underscored by the third captive Gusban lists, "a young Rapace." This captive, whom she lists between the young girl and the old lady, further complicates the letter's mediation of mothering, race, slavery, and freedom. The word *rapace* refers to a specific type of slave. Detailing the logistics of the slave trade on Saint-Louis, René Geoffroy de Villeneuve, second-in-command to Stanislas-Jean de Boufflers, governor of Senegal from 1785 to 1787 (Jones, *Métis*, 26), explains: "When there is not a speck of a European vessel on the coast, often an indulgent master will [allow in] add to his domestic slaves some slaves which he had bought to resell. These are most often children of one or the other sex who will be used for small house details; one calls the boys *rapaces*, the girls *rapacilles*: these children enjoy the same privileges as slaves born in the master's house [hut]."[39] Gusban's third captive, then, is a young boy who was otherwise bound for the Americas but kept instead to be a domestic slave, an act read as indulgence or kindness by the slaveholders in this place. Here, Gusban's ten-year-old daughter, Anne, echoes again in the listing of captives, in age this time rather than gender. In Gusban's listing of her captives emerges a succinct account of the multiple economies and genealogies of unfreedom, blackness, and diaspora produced by the transatlantic trade. That her letter makes explicit the overlapping of these economies and genealogies illuminates the stakes of protecting her child in this place.

Gusban's letter thus reflects the social relationships and recognition of the spiral tensions between race, slavery, and freedom suggested in the written and visual texts that open this chapter. However, Gusban's letter does much more than affirm these tensions. By foregrounding her role as a mother, Gusban's letter resists the discursive narratives that would otherwise frame her subject position solely in terms of her sexual body. That is, popular and academic histories have, necessarily, offered critical examinations of the sexual objectification and commodification of bodies made African, black or mulatta, and female. While recent black feminist scholarship examines how gender has informed diaspora subjectivity and practices outside sexuality by turning to sites of analysis such as women's knowledge production, scholarly and popular examinations persistently emphasize readings of black women in terms of their history as objects of sexual violence. Again, such a focus has been and continues to be necessary in the face of the persistent public and private subjugation of black women's sexual lives. At the same time, we might consider how such an emphasis makes less visible the full and nuanced spectrum of how women marked black and mulatta translated and experienced such commodification and racial violence.

Gusban writes the familial relationship exclusively in terms of her daughter. And by not naming her own relationship to her daughter's father, by not marking his racial status, she asserts an identity outside and beside her sexuality. In contrast to histories and representations of the signares that render primary and most important their sexual relationships and consequent spectacular social status, Gusban's letter asserts the most important kinship relationship to be that between mother and daughter. Indeed, it is her daughter's security that motivates Gusban. In doing so, Gusban shifts the terms of both how we read kinship relationships within diasporic spaces and how we read the sexualized body of the free(d) mulatta concubine.

Gusban's letter makes stark the primacy of mothering in reading diasporic spaces and gendered experiences of diaspora. When we think—imagine—diaspora, we imagine it in terms of motherless children (see Hartman, *Lose*). But Gusban's letter asks us to consider what it means to mother in diaspora. The free(d) mulatta concubine in diaspora is most often presented and read as a sexual agent who gains personally from her sexual relationships with white men. In Gusban's letter there is a reassessment of the stakes of being a subject marked African, female, and black or mulatta in an eighteenth-century slave port. Gusban's decisive emphasis on her role as mother, to the exclusion of telling us how she imagined her own kinship and racial relationship to her daughter's father, resists male claims to possession of her (sexual) body and insists that we also reconsider how we read the social and intimate spaces of eighteenth-century Gorée and Saint-Louis.

Indeed, the stakes of such intimacy are illuminated in how Gusban's daughter acquired this property. In the letter, Gusban refers to the man whose labor earned this property as her daughter's father and, tellingly, not as Gusban's husband or lover. The letter does not explicitly state the unnamed father's racial identity; while it is tempting to deduce that he was white, based on the historical context and Gusban's reference to her husband "serving his country" in the Gambia, assuming the father's whiteness would be falling into the trap of romance and sentimentality that so rigidly frames narratives of the signares and so decidedly erases the economic and political roles of free men of color on the island. Indeed, the absent marker of husband, with the unmarked racial identity of Gusban's daughter's father, parallels the invisibility of free men of color in popular and scholarly histories of the free(d) mulatta concubine. I suggest here, given the heteropatriarchal norms in terms of how power functions and how we understand historical narratives, Gusban's silence on the status or nature of her relationship with her daughter's father and on his racial identity is constitutive of Gusban's unbelonging and casting into diaspora.

Thus, while the question of the father's racial identity is neither incidental nor trivial, what stands out in the letter is that Gusban's relationship with her daughter's father notwithstanding, her attempt to lay claim to the property has thus far been futile. According to Brooks, "At Gorée, a signare's children inherited her possessions, following the Lébou custom that called children to inherit from their mothers without interference from their fathers" (*Eurafricans*, 220). However, as Searing contends, while ultimately, over the course of the eighteenth century, a consistent pattern of property acquisition and inheritance benefiting the signares emerged and solidified, "the relations between this local society and the French merchants of the islands followed no fixed patterns in the first decades of the eighteenth century" (*West African Slavery*, 101). Gusban's letter thus reminds us of the uneven and often contradictory relationships between accepted practice on the ground and official policies. More importantly, it hints at the persistent simultaneity of frustration and anticipation black subjects endured as they navigated rules, regulations, and white sexual and material desire, as well as their own. Indeed, Gusban's appeal to a white patriarchal authority reminds us again how white surveillance and recognition are fundamental to the constitution of black diasporic subjectivity. That is, as a free African woman living on Gorée, Gusban may indeed have had some economic independence and opportunity to build wealth, as evidently many signares did. What her appeal demonstrates, however, is that her authority and ability to do so were produced by and dependent upon the recognition by and intervention of the controlling commercial entity, the Senegal Company. That is, how Gusban writes herself and how she asks her reader to imagine her as a racialized and gendered subject without attachment to a specific, indigenous local ethnic group is determined by how she might make herself most visible and recognizable as a subject before her audience. In cyclical fashion, her legibility occurs because she is produced, legitimized, and recognized by a white patriarchal authority. She may well have embraced the descriptor "Negresse" because it afforded her this recognition and autonomy. Thus, we can understand how "Negresse" makes visible not only how Gusban's diasporic identity is multiply layered in terms of race, gender, sexuality, and geography but also how these multiple layers simultaneously signify her movement and her entrapment. Gusban is free enough, and perhaps even empowered enough, to write to assert the rights of her daughter; that her appeal depends upon the company recognizing neither herself nor her daughter but the labor of her daughter's dead father, and that her appeal asserts that her daughter will starve if not afforded her rights, together insist we analyze both the conditions of and the limits to her tenuous agency.

And then there is this. Gusban closes her letter with an appeal to justice and accountability that belies the power that the "very humble and very obedient servant, A——— Gusban, Negresse," would otherwise hold in the eighteenth-century slave entrepôt. After explaining to her reader the loyal service her daughter's father rendered to the company and that "daring to take her daughter's slaves is like daring to take her daughter's food," Gusban ends her letter with the advisement, "I implore the Company that to consider my representations and acting justly, that one would not be able to say in this country that the Company plunders as does the king Damel."[40] Here Gusban refers to the Kingdom of Kajoor and its regular collection of customs and tax payments from French merchants transporting goods through its territory. Relationships between the Damel, or king, and the French were often tense, as the kingdom used its control of grain supplies as leverage in its trade relations with the French. According to Searing, restricting French access to grain could lead to "famine conditions[, which] ruined the slave trade, as in 1735–6, when there were serious grain shortages in the Lower Senegal. . . . The documents of the eighteenth century reveal a general uneasiness provoked by the daily dependence on trade with Kajoor" (*West African Slavery*, 81, 87).[41] Gusban's invocation of the Damel is striking in its assertion of an authority that exceeds the reach of the company. While Gusban uses the language of supplication, and while her signature of "Negresse" reflects a diasporic dispossession and displacement, her closing also suggests a deliberate negotiation of belonging, power, and possibility in securing the rights of her daughter. She is aware of the conflicting rules of inheritance, and her manipulation of and resistance to these rules is central to her ability to mother her child. Her appeal to the authority of the company simultaneously reminds the company of its own dependencies in the region. Advising the company of the stakes of its reputation on the island conveys a sense that Gusban is, in fact, not a solitary figure but instead part of a larger self-reflective community that sees, knows, and acts.

Because she inhabited a geographic space already defined by an economy of the free(d) mulatta concubine, Gusban's signature of "Negresse" cannot be understood outside of said economy, even as she marks herself as such. Thus, her attempt to secure the rights of her daughter signals her anticipation of the ten-year-old girl's insecurity and potential subjection to this economy; her signature "Negresse" and her focus on her subject position as a mother imply a dynamic resistance to the governing economy of the signares. It is here, in the mother's labor to secure her daughter's rights, that we understand most clearly the stakes of possession for the African diasporic subject. It is in Gusban's appeal to justice that her letter most resonates diasporically. Within this turn of the spiral, Gusban's efforts to protect not only her daughter's rights but also and most urgently her very security illuminate and depend upon a certain incommensurability of freedom in diaspora, for the young rapace and the young négresse is each someone else's child. We must imagine, too, that the old woman could be or could have been someone's mother. The fungibility of each of these subjects (Gusban, her daughter, the seventeen-year-old Negress, the rapace, and the old woman), each of whom is made visible by Gusban's signature, illuminates the desperate stakes of *this mother's* desire to protect her children and haunts *this mother's* ability to speak into and from the archive.

Here again echoes Ezili-Dantò, the dark-skinned, dispossessed, battle-scarred, mute single mother who fiercely protects her daughter. It is here, in the mother's labor to secure the rights of her daughter, that we may understand most clearly the stakes of possession for subjects marked African, female, and black or mulatta. Indeed, the struggle to mother echoes not only across the physical places of racialized chattel slavery but also across the imaginative spaces of diaspora. In Gusban's call for justice, the question of possession reveals itself to be at once public as well as intimate and sacred. Gusban's appeal transcends the limits of her physical authority and informs us of her capacity to imagine her own agency. Reading this letter through the lens of the free(d) mulatta concubine in diaspora and against claims to her possession lays bare the negotiation of race, kinship, and desire that so defines the experiences of subjects marked African, female, and black or mulatta. Just as the habitants' claims to possession and the visual image in Lamiral's text and its (re)iteration in Durand's direct us to consider what diasporic witnesses saw and knew when they encountered the signare in her material setting, Gusban's letter compels us to consider how the subjects marked African, female, black or mulatta, captive or free imagined the possibilities of their existence as they moved in and through the liminal places of Gorée and Saint-Louis.

CHAPTER 4

Mapping Freedom
and Belonging

What is often called cultural "memory," "survival," or "tradition" in both the African Diaspora and at home is, in truth, always a function of power, negotiation, and strategic re-creation.

—J. LORAND MATORY, *Black Atlantic Religion*

After the Door of No Return, a map was only a set of impossibilities, a set of changing locations.

—DIONNE BRAND, *A Map to the Door of No Return*

Where this book begins with the possibilities for imagining diaspora through tracing the free(d) mulatta concubine's echo across diaspora, it ends here with the limits of those possibilities. Within the context of Atlantic slave societies in general and the places I have examined here in particular, the unevenness of the echo's terrain is especially striking in the mid-nineteenth century: in the United States, the 1850 Fugitive Slave Law and the 1857 Dred Scott decision reflected a slave society digging in its heels even as it catapulted toward the Civil War; in Haiti, France's belated (1834) recognition of the black nation's independence carried with it a price tag of 150 million francs, and in 1848 "the very black and illiterate President Faustin Soulouque began the massacre of mulattoes he suspected as [being] conspirators" (Dayan, *Haiti*, 10); in Senegal, the French Revolution of 1848 brought with it emancipation and the abolition of slavery in France's territories, including Gorée and Saint-Louis, and a consequent granting of citizenship to newly freed slaves and then suffrage to all male French subjects.[1] Across such jagged, contradictory terrain, any comparative analysis must necessarily stumble, unwieldy in its awkwardness. As Brent Hayes Edwards, Saidiya Hartman, and others have demonstrated, however, it is the very laboriousness of such comparison that can be most compelling because it illuminates the perpetual process and work of diaspora.

This chapter takes up two very different works from two very different places, each published within ten years of the other, and both within this dramatic midcentury historical moment, in order to reflect upon not only the limits and possibilities of freedom for black and mixed-race women in slave societies but also the limits and possibilities of a black Atlantic framework for understanding how these subjects may have imagined freedom. The first work I consider is an ethnographic tome on Senegal published in 1853, Abbé David Boilat's *Esquisses sénégalaises: Physionomie du pays, peuplades, commerces, religions, passé et avenir, récits et légendes* (Senegalese sketches: Features of the region, peoples, commerce, religion, past and future, stories and legends), a veritable encyclopedia of Senegal. Written by the French-educated and ordained son of a signare mother and French father, "its importance" is, according to Martin Klein, "in part that it was one of the first books on Africa written by an African" ("Review," 449). The book is both an evangelistic ethnographic handbook and, as Bernard Mouralis suggests, an "analysis of the country's future" that "relies particularly on the consequence colonization can have on the economic and political development" of that future ("Les 'Esquisses sénégalaises,'" 822). The second work I examine is Eliza Potter's 1859 narrative, *A Hairdresser's Experience in High Life*. Identified in the archive as a free mulatto from the northern United States, Potter offers an entertaining memoir of her experiences as an independent working woman, first as a nursemaid and then as a hairdresser, as she journeys to France and England, sojourns briefly in Canada, and finally travels across an antebellum U.S. landscape. In important ways, both Boilat and Potter intervene and revise literary genres central to European and American colonial, imperial, and slavery projects. For example, the structure and content of Boilat's work echoes European travelers' narratives of Africa; likewise, Potter deliberately engages the genre and framing of travel as she describes the southern physical and human landscapes made purportedly familiar to her readers by writers like Frederick Law Olmsted and Alexis de Tocqueville. Central to both writers' interventions and revisions are explicit engagements with and deconstructions of stereotypical representations of the free(d) mulatta concubine.

At the same time, as suggested by the mid-nineteenth-century snapshot I sketch above, the stakes of each writer's project cannot be the same. Attending to the echo's fracture is imperative because it is in the "positioning" of these two works alongside and against one another that we can more closely examine, as Stuart Hall writes, that "meaning [that] continues to unfold, so to speak, beyond the arbitrary closure which makes it, at any moment, possible" ("Cultural

Identity," 230). That is, to select this particular moment in Atlantic history, to fix it, is in many ways as arbitrary a choice as any, notwithstanding the decidedly nonarbitrary historical processes that produced such different contexts in each Atlantic site nor the work of historiography and the archive that naturalized such periodization and makes it feel *not* arbitrary.[2] At the same time, however, reading these two texts together is, again following and adopting Hall's example, as "strategic" as it is arbitrary: reading them together produces and thus allows us to examine deliberately that something "left over," that "excess" produced by the "arbitrary closure," here marked by a fixing of dates, historical period, and nation (230). To insist on the arbitrariness of the differences in each work's historical context is not to suggest or advance an unmoored reading of either the works or the histories they reflect but rather to resist a geographic and historical compartmentalization of the transnational and transatlantic intersecting and often mutually contingent processes so instrumental to the subjugation and oppression of black subjects across time and space.[3]

This chapter thus engages two works located in a historical moment where, for black people thrust into the transatlantic economies of race and slavery, freedom's promise had (perhaps) never been more beguiling. I pay close attention to the specificity of that promise for each writer. I suggest that central to each writer's analysis of freedom's promise was a geographically specific revision of the stereotype of the free(d) mulatta concubine. And the distinctions between the shape of that stereotype and the historical subjects and places referenced by the stereotype matter. Thus I examine what does not get repeated across these two Atlantic texts. This chapter does not end with resolution but rather with a refusal to reconcile the differences. This chapter's ending suggests that the echo's persistence paradoxically offers its own evidence of the impossibility of its promise. This chapter thus attends not only to the material limits of diaspora but to its imaginative ones as well.

Mapping

Just shy of five hundred pages, *Esquisses sénégalaises* is divided into twelve chapters, each focusing on a specific place or ethnic group. Boilat complemented *Esquisses* with a separate full-color *Atlas*, an album of twenty-four illustrated plates after drawings Boilat made during his ten-year sojourn in Senegal, depicting a series of individual members of the country's various ethnic groups. The *Atlas* follows the same order of the groups' presentation in *Esquisses*.[4] While *Esquisses* offers prefatory remarks by the author and a brief introduction to Gorée's physical geography and place within European history, both *Esquisses* and the *Atlas* introduce their readers to the people of Senegal with descriptions of the habitants of Gorée. As well, while *Esquisses* offers an overview of the habitants as a whole, the *Atlas* explicitly excludes the male members of this métis class from its visual geography of Senegal.

While *Esquisses*'s written text has received some sustained critical attention, its *Atlas* has not engendered the same kind of analysis. In the one-page preface to the *Atlas*, Boilat offers his illustrations, which he notes are but a sample of the many drawings he made while in Senegal, as evidence for and supplement to the text in *Esquisses*, telling his reader that the illustrations are "indispensable [vital] for a complete understanding of the history I've sketched in my *Esquisses sénégalaises*."[5] His insistence directs his reader not to read the *Atlas* as mere reiteration of his textual explication of Senegalese ethnic groups. As Kay Dian Kriz reminds us, "Images often reinforce and sometimes subvert or complicate certain ideas conveyed in words; but what they never do is simply duplicate the meaning (assuming that one could ever be securely fixed) of a written text" (*Slavery*, 5). Underscoring its distinct object status are the *Atlas*'s unique copyright, separate preface, and explanatory notes for each plate. Furthermore, as with the other images in the visual archive I have traced thus far, the illustrations in the *Atlas* circulate well beyond their material bindings: they not only appear in contemporary books on Senegal but also proliferate in virtual space, abstracted from their physical and textual attachment to *Esquisses*. As complement and supplement to *Esquisses*, Boilat's *Atlas* at once invites a closer examination of his written text and broadens that text's horizon.

Indeed, in its visuality, the *Atlas* exceeds linguistic boundaries. Without fluency in French, one could still discern that the plates depict distinct groups of people. Even the *Atlas*'s structure appears to encourage a reading outside of textual literacy: Boilat first offers written explanations of all of the plates and then presents all of the illustrations. One is thus able to move from one image to the next without interrupting the text, save the brief captions under each plate.[6] Furthermore, if we consider the *Atlas* in terms of the nineteenth-century French definition of the word *atlas*, to be a collection of maps, then we might also read it as a plan for understanding the relationships between the ethnic groups depicted by Boilat. That Boilat also includes a detailed "Carte de peuples du Sénégal" (Map of the people of Senegal) in *Esquisses* that "includes vast areas of land that do not belong to the current Senegalese state (mainly the Gambia and parts of Mauritania and Mali)" underscores the urgency of his mapping project in producing knowledge about his ostensible compatriots (Murphy, "Birth," 57). Boilat's map in *Esquisses* reflects his knowledge of the interior region by marking places outside of France's narrow control of the region, which was at the time of his return to Senegal "limited to Saint-Louis and Goree" (Diop, introduction, 7).[7] Noting the names of islands along the Senegal River and labeling

FIGURE 7.
Signare. L'Abbé P.-D.
Boilat, *Esquisses
sénégalaises: Physionomie
du pays, peuplades,
commerce, religions, passé
et avenir, récits et légendes.
Atlas* (Paris: P. Bertrand,
1853), plate 1. Colored
lithograph.
General Research and Reference
Division, Schomburg Center
for Research in Black Culture,
New York Public Library, Astor,
Lenox and Tilden Foundations.

large spaces in the map with the names of the ethnic groups living in the region, Boilat's map in *Esquisses* offers evidence not only of Boilat's familiarity with the place's physical and human geography but of his authority to produce the geography in the first place. Boilat's command over the terms of how his reader sees Senegal is reiterated and expanded in the *Atlas.* The exquisitely detailed, richly colored images arrest and draw the viewer into Boilat's world. He has made these drawings; his audience must see the people he depicts through his eyes.

Most pressing here is the placement of the signare at the *Atlas's* opening. Boilat's readers must have been startled and slightly perplexed to encounter his signare (figure 7). Unambiguously brown, modestly and simply dressed, unadorned save a small earring, seated indoors in a high-backed chair in front of a fireplace, and holding a small book in her hands, her gaze sedate and direct, Boilat's signare confounds her own stereotypes. Not only did eighteenth- and nineteenth-century European representations of the signare repeatedly emphasize her mixed-race status, sensuality, and vanity, but also by 1853 the spectacle of the near-white mulatta concubine was in strong circulation across the Atlantic world. In offering a portrait of a reserved, relatively unadorned woman firmly ensconced inside a recognizably domestic space, Boilat's revision apparently rejects European assessments of the signares that emphasize their vanity and sexual availability to white men.

If we read the *Atlas* as a collection of maps, we should then consider the signare to mark the point of entry, the threshold one must cross in order to travel and make sense of the geography charted by Boilat. And if maps mark "location, relative position, and routes of travel" (Bassett, "Cartography," 317), then we need also examine the signare's relative position to the other subjects depicted by Boilat in order to understand how she travels across the Atlas. Attending to the visuality of the *Atlas* reveals not only Boilat's mapping of an intimate geography of nation, transnation, and diaspora but, most strikingly, the centrality of his rendition of the signare to said productive mapping.

Staking Diaspora

Born on Saint-Louis in 1814 to a signare mother and a French father, Boilat was orphaned at a young age; he was subsequently sent to France to be educated in a newly established "seminary for African children" that was meant to produce "an African clergy that could minister to the local population in local languages" (Jones, *Métis*, 78, 77). The record indicates that the children taken from Senegal and deposited in France experienced a traumatic rupture. As D. H. Jones explains, "Nineteenth-century Europe was the black-man's grave. About half [of the children brought from Africa to the French seminary] died of tuberculosis and others were recalled by their alarmed parents, until only three, David Boilat, Arsene Fridoil and Pierre Moussa, remained" ("The Catholic Mission," 333). Boilat was ordained in 1840 as one of the "first three Senegalese priests of modern times" (332). In 1842, at the age of twenty-eight, Boilat returned to Senegal in order to proselytize the local population. While Boilat's time in Senegal was marked by conflict and financial problems, he stayed there for ten years, during which time he helped establish a school and traveled extensively throughout the region. In 1852, one year before publishing *Esquisses*, he returned to France, where he spent his remaining years (Diop, introduction, 5–6).

To read Boilat as an African diasporic subject is to trouble the stakes of theorizing a black Atlantic defined by the Middle Passage. Critical attention to *Esquisses* has analyzed and debated Boilat's position and allegiance to the particular French colonial project in Senegal and has thus placed Boilat and his work in terms of how he and it speak to questions of nation.[8] What I would like to consider here is how Boilat's orphan status, dispersal to France, and survival in that hostile climate place him within a specific relationship to diaspora. Boilat did not experience the unique horror of the Middle Passage. However, surely the thirteen-year-old orphaned boy sent to a foreign and hostile climate would have experienced some sort of terror. With no parents to request his return home, witness to the deaths of half of his classmates, subject to a religious education that likely emphasized his racial inferiority and spiritual poverty, Boilat entered a diasporic space that was both unique and embedded in the social and economic systems inextricable from the transatlantic slave trade.

The very purpose of Boilat's displacement meant that he and his fellow students shared language and culture and were likely mandated to retain and practice their indigenous languages. That several of the children's parents retrieved them from the evangelical experiment underscores both the apparent volition and the intended temporariness of their displacement. Indeed, the whole endeavor was grounded in the premise that the students would return to Senegal as emissaries to their own people. The project's success thus depended upon that which diaspora would otherwise foreclose. To assert Boilat's diasporaness, then, is to emphasize, rather than flatten, the multiple experiences of and relationships to diaspora within the economies of the transatlantic trade. To highlight the privilege of his background against the trauma of his individual experience is to posit a point of departure for thinking about how this diasporic subject in this place and time imagined and produced a geography of nation and belonging against his own dispossession.[9]

Hartman's rumination on diaspora instructs and troubles: "It is only when you are stranded in a hostile country that you need a romance of origins; it is only when you *lose your mother* that she becomes a myth" (*Lose*, 98, emphasis in original). As with (but emphatically not "like") those in an American African diaspora, Boilat lost his mother and was subsequently taken to what, from the evidence of the fate of his nonorphaned peers, was very much a hostile place. (And whether he, invested in his Frenchness, found Senegal differently hostile is a question.) And it is not an aside to emphasize that unlike those in the Americas and some others living in the very place of his return, Boilat was never enslaved. To insist that he has lost his mother, has been displaced, is not to suggest that his experience in diaspora is akin to that of those black subjects produced by the Middle Passage. It is to say that his entry into diaspora is driven by the same logic and economies of power, race, and capital that enacted transatlantic slavery. It is to understand his mapping of Senegal through this signare in this *Atlas* to be full of a specific kind of desire, longing, to be a map that charts a "romance of origins" that *begins* in myth. It is to consider Boilat's *Atlas* to participate in a ritual constitutive of diaspora, a piecing together, a tracing and retracing, an insistence that fragments, echoes, fleeting repetitions mean *something*. And it is to recognize, through this stringing together, marking of continuity, and connection among the peoples of Senegal, how decidedly *uncollective* an experience of diaspora can be.

Threshold

As discussed throughout this book, particular attention to the signares' sartorial choices, especially their distinctive headwrap, flows through travelers' insistence on the signares' inscrutability and unfixability within the racial and national binaries central to the coherence of European presence in Africa. In the *Atlas*, so too does the signare's clothing and headwrap mark a certain otherness to her social identity. At the same time, Boilat's signare is inextricable from French civilization. Thus, Boilat infuses her skin, headwrap, and clothing with the same vibrancy that he does the high-backed chair upon which she sits. The markers of the signare's distance from a legitimate French subject position—her unambiguously brown skin, the heavy layer of fabric she drapes over her simple dress, her towering headwrap—are countered by her poise on the highbacked chair, her ease and comfort inside a carefully marked European-style interior. In intensity of color and placement within the frame, the high-backed chair is as much a focal point as the signare herself. And although less prominent, the clearly distinguishable fireplace, the heavy drapes, and the framed art in the background all work against the pervasive signs of the natural world in portrayals of free women of color across the Atlantic world—those palm trees and other fauna that mark the women as exotic, possibly savage, and definitely Other.

It is possible that Boilat's portrait of the costume of the signare may be read as an echo of the ethos of "refinement" found in European artists' depictions of the Americas. In her examination of Italian artist Agostino Brunias's prolific eighteenth-century depictions of free women of color in the British West Indies, Kriz contends, "It is precisely [the free(d) mulatta's] ambiguous social and racial status—her in-betweenness—that Brunias exploits in order to represent civilized society under development in a place 'in-between' civilized Europe and savage Africa" (*Slavery*, 45). In Brunias's scenes, the well-dressed mulatta is the "sort of woman . . . best able to represent the prosperity and promise of the newest British colonies in the West Indies" (57). Given Boilat's endeavor to argue simultaneously for the inherent value of Senegalese culture and the colonial enterprise of the French, it would not be a stretch to imagine that his depiction of the signare invites the same imagining of possibilities as do Brunias's illustrations of mulatta women.

However, Boilat's explanatory text, especially within the distinct sociohistorical context of Gorée and Saint-Louis, troubles such an interpretation. In terms of Brunias's depictions, Kriz argues: "Within the racial hierarchy of West Indian sexual relations, white men were widely acknowledged to be the winners of the contest with black men and men of color over possession of the bodies, if not the hearts of the *mulâtresses*.... The promise of refinement offered here by well-dressed mulatto women shopping for linen goods does not preclude, and in fact, is fueled by, the fantasy of rude sexual pleasures that the mulatto woman presented to white men in the West Indies" (*Slavery*, 51). As discussed in the previous chapter, by the beginning of the nineteenth century, the habitant populations of Gorée and Saint-Louis had reached demographic "maturity": the male habitants had emerged as the political and economic leaders of each island. Furthermore, in contrast to Brunias's depiction of "foppish, ineffectual mulatto men" (Kriz, *Slavery*, 51), Boilat boldly asserts the male habitants' equivalence to French men, writing, "I have no point in giving the costume nor the racial characteristics of the men of color, called the habitants of Senegal; their racial characteristics are Caucasian, and their way of dress is absolutely French."[10] As with the habitants' 1789 petition, Boilat's insistence on the habitants' nearness to a French identity simultaneously appeals to and subverts French authority over the men. Unlike the petitioners, Boilat's explicit project in *Atlas* does not seem to be proving the habitants' worthiness for French subjecthood. Instead, he takes the men's proximate French identity as a given, a point of departure.

Boilat then offers the signares as contrast to the habitants' near-absolute racial and cultural assimilation into French identity. Informing his reader that, unlike the men, the signares "still retain their distinctive dress," Boilat states that the woman presented in the *Atlas*'s first plate is dressed as the signares would be in "their interior." Noting, almost as an aside, that the "signare ladies are housed nearly the same as in France, their homes built in brick or stone," Boilat implies that the signares would be just as comfortable, just as at ease, in France as in Senegal.[11] At the same time, by focusing on how the signare is dressed and framing her dress within the privacy of her home, perhaps even playing on the multivalent word "interior," Boilat asserts a knowledge that both presupposes and produces his readers' unfamiliarity with the details of the signares' domestic and intimate lives.

The balance of his two-page explanation of his illustrated plate of the signare is spent detailing how decidedly non-French are the cultural practices of the signares. For example, he explains how "the signares divide themselves by societies or companies known as *mbotaye*." Important also for Boilat is the signares' subversive accommodation to the French Civil Code. Because the code requires immediate reporting of births, the habitants and signares can no longer follow their traditional practice of waiting until the eighth day of life to name a newborn (Boilat, *Atlas*, 6). Rather than abandon the ritual altogether, the signares

have developed a new tradition: "the first outing of the infant." Describing the
celebration, Boilat details how the signares, organized in their mbotaye, send
food and drink to the family. Visits to the family are grand productions, with the
signares accompanied by "parents and friends, each followed by many servants,"
and dressed extravagantly in *mboubes*, or caftans, that are "embroidered with finesse and with artistry, the neck, the ears, the arms, and the feet adorned with
gold jewelry."[12] Significant, too, is that the first time he mentions the mboube in
Esquisses is in describing the dress of the black population, a category he marks
as separate from that of the habitants (Boilat, *Esquisses*, 8). Boilat's explanation
of the plate thus details the signares' deliberate and recalcitrant attachment to
black African cultural practices.

Against his readers' expectations of depictions not only of the signares specific to this place but also of the free(d) mulatta concubine across the circum-
Atlantic, the brownness of Boilat's signare reflects and enacts Boilat's subversive rendering. Against the preponderance of representations of the signares as
free(d) mulatta concubines, where the near whiteness of their skin color makes
visible a presumption that white European men are "the winners of the contest
with black men and men of color over possession of bodies" of the women, Boilat's depiction of a brown-skinned signare challenges that claim to victory and
stakes its own claim. In this *Atlas*, the signare, brown-skinned, African in culture and dress, rooted in a female-centric society of mothers, sisters, and friends,
appears to achieve on this side of the Atlantic that gender-specific recupera-
tion of will and agency that, as Pier Gabrielle Foreman insists, black women in
the nineteenth century had to "work to steal away": on Gorée and Saint-Louis,
whether stolen, negotiated, or bought, the signares in this geography appear to
exercise what Foreman describes as a "black female motive will and active desire
as well as . . . an economically, legally viable and racially inflected motherhood"
("Who's Your Mama," 507). The contest is not between black or mulatto or white
male claims to possession of the free(d) mulatta concubine. The contest here, its
results conveyed through the unambiguously brown color of the signare and her
insistently African rituals of dress, birth, and celebration, is about the women's
own claims to their own bodies and lives.

It may seem contradictory to spend so much time on an analysis of Boilat's
text in pursuit of a claim about the significance of the *visual* work of the *Atlas*.
To do so, however, is to underscore that the plate's accessibility across language
depends on and even demands diaspora literacy; here, that means a certain understanding of the transnationality of blackness within and across the physical
and human geography Boilat maps in the *Atlas*. As well, and interconnected
with this first point, is again the question of evidence in any account of African diaspora. Boilat's textual explication thus works doubly: for his reader—the

intrigued or disinterested French subject—Boilat's textual explanations of his plates teach one *how* to see the plates; for the diasporic subject, perhaps even for Boilat, the text offers legitimating evidence that the visceral and geographic encounter with and across the subjects depicted in his visual archive makes sense.

Thus placed at the threshold, liminal in her simultaneous nearness to and distance from Frenchness, the signare is the point of entry for reading the *Atlas*'s human geography of Senegal. And here, too, seeps through the work in diaspora of making sense of what has happened and imagining possibilities for something else. For within this echo traced herein, the *Atlas*'s synthesis of visual and textual signposting, in concert with the appearance of its most in-between figure at its threshold, evokes the work performed by the vèvès in vodou. Let me state clearly: I am not suggesting that the portraits in the *Atlas* are akin to the vèvès. Nor am I speculating that the evangelical Catholic Boilat used his drawings, like vèvès, to open the crossroads between the earthly and divine, to "praise, summon, and incarnate all at once" the presence of the sacred (Thompson, *Flash*, 188). Rather, what compels me is how the signare's location in the *Atlas* and the multiple and variable signs of her cultural identity underscore both the opposition between two vastly different worlds and worldviews and the signare's unique ability to inhabit the space between the two worlds and serve as a conduit between them. To read this portrait specifically in terms of the vèvès, then, is not to ascribe a subversive Afro-diasporic religious intervention on Boilat's part. Rather, it is to emphasize the ontological labor of finding one's place in diaspora and the centrality of this figure, the signare, placed at the threshold of the *Atlas*, and her multiple incarnations on *this* side of the Atlantic to that labor.

Anticipation

To enter the *Atlas* through the signare is to consider her the point of entry into a human geography of diaspora that marks moments, identities, ways of being not before but rather *away* from the point of departure, the point of irretrievable rupture and dispersal. That is, if the echo of the signare across the Atlantic in Ezili signals how captive (and noncaptive) Africans passing through these parts may have seen, made meaning of, and remembered the signares' practices of freedom, then perhaps her echo backward, away from the Door of No Return, toward places encountered *before* arrival on the coast, invites us to consider the *anticipation* of her presence at this point of departure.

The sequence of plates in the *Atlas* reiterates Boilat's plotting of the landscape in *Esquisses*: having located the habitants on the island of Gorée, he begins with the Serer, the group he has marked as farthest west, and moves east, toward the interior. Even as each plate offers a representation, or something representative, of each ethnic group, so does each plate offer a portrait of an individual. Furthermore, the *Atlas*'s material form means that none of its plates may be viewed simultaneously; until the very recent digitalization of the work, none of the full-page plates could be seen side by side. To move across the human landscape produced by Boilat, to make connections between each figure, one must rely on something seen and remembered, turn pages, retrace movement, and turn back again to discern what, if anything, holds the *Atlas* together. That the landscape in each plate changes so dramatically and pointedly as one moves across the *Atlas* underscores the plates' resistance to a facile navigation, to an easy familiarity with its subjects.

And still, there is a distinctive repetition, a careful signposting of dress and landscape that marks connections and differences between the figures. Across the groups he surveys, the Serers, the Wolofs, the Moors, the Mandingos, the Toucouleur, the Sarackoullé, the Peules (Poulard), and the Bambara, Boilat explains not only the general characteristics of each group he represents but also the circumstances of the individuals who sit for his portraiture. In these small stories, in the persistent presentation of solitary figures, what emerges alongside Boilat's reiteration of travelers' narratives that stereotyped groups of people is a sense of Boilat's desire to connect. As Mark Hinchman contends in his examination of the *Atlas*, "Boilat made an important observation: the people represented in his book showed their representations to their friends and relatives. . . . He indirectly implies that the people represented saw themselves in his portraits. This underscores that African viewers and readers of the *Esquisses* saw in Boilat's portraits, textual and visual, something familiar" ("When Stereotypes").[13] Hinchman's assertion helps illuminate Boilat's efforts to make visible his individual relationships with the people he sketched. What matters to me here is how Boilat's portraits reflect an intimate understanding of how each individual inhabited and navigated an African landscape within an Atlantic geography.

Even as the *Atlas* conveys familiarity and intimacy across the human landscape Boilat has produced, so does it lead the reader away from the contact zone of Gorée and the West African coast and into the hinterland, those parts of Senegal not controlled by France. Thus, if we enter the place mapped by the *Atlas* through the signares, we exit it through the Bambara woman, the last figure portrayed in the *Atlas* (figure 8). The portrait is resplendent. Seated on a straw mat, her legs tucked underneath and slightly to her left, the figure gazes directly at the viewer. Noticeable and striking are the three vertical marks on each cheek. The woman's clothing is perhaps the most sumptuous of all the women presented in the *Atlas*, including the signare and the Wolof queen of Walo. As Boilat's explanatory text describes, "She is in holiday clothing; her costume is very rich; the scarves on her head are beautiful madras, and her mboube is silk.

FIGURE 8.
Femme Bambara. L'Abbé
P.-D. *Boilat, Esquisses
sénégalaises: Physionomie
du pays, peuplades,
commerce, religions, passé
et avenir, récits et légendes.
Atlas* (Paris: P. Bertrand,
1853). Colored lithograph.
General Research and Reference
Division, Schomburg Center
for Research in Black Culture,
New York Public Library, Astor,
Lenox and Tilden Foundations.

Her necklace ends in carefully made straw rings."[14] The woman appears to be wearing three layers of fabric: while only a portion of her costume's skirt is visible, its multiple folds indicate its fullness. Yellow in background, the striped skirt alternates thick red lines, narrow pairs of green lines, and a muted line of dark gray rectangular shapes. Over the skirt but under the top layer of clothing falls a substantial width of white fabric, its folds again suggesting its fullness as it grazes the tops of her knees. The top layer of her mboube is white in background and boldly striped in green, blue, and red lines, with a crisscrossed white edge bordering the shirt's bottom, falling at midthigh on the seated woman. In addition to her necklace, adorning the woman are simple bangles, two on her wrist and one around her ankle, and medium-sized gold earrings. Atop her head is an intricate headwrap of two distinct fabrics, both with rose background, one decorated with black dots, the other with darker rose crisscrossed lines; her headdress towers (but not in the particular cone shape, like that of the signare) and is tied in a distinctive knot in the front.

If the *Atlas's* signare sits at the threshold of diaspora, if she is Boilat's point of entry for mapping belonging and authority, then the Bambara woman who closes the *Atlas* marks the heart of the matter. Farthest from the coast in Boilat's geography, inhabitants of the African interior, the Bambara occupy a prominent place in African diasporic history and imagination. As Gwendolyn Midlo Hall details, the Bambara were brought to the coast as captives and served key roles for the French on Gorée and Saint-Louis, laboring as domestic workers, river guides, and interpreters for the French (*Africans*, esp. chap. 2). Indeed, the appearance of the Bambara in the histories of these islands underscores the island's diasporic geographies. By the mid-eighteenth century, "'Bambara' was variously used in the eighteenth century to refer to a slave, especially at Galam and on the island of Gorée; to a captive from east of the Senegal river; to a slave soldier; to the ethnic group of an individual's captor; or to a pagan or non-Muslim" (Caron, "'Of a Nation,'" 102; see also Hall, *Africans*, 42). The French application of "Bambara" to any captive laboring on the islands thus reflected the violent erasure of specific and autonomous African social, ethnic, and national identities so central to the mechanics of slavery and colonialism. In this context, Boilat's inscription of the Bambara generally and the Bambara woman specifically underscores the tension in official histories and archives in telling diasporic histories.

At the same time, Hall's history of the roots and evolution of Afro-Creole culture in Louisiana indicates the persistence of an identifiable Bambara identity against the stereotyping of the French. Drawing from records from Louisiana that indicate that the Bambara formed a significant number of captives brought to that colony, Hall argues that the Bambara "played a preponderant role in the formation of the colony's Afro-Creole culture" (*Africans*, 41). Addressing the concern that French understandings of African "national and ethnic identities" did not necessarily reflect how those Africans so marked understood their own nationality, Hall mines the written and oral histories for linguistic, social, cultural, and political evidence to support her assertion that "there is little doubt that the Bambara brought to Louisiana were truly ethnic Bambara" (42; see also Caron, "'Of a Nation,'" 99). Perhaps most importantly, within an African diasporic landscape, in colonial Louisiana slaves marked in the archive as Bambara were key actors in individual and group resistance and rebellion (see Hall, *Africans*, esp. chap. 4). Indeed, a fascination with the Bambara as emblematic of resistance and survival permeates Louisiana and African diasporic history.

As an isolated figure, the Bambara woman in the *Atlas* echoes the stereotypical representation of her ethnic group as a generic term for Africans viewed as sufficiently Other to be held as slaves. The uniqueness of her necklace, the visible presence of her gold hoop earrings, the nakedness of her feet, the tropical landscape behind her (a palm tree in the distance), her straw mat, her colorful clothing, her headwrap, and, perhaps most damning, the scars that mark her face work to cast her as intractably African as possible, as far from French womanhood as the interior trappings of the signare's home move her toward it.

Furthermore, twice in his textual explanation—once in *Esquisses* and again in the *Atlas*—Boilat informs his reader of the Bambara woman's near-slave status within her own ethnic group. In his description of the plate depicting the Bambara man, which immediately precedes that of the Bambara woman, Boilat laments: "The greatest fault [of the Bambara] after that of having nothing of religion, is that they have no kind of affection for the family. For them, the woman is nothing but a slave who one employs as long as she is useful and whom one gets rid of when one no longer wants her. It happens frequently that a Bambara man, after three or four years of marriage, sells his wife and their children into slavery, and remarries a younger wife." Boilat's characterization thus underscores the barbarity of the ethnic group most representative of captive Africans on the Senegambian coast. Most striking is the gendered specificity of the Bambara woman's vulnerability to the abuse and slavery. The Bambara woman, her "great intelligence [and] jovial character" notwithstanding, embodies the barbarism of a tribe farthest away from both Boilat's own ethnic group and any potential for French legibility.[15]

Read against and alongside the signare, however, the Bambara woman might be understood to represent something else, too. For if she signifies the limit of what it means to be African, if she is the final example of the specifically gendered vulnerability of African women across a Senegalese landscape, she also indicates the tenuous liminality of the signare's privileged position in diaspora. That is, if the signare sits at the threshold, literally and geographically occupying a liminal space, then the Bambara woman, placed as she is in Boilat's *Atlas*, demands we consider what lies on both sides of that liminality.

The signare's hypervisibility and social and class status may appear to undermine an insistence on her liminality. For example, in Victor Turner's classic formulation, "the subject of the passage ritual is, in the liminal period, structurally, if not physically, 'invisible'" ("Betwixt," 97). Furthermore, the status of liminal subjects is profoundly marked by absence: they "are symbolically either sexless or bisexual" and "*have* nothing. They have no status, property, insignia, secular clothing, rank, kinship position, nothing to demarcate them structurally from their fellows" (99, emphasis in original). Following this definition, the signares are everything but liminal.

However, the signares' liminality is a geographic one. This geographic liminality was perhaps most evident during the height of the transatlantic slave trade. By the time of Boilat's *Esquisses* and *Atlas*, certainly the status of the habitants and the signares had achieved more than a modicum of stability; they had created their own social order that in itself was not liminal, even as they sought to secure the benefits of being French subjects. However, what the presence of the Bambara woman demands we remember are the contours and the stakes

of the signares' privilege. They inhabited a place where it appears it was accept-
able for some black and African men to sell their wives into slavery when the
women became useless to their husbands.[16] And here, too, we must remember
that, according to Lamiral, the French men living on the islands followed the
same practice of selling wives no longer useful into slavery. And finally, the signares inhabited a place where a "clandestine" slave trade in young girls persisted
into the beginning of the twentieth century, well after the abolition of slavery
(see Klein, *Slavery*, 29).[17]

Within this context, against the specificity of the gendered and sexualized
nature of the persistent slavery in this landscape, the liminality of the signares
also lies in the precariousness of their position in diaspora. Again, as a class, as
part of the habitant ethnic group, and within a Senegalese context, the signares
appear to have enjoyed the privilege and status of their subject identity; indeed,
the visceral enjoyment of this status is marked by their lavish ritual celebrations
of birth and marriage as described by Boilat and in their ostentatious displays
of wealth and property via their adornment and "an entourage of slave women
to accompany them on public outings" (Jones, *Métis*, 49). However, if we consider them in terms of diaspora, then we must consider such enjoyment in terms
of their status as African women in a landscape where "female slaves *remained*
in high demand throughout the nineteenth century" (49, emphasis added). To
consider the signares in terms of diaspora is to consider the tenuousness of the
thread that links the disparate and often mutually hostile ethnic groups mapped
by Boilat in *Esquisses* and the *Atlas*. It is to consider what it means to be free,
what it means to be safe when such freedom and security depend on one's ability to transform sex into wealth and power. It is to consider that to remain free
and safe demands that one is anchored to a port, an entrepôt, one is always connected to water, one is always in the place where departure and return are only
possibilities full of treachery. To be in such a place secure only in one's connection to property and respectability, to always be on display, to be, in one's
body, evidence of the possibility of freedom and the costs one must pay for that
possibility. (Perhaps, then, to be a signare in the time of slavery was to inhabit a
precarious refuge.)

Crossing

If eighteenth-century Gorée and Saint-Louis were liminal in their geographies, antebellum New Orleans was marvelous.[18] Situated on the banks of
the Mississippi, antebellum New Orleans was a bustling shipping port that attracted commerce, immigrants, and visitors from the Caribbean, Europe, and
North America. The city's physical landscape and tropical climate astounded

white European and Anglo-American visitors well into the nineteenth century. Charles César Robin's 1807 account of his entry into New Orleans via the Bayou St. John is emblematic of and sets the tone for other nineteenth-century travelers' encounters with the city and is thus worth quoting at length:

> These stagnant waters swarm with reptiles, especially alligators and are divided into so many channels that it is easy to lose one's way in them. They are shaded by tall trees which are, however, crowded and deformed and covered from their tops to the ends of their branches with a lugubrious covering of a plant parasite, a kind of grayish moss which hangs down in festoons up to seven feet long, which causes the branches to bend under its weight. This covering conceals much of the foliage and gives to these wild places a strange air of sadness. (*Voyage*, 30)[19]

The viscerally "stagnant" and festering swamps that "swarm with reptiles, especially alligators," convey the menace with which New Orleans's landscape accosted its visitors. The maze of waterways and the "deformed" trees burdened with a "lugubrious covering of a plant parasite" worked together to produce a disorienting, marvelous site for white European and Anglo-American travelers about to enter New Orleans. Early and mid-nineteenth-century travelers' accounts thus regularly expressed varying degrees of surprise and consternation in their initial encounters with the city. Frances Trollope's account of her entry into New Orleans in 1827 describes "the most unnatural appearance imaginable" (*Domestic Manners*, 5). And Frederick Law Olmsted's description implies a deliberate deceit in the city's geography: "I had expected to be landed at New Orleans by the boat, and had not been informed of the rail-road arrangement, and had no idea in what part of Louisiana we might be" (*Journey*, 579–80). For these travelers, the city's singularity—literally spectacular—is rendered almost organic, an inherent consequence of its natural landscape and geographic location.

Just as New Orleans's topography disoriented its visitors, its human pageantry enthralled them. Ostensibly part of the United States, and despite a consequential Yankee population, the city overwhelmed European and Anglo-American visitors with a French colonial past and a resilient Creole culture fortified by nearly ten thousand refugees from Saint-Domingue by way of Cuba.[20] Central to the antebellum city's exotic scenery were the notoriously beautiful near-white quadroon women.[21] As Emily Clark details, descriptions of the women's licentiousness were "wildly inaccurate and borrow[ed] freely" from descriptions of colonial Saint-Domingue's mulâtresses (*Strange History*, 52).[22] Furthermore, European and Anglo-American travelers' accounts consistently assign responsibility for quadroons' "wantonness" and relationships with white men to the women; as suggested in chapter 2, the quadroons thus appear to inhabit a sexualized agency otherwise incongruous in a slave society. Even those writers who acknowledged illicit sexual unions in other U.S. cities found in New Orleans something particularly compelling. For example, Olmsted's passage through Virginia includes a single paragraph-length description of "colored ladies" whose dress and "carriage was more often stylish and graceful than that of white ladies who were out" (*Journey*, 28). In contrast, his encounter in New Orleans inspires six pages detailing the social status, economic operations, and sexual lives of the city's famous "colored women (mulattoes or quadroons)," including a declaration that, "their beauty and attractiveness being their fortune, they cultivate and cherish with diligence every charm or accomplishment they are possessed of. Of course, men are attracted by them, associate with them, are captivated, and become attached to them" (594).[23] Liminal in its geography and libertine in its sexual and racial mores, antebellum New Orleans offered Anglo-American and European visitors spectacles unimaginable outside the city's borders.

For enslaved and free(d) African Americans, however, antebellum New Orleans epitomized the slave South and provoked visceral terror. Fugitive slave narratives often included allusions to, if not experiences in, the New Orleans market. William and Ellen Craft encountered a "rough slave-dealer" who admonished William's "master" (a disguised Ellen) not to take William north but rather "sell, and let me take him down to Orleans" (*Running*, 24–25). In his own narrative, Henry Bibb presents the threat of the New Orleans market as the ultimate punishment for his multiple escapes. Whether sold down the river or sent to the New Orleans market, the passage of black captives through the city signified inevitably tragic and often horrific endings inextricably linked to the specter of New Orleans over the U.S. landscape.

Nor were free black people immune to the menace of New Orleans. According to Ira Berlin, while the city's free people of color enjoyed relative and often exceptional liberties, including freedom of movement and the "right to testify in court against whites," and experienced "relatively high status," they endured daily threats against their liberty (*Slaves*, 129). The 1830s, 1840s, and 1850s witnessed an escalation of oppressive laws against free people of color that ranged from forbidding the immigration of free black people to arresting black seamen who had the misfortune to dock in New Orleans. Extralegal measures against free black people included kidnapping and enslavement.[24] Even the intrepid Nancy Prince, a free black northerner who published her own travel memoir in 1850, refused to disembark at New Orleans. And while Prince suffered a similar experience at Key West, it is her encounter in New Orleans that receives extensive narrative attention; she describes "poor slaves, who were laboring and toiling, on either side, as far as could be seen with a glass" (*Narrative*, 78). For black Americans, slave and free, to encounter New Orleans meant to encounter a place "where we could neither escape ourselves, nor instruct others the way" (Bibb, *Narrative*, 51).

If Gorée, Saint-Louis, and the signares suggest a paradigm for theorizing how black subjects in diaspora may have imagined the possibilities for and freedom through the figure of the free(d) mulatta concubine, antebellum New Orleans may very well suggest the limits of such possibilities. The city's hostile geography and unique demographics, and consequent racial and social fluidity, particularly in the colonial period, helped to produce a place where "Africans and their descendants were competent, desperately needed, and far from powerless" (Hall, *Africans*, 155). Antebellum New Orleans was a place where enslaved Africans could congregate publicly in Congo Square, described by Shirley Thompson as a "market and a ritual performance space for New Orleanians of African descent" that "foster[ed] a limited economic and cultural resistance to increasingly restrictive laws governing slavery and interracial and interstatus mingling" (*Exiles*, 132, 133). The tertiary racial structure codified under French and Spanish rule persisted well into the nineteenth century, and the city's free people of color, by now many of whom had roots in Saint-Domingue, occupied a distinct racial, social, and legal status. Antebellum New Orleans was thus a place that witnessed extraordinary examples of black authority and self-determination in the face of the racial and sexual economies of slavery.

At the same time, the city was the site of the largest antebellum slave market in the South. The city was also infamous for its fancy trade, where slave traders and slaveholders bought, sold, and displayed publicly girls and women "for sex or companionship" (Johnson, *Soul*, 113). And while free black people faced increasing restrictions on their liberty within the city, so did free people of color hold others in bondage. While the historical narratives of the signares and habitants emphasize that class's familial (although not blood-kinship) relationships to those they enslaved, frameworks for theorizing black ownership in the United States must necessarily be more ambivalent. Speaking specifically about free(d) women of color, Wilma King notes, "Color appears to be less significant in assessing the treatment of slaves than the reasons for owning slaves" ("Out of Bounds," 132). Thus, while some free(d) people of color held legal ownership of family members and treated them as such, in other cases observers, including Eliza Potter, noted the particular cruelty of black slaveholders.[25]

Whether represented by white travelers as a site of spectacular black agency or experienced by African Americans as a place of extreme brutality, for white European and U.S. subjects, New Orleans provided what Joseph Roach calls "a constantly visible yet constantly receding perimeter of difference" necessary to maintaining the "myth of coherence at the center," in the case of the antebellum

United States, a racially and sexually coherent landscape (*Cities*, 39). As Emily Clark contends, the proliferation of exaggerated and spectacular literary repre-sentations of the New Orleans quadroon appeared in response to the specter of the Haitian revolution and the threat that the black rebellion there would invade the United States. Regarding the unabashed duplication of eighteenth-century depictions of Saint-Domingue's free(d) mulatta concubines in ante-bellum descriptions of New Orleans's quadroons, Clark observes: "If America was to be exposed to the reverberations of the Haitian Revolution, however, the *mulâtresse* was preferable to the alternative of unbridled black violence. Directing the gaze of the American public toward the *mulâtresse* drew attention away from the more terrifying danger of the black rebellion that might escape the island's boundaries to far more devastating effect" (*Strange History*, 53). For antebellum travelers to the city, then, obsession over the agency of the free(d) mulatta con-cubine was central to a geography that rendered New Orleans the "perimeter of difference" that maintained the U.S. landscape racially and sexually coherent and thus ultimately, utterly secure for free white subjects.

Against this context, Eliza Potter's opening of the penultimate chapter of her 1859 narrative, *A Hairdresser's Experience in High Life,* appears to reiterate the preponderance of white European and Anglo-American antebellum descrip-tions of the Crescent City. She begins the chapter with the following disclaimer:

> I have spent many seasons in the South; sometimes I was in Natchez and Vicksburg, and at the plantations along the coast, but generally the greater por-tion of my time was spent in the city of New Orleans. I have been witness to many queer scenes in this southern country, the relation of which shall oc-cupy this chapter. They were all written long after they occurred, and in the order in which they presented themselves to my memory; so that this portion of my narrative will, perhaps, be more desultory and unconnected than any other. (Potter, *Hairdresser's Experience*, 144)

At first glance, Potter's description echoes those depictions that consistently por-tray New Orleans in spectacular terms, narrating a space that arrested the senses and engendered a visceral experience of strangeness by all who encountered it.

Eliza Potter, however, was no ordinary antebellum traveler, and her inscrip-tion of New Orleans does not simply reiterate the city's image within the U.S. racial imaginary. A free, colored, French-speaking hairdresser from the North, Potter, as Xiomara Santamarina argues, "exploited hairdressing's structural rela-tions of 'anonymous friendship' to inscribe herself not as the gossipy and socially inferior servant but as an expert in her clients' shortcomings as ladies" (*Belabored Professions*, 112). Potter moved easily through the private rooms of her clients and thus occupied a unique insider/outsider position in the "high life" society of

New Orleans. At the same time, her "many seasons in the South" coincided with increasing restrictions on the liberties and mobility of free African Americans in the antebellum United States. Just as her chapter on New Orleans satisfies her readers in its scintillating descriptions of interracial sex and marital indiscretions, it also, as Rafia Zafar describes, "abounds with tales of horror, from the chained, beaten slave who fights back and kills his master to colored, and cruel, slave owners" (*We Wear*, 168). A city as infamous for the size of its slave market as for its spectacularly visible interracial sexual economy could not function merely as a discursive site for Potter, a colored woman traveling alone.

Indeed, Potter consistently reminds her reader of the terror faced by any black woman, slave or free, moving across a U.S. landscape. While she explicitly frames her travel within the lexicon of choice, desire, and will, Potter also exposes and revises travelers' geographies that narrate New Orleans as a container for the excesses of a binary racialized slave society and a site of black female agency. At stake in Potter's revision of New Orleans are two issues, both of which center on the bodies of enslaved and free(d) mulatta concubines: the disavowal of the libidinal economy of slavery that at once denies white sexual desire for black subjects and enables the subjection of black subjects to that desire; and the disavowal of the brutality of such subjugation that simultaneously denies the sexual violation of black women and enables rationalization for this violence. Potter threads her narrative with a series of encounters with enslaved women whose relationships to travel at once mirror and threaten Potter's own. By insisting that the freedom of her own mobility and the impossibility of this same freedom for the enslaved black women she happens upon along her travels are linked inextricably by the specter of New Orleans, Potter produces a subversive geography that challenges the possibilities of freedom for a black female subject, even a mixed-race one, moving across a landscape marked indelibly by slavery.

Terror

Potter's subject position vis-à-vis her travel is central to her geography. While literary critics foreground Potter's autonomy as an independent woman traveler, what such analyses implicitly acknowledge is that one cannot presume Potter's status as a freely traveling subject. As Santamarina asks, "How could a Black woman author represent herself as an independent working woman who proclaims her 'liberty' in the book's first paragraph and not a goal to be reached at its end?" ("'So You Can See,'" 172). A free colored woman marked as a mulatto by at least one census taker, Potter inhabits a subject position threatened as easily as it is enriched by its location in the tertiary racial society of antebellum New Orleans.[26] The intersection of Potter's race and gender with the southern city complicates assertions that "by economic skills Potter gains geographic freedom" (Zafar, *We Wear*, 158) and that Potter's work "makes no reference to racial injustices" (Santamarina, "'So You Can See,'" 171). Through the construction of her travel, Potter reveals how the mythology of a sexually powerful and seductive free(d) mulatta concubine and the attachment of this mythology to New Orleans perpetually threaten the peace and safety of a free black woman traveling across the antebellum landscape.

In the first pages of her narrative, Potter declares, "Being at liberty to choose my own course, I determined to travel, and to gratify my long-cherished desire to see the world" (*Hairdresser's Experience*, 11). Through this initial description of the commencement of her travels, Potter inscribes her narrative into a canon of those whose travels are born of privilege rather than necessity. Eliza Potter's rather detached preface to her own description of the city underscores her uneasy fit within traditional readings of nineteenth-century African American literatures. Her assertions regarding travel further highlight her difference from other antebellum black authors.[27] Potter's ambition to "gratify [her] long-cherished desire" to travel separates her from both antebellum fugitive slaves and her more famous contemporary, the free northern black female traveler, activist, and writer Nancy Prince. Documenting her experiences from Boston to Russia and Jamaica, Prince also frames herself within discourses of travel and respectability. However, while Prince's travel was voluntary, it was motivated by a need to escape dire circumstances, as she states, "After seven years of anxiety and toil, I made my mind to leave my country" (*Narrative*, 20). In contrast, Potter emphasizes her choice to travel in terms of desire rather than necessity and deliberately appeals to an audience that "reached beyond the racialized norms of abolition and sentimental reform" (Santamarina, *Belabored Professions*, 124).

At the same time, Potter's repeated statements about her freedom to travel acknowledge what she leaves unstated: she is a black woman whose ability to travel is constantly threatened and increasingly circumscribed as the United States moves toward a civil war. Indeed, perhaps most remarkable is Potter's characterization of her marital status in the opening of her narrative. Describing her early years, she recalls: "At Buffalo, however, my journey was suddenly arrested by a sort of ceremony called *matrimony*, which I entered into very naturally, and became quieted down under it for a length of time *just as naturally*. I have seen other persons do the same thing, and so, I suppose, I need not be ashamed to own having committed a weakness, which has, from the beginning of time, numbered the most respectable of the earth among its *victims*" (Potter, *Hairdresser's Experience*, 11–12). As Santamarina notes in her annotations to Potter's narrative, Potter's "gesture of nonconformity resembles those of other [nineteenth-century] African American female writers, including Harriet Ja-

cobs ... and Harriet Wilson ... who refused, in their own narratives, to represent marriage as the culmination of their lived experiences" (introduction,
200n4). Potter's dispensation of marriage here is not only discursive: when read
in anticipation of how her memoir uses the visibility and vulnerability of enslaved and free(d) mulatta women to repeatedly underscore the terror of her
travel, her declarations of her marriage and her evident escape from that marriage hint at the limits of respectability as protection for a free woman of color
traveling across a U.S. landscape.[28] Thus, rather than a celebratory description
of her independence in labor and travel, Potter's opening pages offer a critical
commentary on the precariousness of autonomy for a free black woman moving
alone across antebellum North America.

Having introduced herself to the reader, Potter proceeds to describe the initial
leg of her journey, wherein she finds herself nearly isolated on a steamer bound
for Canada. She then details an encounter with a slave coffle on a ship headed
south on the Ohio River. Finally, Potter culminates her opening discourse on
travel with an episode featuring the escape of a near-white female slave. While
we do not know what Potter looked like, and while Potter herself never explicitly
identifies her own race or complexion, her deliberate identification with both of
the enslaved women she encounters as she embarks on her journey "to see the
world" reveals Potter's investment in the visible economy of slavery and hints
suggestively at the racial markings of her own body.

These incidents happen well before her chapter on New Orleans. They are
important, however, for assessing Potter's disruption of the myth of New Orleans as a site of agency for the free(d) mulatta concubine in that they establish
Potter's subject position vis-à-vis the sexually available black female commodity
upon which that myth depends. Across her encounters, the specter of New Orleans's libidinal racial economy constricts that which Potter so fervently desires,
the freedom to travel. In order to authenticate her agency, Potter confronts and
marks this specter head-on.

After detailing her freedom to venture forth into the world, Potter's first
chapter documents her initial encounter with the travel she has so "long-
cherished." Potter's account of her experience on a steamer bound from New
York to Toronto vividly demonstrates bell hooks's assertion that "from certain
standpoints, to travel is to encounter the terrorizing force of white supremacy"
("Whiteness," 174). Potter recollects: "I was alone in the world—self-exiled from
home and friends, to be sure—but it was not until we were out some distance
upon the rolling waters of the lake, that I realized my isolated condition. I sat
upon the deck, surrounded by people; but being a stranger among strangers,
I had no claim upon the notice of any one; and I gazed out, with somewhat
saddened feelings, upon the waste of waters before me" (*Hairdresser's Experi-*

ence, 12). Potter introduces her reader to the particular hazards of her travel as she recognizes her precariousness in the "waste of waters before" her. For African Americans in the antebellum United States, Canada represented one of the nearest sites of true freedom, outside the reach of the Fugitive Slave Acts of 1793 and 1850.[29] Yet, the very promise of refuge troubles the waters. The ship, full of strangers, threatens to strand the traveler as much as it offers relief from the limits of society. Potter's reassertion of her own agency, "self-exiled . . . to be sure," ironically disturbs that very choice. While Potter claims an authority to move freely, her assertion that she "had no claim upon the notice of any one" underscores her subjection to the authorizing gaze of her fellow passengers, none of whom share her "isolated condition."

Of course, any working woman traveling alone in the antebellum North would likely express similar anxiety; Potter's description, however, marks the specificity of her situation and, more importantly, comments on how her fears are shaped by a racialized geography. The "Governor-General of Canada" notices her discomfort and invites Potter to join him and his family at their table for dinner (*Hairdresser's Experience*, 12). Initially uneasy because she has "never before associated with those who considered themselves [her] superiors—*at table*" and because she understands that these same people, "had they been educated in [her] own country, would have indignantly repudiated any such arrangement," Potter is eventually persuaded to sit down (12–13). That Potter's discomfort may arise from her racialized position is a matter of speculation. Throughout her narrative, Potter marks her relationship with the newly formed middle class she describes primarily through her work in service to them; even without marking her racialized position, this difference in labor status could be sufficient to distinguish her from those who she contends would "consider themselves [her] superiors." Through the specificity of the "Governor-General of Canada" and her assertion that "had they been educated in [her] own country," however, Potter highlights her border crossing and thus alludes to fundamental differences between an oppressive United States and an apparently freer Canada.

Potter's description of her experience on the Toronto-bound steamer does not simply detail the fear and anxiety of a black woman under the scrutiny of strangers; it indicts the geographies of a white gaze on a black female traveling subject. Potter's most explicit reference to her own racialized position follows immediately in her satisfied declaration that "well-bred people perfectly understand the art of making all comfortable around them, no matter what their color or condition might be" (*Hairdresser's Experience*, 13). While "condition" may mark any one of a variety of social or legal statuses, Potter is a stranger to her fellow passengers; thus, one might safely assume her distinct "condition" to be readily recognizable.[30] While Potter's ensuing critique of "*parvenu* ladies and gentlemen" illustrates the contemptuous tone she employs throughout her narrative, her repeated declarations of her unease amongst wealthy whites who "considered themselves [her] superiors" underscores a pervasive fear of any potentially wrong move on her part (13).[31]

With her next riverboat adventure, Potter makes explicit the precariousness of her liberty and implicitly links it to the specter of New Orleans. After a brief stay in Toronto, Potter heads west to Cincinnati via a southbound steamer from Pittsburg on the Ohio River.[32] Her experience aboard the *David Marshall* is at first marked by a sense of community and self-confidence. Almost immediately, however, the ship is delayed, and a "*negro trader*" embarks with "a number of unfortunate beings in chains and shackles" (Potter, *Hairdresser's Experience*, 15, emphasis in original). Potter describes the chattel as "all confined, with the exception of *one*—a good-looking, well-formed girl, for whom he had obtained a *cabin passage* and who was treated better than her unfortunate companions. Why? Because the trader doomed her to *ignominy*. He knew he would be paid for his trouble and expense. She had beauty enough to arouse the *base lust of some southern buyer*" (15, emphasis in original). Here, Potter alludes to the fancy slave trade; as Deborah Gray White notes, while one found fancy girls throughout the slaveholding South, "New Orleans seems to have been the center of the trade" (*Ar'n't I a Woman?*, 37). Just as travelers passing through New Orleans regularly described quadroon balls and plaçage, so did they offer accounts of the fancy trade, though rarely did they link the two together.[33] The slave trader's embarkation while the ship is still in the North thus functions multiply: it literally arrests Potter's pleasurable journey, reminds the reader of the precariousness of her liberty even in free states, and links this precariousness to the specter of New Orleans's narratives of sex and race. With the entrance of the "well-formed girl" and the "trader [who] doomed her to ignominy," Potter's critique of race, geography, and the impossibility of desire confronts the commodities of sex and fantasy in the libidinal economy of slavery.

Although Potter does not describe the girl's color, the preponderance of nineteenth-century depictions of the fancy trade consistently focused on the enslaved subject's proximity to whiteness. In print media as varied as antislavery novels, travelers' journals, fugitive and ex-slave narratives, and correspondence between slave traders and buyers, descriptions of "fancy girls" or "fancy maids" emphasized the light and often near-white skin of the women traded. Edward Baptist's delineation of the fetishization and disavowal at work in slave traders' letters illuminates Potter's intervention in these narratives: "The value of a fancy maid . . . was lewdly plain. . . . She was neither precisely black nor white . . . but rather the 'fancy' of the market for selling the right to rape a special category of women marked out as unusually desirable" ("'Cuffy,'" 1642–43). Baptist argues that "fancy girls" were commodities and sexual fetishes; white slaveholders' descriptions of the girls as desirable because of their proximity to whiteness enabled disavowal of the planters' "creation of the 'impassioned object' [the fancy girl]" while he "returns compulsively [and] pleasures the self with the unacknowledged remembrance of a transgression without blame, an ambiguity controlled and fixed, a memory displaced and encoded in the fetish object" (1625). The repeated emphasis on the near-white appearance of "fancy girls" enables an acknowledgment of sexual attraction to a body otherwise marked as black even as it rejects the possibility of sexually desirable black women. Baptist thus theorizes that near-white fancy girls enabled two kinds of disavowal central to white patriarchal ideology: simultaneous acknowledgments and denials of racial difference and of the libidinal economy of slavery.

Potter's introduction of the "well-formed girl" simultaneously invokes the narrative of the fancy trade and disrupts its fetishization of near whiteness. Her description of the "privileging" of the unnamed girl against the ends to which she is condemned and her emphasis on the humanity of the girl (through inscribing the possibility of "ignominy" onto the captive body) provide a counternarrative to descriptions of the fancy slave trade that "depicted the enslaved in mystical terms as standardized objects" (Baptist, "'Cuffy,'" 1622).[34] In contrast to nonfictional and fictional accounts of the fancy trade, Potter does not explicitly mention the enslaved girl's complexion. Rather, she describes the girl's degraded subject position and links it to the libidinal economy of slavery. By not describing the skin color of the girl and by emphasizing the "base lust" of some southern buyer, Potter not only erases any fantasy that the girl has some agency but also resists her reader's assumption that it is because the girl is light that her sexuality is a commodity. Potter's refusal to mark explicitly the girl's skin color and insistence on the conditions of the girl's captivity thwart the construction of white male desire as being predicated on the near whiteness of the otherwise black female body and lay bare the sexual economy of slavery.

Potter's ensuing description of her own interaction with the "negro trader" and the "well-formed girl" illustrates and critiques how romanticized narratives of the fancy trade extend from the "Southern market" of New Orleans to impact Potter's own efforts to travel freely. When the trader insists on a "cabin passage" for the girl, Potter recounts, "I objected to sit at table with her . . . and it grieved me to contemplate the *cause* of the distinction shown between those who had been equally bought, and were alike to be sold" (*Hairdresser's Experience*, 15–16, emphasis in original). Her objection to "sit at table" with the girl recalls and inverts Potter's singular status in her previous voyage aboard the Canada-bound steamer, when she expressed surprise that the governor-general invited her to sit "at table." Potter's emphasis on the "*cause* of the distinction" reminds her reader that the terror of the girl's travel and the precariousness of Potter's own are linked by an economy of the fancy trade that exceeds the boundaries of the "Southern market" of New Orleans.

Finally, underscoring the precariousness of Potter's safe travel is a complex disavowal that results from her careful negotiation of her and her reader's gazes. In order to critique the terror that the libidinal economy of slavery holds for any traveling black woman, Potter must acknowledge her identification with the "well-formed girl." However, so that she can maintain her own tenuous safety, Potter must simultaneously distance her position from the girl's, which she does when refusing to "sit at table" with her. Potter's concomitant mirroring and dis-identification at once recognize and resist the fungibility of black women's bodies in a nearly futile effort to find a safe space in the free North.

And here, though she is emphatically not a concubine and only tenuously a mulatta, Potter's rhetorical mirroring invites us to speculate an intentional resistance to being seen as a free(d) mulatta concubine. That is, it is not only the poor girl's slave status that underscores Potter's terror in travel but also the specter of sexual licentiousness: if the passengers and reader might ascribe a threatening sexual agency to the enslaved girl, then they should also imagine that Potter risked being placed within the same economy, especially given antebellum stereotypes of black women's sexuality. Read within an African diasporic context, Potter's careful negotiation is even more haunting. Here again echoes Lasirèn and her insistence on unknowability as a tactic of resistance. Here again, in Potter's occupation as hairdresser, in her financial independence's dependence upon the simultaneous promise and peril of waterways, echoes Mami Wata. And if Lasirèn specifically and Ezili more categorically suggest how black Atlantic subjects may have imagined the possibilities for freedom, may have theorized the sexual and racial economies of those possibilities, Potter's travel on a ship that moves toward the largest slave market in the South, her insistently willful travel aboard a vessel that carries a fancy girl, demands those of us invested in the question to consider whether it is possible to imagine, articulate, and inhabit freedom without recourse to insisting on one's difference from those who are legitimately, in the most technical sense of the word, enslaved.

Remapping

In its apparently abrupt appearance and its prolonged focus on the sexual relations of slavery, caste, and skin color, Potter's chapter "Natchez–New Orleans" mimics travelers' narratives whose depictions of New Orleans operate in drastic contrast to their descriptions of the rest of the U.S. landscape. Between her opening chapter and this penultimate chapter, putatively devoted to New

Orleans, Potter spends the overwhelming majority of her narrative with her eye trained on her well-heeled clientele. Throughout the work, as Santamarina and Zafar argue, Potter foregrounds her paid labor in authenticating her authorial gaze. By the time her narrative arrives at New Orleans, Potter's early negotiation of race, sex, desire, and agency seems to have faded into the background of both her writing and her travel. In its decisive shift in focus, "Natchez–New Orleans," a cacophony of sexual and racial transgressions, impersonations, and deceptions, fulfills and even exceeds readers' expectations of literary representations of New Orleans.

However, the chapter also recovers and extends Potter's critique of the limits of her own travel. Just as her opening chapter's focus on travel through a supposedly free landscape produces an exegesis of the permeability of that space, Potter's examination of the workings of race, sex, desire, and freedom in New Orleans reveals the impossibility of containing the brutality of a specifically sexualized economy of slavery within a liminal city or limiting discussions of that economy to the spectacle of the free(d) mulatta concubine. Even the chapter's title, "Natchez–New Orleans," tethers New Orleans to another North American city and invokes movement between the two, thus reminding her reader that New Orleans is, by 1859, inextricably part of the United States rather than tenuously attached as that disorienting and exotic space evoked by other travelers.

Not only does Potter mark New Orleans familiar within a U.S. landscape, but the anecdote that opens "Natchez–New Orleans," detailing the killing of a white slaveholder by his mixed-race enslaved body servant, subverts dominant representations of New Orleans that largely erase New Orleans's mixed-race men from the imaginative landscape. For example, while Olmsted's extensive description of quadroon women and the system of plaçage begins by "refer[ring] to a class composed of the illegitimate offspring of white men and colored women," his account focuses exclusively on the women of this class. In passing, he notes, "What becomes of the boys, I am not informed" (Olmsted, *Journey*, 59–97). As explored in chapter 3, invisibility of free men of color in travelers' accounts is striking given the prominent role these men played in New Orleans's political, economic, and artistic life. As with the erasure of the male habitants of Gorée and Saint-Louis in European depictions of the signares, however, the absence of New Orleans's free men of color should not surprise. Race, gender, and sexuality are mutually supportive social constructions whereby patriarchy represents itself as stable in its whiteness, masculinity, and heterosexuality.[35] Whereas fetishization of near-white women, be they "fancy girls" or free quadroons, enables a disavowal that affirms heterosexual ideologies that help uphold patriarchy, the acknowledgment of white male or female sexual desire for mixed-race men would undermine the very definition of white masculinity.

Thus, as "Natchez–New Orleans" unfolds, its subversive opening anecdote belies the humility of Potter's prefatory remarks. The first pages of the chapter describe "Mr. H.," a Natchez resident who "treat[s] [his body servant] as a companion" (Potter, *Hairdresser's Experience*, 145). Potter's emphasis on the intimacy between the two men, whom she describes as "inseparable," implies a sexual relationship between them, albeit lopsided and qualified by the fact that Mr. H. "did not eat, drink or sleep with him" (145). And of course, underlying the "companionship" is the profound imbalance of power between master and slave, so that when "after a while a change [comes] over Mr. H.," he begins to abuse his property (145). Potter's account of his body servant's response is remarkable in its succinct assessment of the violent sexual and racial economy of slavery:

> It happened that, from some cause unknown, Mr. H. fell out with his body servant and chained him to a log of wood, and whipped him severely. He went out the next day to repeat the dose, when the despised slave, enraged at the treatment, broke loose from the log, seized it, and dashed Mr. H.'s brains out before the eyes of his family. It appears that, although a slave, he was descended from one of the highest southern families, and inherited all the proud feeling and independent spirit the Southerners generally pride themselves on. (*Hairdresser's Experience*, 145–46)

That Potter makes visible the presence of mixed-race men through an account of a murderous male captive lays bare the instability of white masculinity. The stakes of Potter's intervention here, against Boilat's own revision of mulatto masculinity, underscores the unevenness of the terrain traveled by the echo. While the habitants argue for inclusion into French nationhood, Potter illuminates the incommensurability of nation, race, and sexuality in the U.S. landscape. Her insertion neither beseeches nor stakes claim; it indicts the very terms of national belonging. While travelers' romances focus on love triangles between wealthy white men, seductive quadroon women, and respectable white women, all free subjects, Potter's account of the relationship between a married planter and his captive body servant explicitly delineates the dangerous corporeality of mixed-race men to the authority and vitality of white heteropatriarchal ideology.

It is precisely the man's enslavement that places him in an intimate bond with Mr. H. The intimacy of the relationship, the suddenness of its dissolution, and the violence of its conclusion mark it a sentimental romance. Consequently, the mechanics of the slave's murder of Mr. H. are central to Potter's intervention into romantic discourses of interracial sex. The "log of wood" is literally attached to the enslaved man's body. It is the site of Mr. H.'s assault on the captive slave and becomes in the hands of the self-freed slave an extension of his body. That the log of wood is transformed into an exaggerated and deadly black phallus that both imprisons the captive slave and murders the slaveholder renders the disavowal enabled by representations of the quadroon untenable.[36] Potter's portrayal of the graphically violent culmination of a white male slaveholder's homosexual desire for an enslaved black man and her explanation of the captive's mixed racial heritage make impossible the forgetting of the sexualized brutality of slavery's material conditions. Finally, as Potter is careful to note, the relationship between Mr. H. and the unnamed slave was common: "Almost all gentlemen in Louisiana and Mississippi have favorite body servants, and they are always very kind to them, more particularly than any other servant" (*Hairdresser's Experience*, 145). Rather than echo depictions of interracial sex in New Orleans that indulge in fantasies of seduction, exoticism, and public agency of free(d) near-white female subjects, Potter's introduction of New Orleans offers a portrayal of interracial sex permeated by intimate violence, the mundane, and individual desperate acts, each and all of which reveal fissures in the stability of white heteronormative patriarchal identity.

Following Potter's account of Mr. H. and his body servant are a series of vignettes that satisfy and exceed her reader's expectations of literary representations of New Orleans. These anecdotes include descriptions of heterosexual consensual interracial relationships between white women and mixed-race men across state lines and "hundreds of mulattoes who are married to white men" in Potter's adopted hometown, Cincinnati (*Hairdresser's Experience*, 155). Crossing state and geographic borders within a chapter putatively devoted to New Orleans, Potter thus reiterates her contention that the romantic narratives of interracial sex are neither exclusively between white men and quadroon women nor contained within the city of New Orleans.

Having at once satisfied and frustrated her reader's desires, Potter turns to New Orleans's iconic phenomena, plaçage and quadroon balls. In contrast to travelers' accounts that cast New Orleans's free(d) quadroons as extraordinarily agential, Potter's descriptions of plaçage and quadroon balls foreground the slave economy that anchors sexual relations between white men and women of African descent, whether bonded or free. Noting that free women of color are often proprietors of boarding houses in New Orleans, Potter introduces her reader to one such woman who is "very beautiful and very wealthy" (*Hairdresser's Experience*, 160). Discussing the woman, Potter writes, "She inherited this property by her husband and master, he emancipated her . . . he died, leaving her in possession of all his wealth" (160). Potter's attention to the fact that this woman was made wealthy by "her husband and master" firmly locates the sexual economy of the beautiful free(d) mulatta concubine within a slave economy of property and subjection.

Not only does Potter emphasize the slave economy that frames the system of plaçage, but she again refuses the disavowal of white male desire for black women enabled by elaborate descriptions of the near whiteness of quadroon women. By introducing this woman not as some ephemeral and racially ambiguous quadroon beauty but instead as a "colored lady," Potter reiterates her assessment of not only the slave economy of plaçage but also the visible economy of desire (*Hairdresser's Experience*, 160). When Potter offers a more elaborate description of quadroon balls and plaçage, she mirrors popular representations: she details the extravagant display of wealth, from the hall's furnishings to the women's clothing and jewelry, and observes the spectacular beauty of the women. However, while she observes one woman "who looked as though she might be white," she also informs her reader that this woman's mother is "a colored creole, a brown skinned woman" (189), a gesture that echoes Boilat's revision of the signares and anticipates Oscar Felix's insistence regarding Marie Laveau's unambiguous brownness. Potter proceeds to describe another attendee, "a most beautiful brown skinned woman, elegantly dressed in pink brocade, and a full set of diamonds.... She looked to me more like an African princess than a Louisiana creole" (189). Her assertion that the woman in question "looked more ... like an African princess than a Louisiana creole" mocks the authority of other travelers who marvel at the near whiteness of New Orleans's famous quadroons. While Potter's marking of the ball and its attendees as "creole" reinforces the foreignness of the space, her repetition of "brown skinned" disrupts the phantasm of New Orleans: it does not magically transform black women into ethereal, racially illegible bodies.

At the same time, Potter's invocation of an "African princess" is suggestive in its ascription of the woman's beauty, wealth, and agency to a diasporic genealogy and geography that exceed the physical and national boundaries of New Orleans. Against Potter's carefully analytical and decidedly *un*romantic depictions of interracial sex seeps that romance of origins so pervasive in diaspora. While Potter makes undeniable the economy of slavery in the production of quadroons, she also disrupts presumptions that any agency the women may have held lay in their proximity to whiteness by locating the woman's beauty and power in an imagined royal African lineage. Potter's invocation of her own fantastical representation as a counternarrative to the mythology of the quadroon ball suggests a playfully subversive stance vis-à-vis the dominant archive on the free(d) mulatta concubine that depended so much on myth and exaggeration: why not an "African princess," then?

And here again, the echo falters. For while Potter invokes a diasporic genealogy in her disruption of the myth of New Orleans quadroons, she resolutely does not suggest, as she has with the enslaved near-white girls above and below, an affective or rhetorical affinity with the women she sees at the quadroon ball. Instead, Potter confronts the cost of their freedom, not only what it costs the women, but also what price other black subjects must pay for this particular freedom. Thus, just as she introduces her initial depictions of interracial sexual unions through tales of intimate violence, Potter frames her account of quadroon balls and plaçage with portrayals of women debased, one way or another, by slavery. She thus precedes her description of the quadroon ball with an account of an enslaved woman, Julee, who lives on a plantation where the slaves receive "for the whole week but a pint cup of buttermilk and a slice of bread" (*Hairdresser's Experience*, 187). Potter then follows the quadroon ball with a reference to a "creole" woman slaveholder Potter meets at the ball who is "one of the most cruel women [Potter] had ever seen or heard tell of" (190). Potter exclaims: "I told her I did wish her up in our state a little while, when she would wish she never had owned a slave, or never seen one. I got so outrageously angry at her proceedings, that I got a petition drawn up by an old citizen, and signed by a goodly number of the most influential citizens, which I determined, myself, to present to Congress, to prevent the colored people from owning slaves unless through some change in law" (190–91).[37] Potter's righteous anger here refuses a romance not only to the white traveler but also to the black subject who might otherwise be seduced by the promise of individual freedom, whatever its costs. For Potter, the economy of interracial concubinage is neither liberatory nor romantic but rather entrenched in the brutal violence of slavery. New Orleans, therefore, cannot be that site of remarkable agency for women of color imagined and depicted in travel narratives. Indeed, while Potter endeavors to render New Orleans domesticated within the nation, she insists on articulating the particular terror the city engenders for black female subjects, free and enslaved, herself included.

Revision

Before she acknowledges and assesses the spectacles of quadroon balls and plaçage, Potter relates an account that forces her reader to consider the precariousness of freedom for women like her. While in New Orleans, Potter describes a heated debate with two clients, both slaveholders, over the practice of sexual servitude in the South. Infuriated by the conversation, Potter "dash[es] down the stairs" (*Hairdresser's Experience*, 171). She hears a "great shout" that arrests her descent and "look[s] down in the rotunda, and there was a slave-market" (171). While Potter has discussed her views on slavery and abolition throughout her narrative, this passage marks her first direct encounter with that "Southern market" to which she first refers in chapter 1 of her work. Gazing down on the rotunda, Potter recalls, "On the stand was a young girl who, it appeared, had been born in New York, and had gone traveling with an unprincipled family, who had undertaken to sell her" (172). The visual and rhetorical resonance is striking. The "young girl" standing on the auction block has led a life nearly parallel to Potter's: both are from New York, both traveled with their employers, and both arrive in New Orleans, one freely, one subjected to the horrors of slavery. The "young girl" withstands a public display of her undressed body and the threat of violence from the winning bidder. Potter describes how, in the midst of this terrifying scene, the young girl "asked a friend who stood behind her for a pen-knife, and ripping open her corset, took out her free papers, and, holding them up, demanded who dare insult her, or use such violence anymore" (172)!

Potter's readers may have been aware of a similar incident. In the 1840s Salomé Müller, a free German-born girl who had been forced into slavery, was subjected to a public inspection of her undressed body and granted freedom only when the white midwife who witnessed her birth affirmed Müller's whiteness. The court case, which took place in New Orleans, was well known enough for William Wells Brown to recount it in *Clotel; or, The President's Daughter* (145–48; see also Craft, *Running*, 4–5). In Potter's retelling, rather than benefit from a genealogy of whiteness as her claim to freedom, the young girl has recourse only to her "free papers."

Potter's revision of the Salomé Müller incident is a remarkable culmination of Potter's careful negotiation of her reader's gaze in her indictment of the simultaneous fetishization of New Orleans and the quadroon female body. Lindon Barrett's argument regarding what he calls the legibility of the enslaved subject helps illuminate Potter's intervention: "The story of Salomé Müller illustrates the manner in which African American bodies are taken as signs of nothing beyond themselves—signs of the very failure of meaning—for these bodies are able to signify, in their obdurate physicality, only a state of obdurate physicality" ("Hand-Writing," 322). In the white slave narrative, the black body can only become a human subject when it acquires or is "grafted to" other signs that translate the body's signification into something other than black. One of these signs is "attaining literacy," which, as Barrett argues, "becomes equivalent to extending oneself beyond the condition and geography of the body" (324).

Potter's substitution of free papers for a white witness resists the "obdurate physicality" of the black body by invoking literacy as its own testimony. That is, the black body becomes a free(d) subject through its own agency rather than the whim of an authorizing white gaze. And while one might argue that the free papers function as surrogate for that white witness, Potter's revision resists the humanizing narrative of the white slave by retaining the girl's racial blackness. The girl in Potter's narrative, unlike Salomé Müller, deserves freedom not because she is suddenly white but because she is free. That she "rip[s] open her corset" to reveal neither her whiteness nor her blackness but her free papers provides a fleeting moment of authority as she seizes, however briefly, control over the display and signification of her unclothed body in a roomful of white male traders and speculators. The revelation of her free papers rather than her exposed breast thwarts attempts to render her near whiteness an exchangeable commodity and thus removes the girl from the fetish economy of white male desire even as the act of "rip[ping] open her corset" acknowledges that same desire. Rather than indulge in supplanting the subjugation of an enslaved black body with that of a more recognizably human white body, Potter's revision emphasizes the precariousness of liberty for free black women traveling in the United States.

Potter's description of the near sale of a girl whose background mirrors her own entails considerable risk: drawing her reader's attention to the parallels between herself and the wrongly enslaved girl threatens to undermine her own "sense of place" as a freely traveling subject. The spectacle of the slave auction concretizes the objectification of the black subject. As Katherine McKittrick argues, "The black female purchased on the auction block is rendered a public, rape-able, usable body-scale through which a distinct, or resistant, or human sense of place is obscured" (*Demonic Grounds*, 81). It is thus remarkable that Potter maintains her authority in her spatial relationship to the slave auction: having emerged from the protected private rooms of the hotel, she is above the rotunda, out of sight of the spectacle below her. As with her refusal to sit "*at table*" with the "well-formed" fancy girl, Potter's sudden halt at the top of the rotunda preserves a physical and rhetorical distance from the "young girl" from New York. Potter thus resists making her own body publicly available and preserves the autonomy of her travel even as the similarities between her and the young girl on the auction block lay bare the terror of a racialized and sexualized slave geography that stretches from New Orleans to New York.

The recognition of the "young girl" for sale resonates because Potter has invoked this mirroring before, when she encounters the "well-formed girl" destined for life as a fancy girl. Significantly, both girls temporarily impede Potter's ability to move freely across a U.S. landscape. The "well-formed girl" threatens Potter's hard-earned ability to "sit at table" with the ship's other passengers, while the girl in the rotunda reminds Potter that her own northern roots and freedom cannot protect her liberty. While Potter never explicitly refers to race or color in describing herself or either of these girls, that each iterates a crucial aspect of Potter's desire and ability to travel freely suggests that all three inhabit a geography distinct from that available to the other travelers Potter encounters through her adventures in "high life." That Potter portrays each of these girls within a narrative frame of sex, race, and desire and links each to the space of New Orleans suggests that the city casts a long and menacing shadow over the geography of her travels.

For Eliza Potter, New Orleans is at once a singular and a mundane space. Its hypervisibility in a North American imaginative landscape allows her to use the city rhetorically in order to unmask the terror produced by a racialized slave society. In one sense, using the city of New Orleans certainly replicates the city's hypervisibility as a "perimeter of difference" that enables the myth of a coherent, domestic U.S. racial and sexual order and the fantasy of extraordinary black agency. Potter's rhetorical strategies, however, dislodge New Orleans from an imaginative exoticism and expose the normalcy of the city within a national landscape terrifying to the free black woman traveler. When Potter tells her reader that the "very beautiful and very wealthy" woman who chooses her white male lovers "inherited this property by her husband and master," she reiterates the inextricable link between sexual subjugation and material agency for free black women. McKittrick insists, "If *who* we see is tied up with *where* we see through truthful, commonsensical narratives, then the placement of subaltern bodies deceptively hardens spatial binaries, in turn suggesting some bodies belong, some bodies do not belong, and some bodies are out of place" (*Demonic Grounds*, xv). Through her textually complex resistance of the readers' desiring gaze and her unmasking of the romance of the free(d) mulatta concubine, Eliza Potter demands her reader reassess "whom we see" and "where we see" the sexualized violence of an Atlantic slave society.

Breath

On the one hand, it would seem that Potter and Boilat share, unexpectedly and serendipitously, much across their individual projects. Both, after all, take up familiar literary genres in order to claim knowledge and authority about the places and peoples they describe. Both subvert dominant geographies of the spaces across which they travel. Both invoke notions of diaspora specific to their locations. And most importantly here, both center a revision of the stereotype of the free(d) mulatta concubine in their respective meditations on desire, freedom, and belonging.

Ironically, however, these very same shared details reveal the tenuousness of their collective enterprises. For what comes across most clearly is the utter solitude of each writer. The orphan Boilat fails in his return to his homeland, only to spend the balance of his life in the hostile climate of France. Potter repeatedly asserts her single bearing in the world, never alluding to her second marriage or stepchildren (see Santamarina, "Introduction [Appendix A]," 180). This solitude, too, permeates the echo throughout. Indeed, even Ezili, tended to by devoted serviteurs whose appearance offers evidence of the collective experience of Haitian women, rages and sobs, feeling unloved, or suffers the desertion of her lovers and her people. Indeed, when the echo has exhausted its reverberation, what is left but the sense of smallness in the wake of its silence? The echo of the free(d) mulatta concubine in diaspora is not only a remembering but also an act of hope for the future, for a possibility of a freedom, one beyond what these two subjects, free and black in a moment that was supposed to be most full of possibility for an African diaspora across Atlantic spaces, ever experienced. The echo between Potter and Boilat, between the signares and Ezili, between these places in diaspora fractures and falls away.

EPILOGUE

The archive seduces. In a history of an African diaspora produced by and through the transatlantic slave trade, the dominant archive's obscene wealth of evidence—ships' logs, inventories, bills of lading and bills of sale, legal edicts and colonial codes, baptismal records, official minutes, letters and petitions, travelers' journals, newspaper accounts, engravings, paintings, and other illustrations, account ledgers, court records—is tantalizing. It compels even the most skeptical and critical of scholars of the African diaspora to search it, scour it for scraps, beseech it to give up stories it has no interest in telling. As with the free(d) African mulâtresse aboard the slave ship *La Galathée*, the letter from the mother Gusban, and the portrait of Marie Laveau, the archive titillates in offering the briefest of glimpses, promising but not offering anything more than a flash of a fragment.

And so we who desire more than what the dominant archive can and will tell, we who desire some sort of repair, redress, recognition, we perform rituals to coax the archive into giving up what it refuses. We read against the grain. We turn away from the official archive and look for and to other kinds of evidence. We imagine. Saidiya Hartman suggests "critical fabulation" as one such move: "advancing a series of speculative arguments and exploiting the capacities of the subjunctive," thus engaging in "a critical reading of the archive that mimes the figurative dimensions of history ... both to tell an impossible story and to amplify the impossibility of its telling" ("Venus," 11). Colin Dayan invokes "vodou practice, its concreteness, its obsession with details and fragments" and insists the Haitian religious practice "be viewed as ritual enactments of Haiti's colonial past, even more than retentions from Africa" (*Haiti*, xvii). Such inventive engagements with the archive have produced revelatory readings of black Atlantic histories. At the same time, as Hartman cautions, doing such work risks "[replicating] the very order of violence that it writes against by placing yet another demand upon the [captive subject], by requiring that the [captive subject's] life be made useful or instructive, by finding in it a lesson for a future or a hope for history" ("Venus," 14). And as Dayan warns in her critique of Paul Gilroy's *The Black Atlantic*, reading against the archive, working to shift paradigms, risks reducing a brutal, real, lived history *and* present to mere metaphor. And yet and again, "the question must be asked." I have no desire to resolve this tension. Rather, in these pages I have endeavored to place even more pressure on it.

The dominant archive is perhaps most seductive in its promise of coherence. It provides dates and points of embarkation and disembarkation. It records transfers of property, colonial power, and human chattel. It records deaths, even if it does not always record the dates of those deaths or the names of those dead. It composes its documents in orderly files and boxes, and it catalogs them in ways that make sense. It dictates and maintains the lines between slavery and freedom; it defines the possibilities for movement from one category to the other. From this perspective, from the dominant archive's insistence on points of origins and linear trajectories, to encounter the free(d) African mulâtresse traveling on a slave ship garners but a quick glance, an acknowledgment of her use for evidence for something already noted. From this perspective, to encounter Ezili is to imagine that she may be a memory of the signares, perhaps thrilling, but no more enlightening. From this perspective, to encounter the free(d) mulatta concubine in diaspora is to encounter the expected, the utterly mundane.

And yet. The free(d) mulatta concubine is one of the least coherent of black Atlantic subjects. The color of her skin, which marks her privilege, also offers evidence of the violence of diaspora. Indeed, her body serves as a sort of doubling of the vulnerability and culpability of the black subject. She is at once a reminder of rape and conquest and a perceived coconspirator in the giving of her body to the European conqueror. Her historical and mythical genealogies engender elision, debate, and consternation. Her hypervisibility in the official archive belies her unknowability. It is precisely in her unknowability, her resistance to coherence, that she is most generative. And it is also true that the fact of her freedom, that she enjoys a particular visibility across archives, does not lessen the matter of care, the potential for violence, in excavating her story. Thus, rather than offer closure to my reading of the free(d) mulatta concubine across a black transatlantic, I leave where I began. The point here is not to recover a lost fact. It is, rather, to resist coherence, to disrupt or even distort the very frame through which we read the evidence.

In 1728 a free African mulâtresse boarded the slave ship *La Galathée* at Gorée Island. She and her three slaves arrived in New Orleans in 1729. As Gwendolyn Midlo Hall recounts, the details of the ship's journey are as horrific as they are mundane within a history of the black transatlantic. Of the "400 *captifs*, men, women and children" held on the ship at its embarkation in Gorée, 260 landed in Louisiana (Hall, *Africans*, 82–83). Drowning and death from sickness at sea and delivery of sick captives at port in the Americas before landing at New Orleans accounted for the loss of human cargo (82–83). The ship's crew did not escape sickness: eleven, roughly one-fifth, of the crew members died as well (83). The survival of the mulâtresse, en route to join her French gunsmith husband, and her three slaves bears consideration. What were the conditions of her passage aboard the slave ship? Would the captive Africans bound in the ship's hold have seen her or made meaning of her presence aboard *La Galathée*? If, as Stephanie Smallwood insists, "in one another's eyes they saw the reflection of their own traumatic alienation," what did the captives see in the face of the free(d) mulâtresse (*Saltwater*, 121)?

More mundane but just as urgent in this moment is the question of why and how she and her three captives survived a voyage that decimated more than one-third of the humans aboard. How does her story of survival fit into an understanding of African diasporic history and memory? How did she calculate the costs of her own survival? Smallwood's evocation of the "anomalous intimacies" of the slave ship might extend beyond the ship's cargo and demand that we consider the unthinkable, unimaginable, unspeakable of how she may have enacted her own survival. Indeed, following Smallwood, the unnamed free(d) mulâtresse's presence and survival suggest a production of diaspora not as a community but as a diversity of subjects and their multivalent responses to a set of terrifying conditions that governed the most intimate of relations and relationships across Atlantic slave societies.

Finally, if we might imagine her genealogy to resonate in Ezili—a goddess who demands fidelity, revels in luxury, promises wealth, whose skin bears the markings of the trauma and rupture of diaspora, whose connections to waterways hold both promise and peril, whose devotion to her children is fierce—if we imagine her genealogy to resonate there, then we might attend to that which exceeds our apprehension. Because surely, if, if the African mulâtresse boarded the slave ship of her own volition, if she indeed "followed her gunsmith husband," surely we can theorize that perhaps she understood that things might be better for her in this new place, colonial New Orleans, a place just a decade old, than they would have been, after the forced departure of her criminal French husband, in Gorée had she stayed.

To imagine her reasons for following her husband means both to confront the precariousness of her freedom and safety in a place where women like her and their children would establish an elite social and political class and to speculate wildly so as to "amplify the impossibility" of knowing, that she might have thought not only of her own possibilities but also of those of her children. Even as I want to resist naturalizing a desire for motherhood, particularly for black and mulatta women living in slave societies, I contend the multiple and diverse archival traces of the free(d) mulatta concubine invite repeating in their revelations of how questions of mothering, matrilineal lines of descent, and desire intersect and run through each of the case studies examined here. Thus, while the record thus far does not indicate she traveled with children, it also does not tell us whether she eventually became a mother. It cannot tell us whether she desired to do so. But what if she had so desired? What if she had so desired, and had imagined it might be better, in 1728, to bring her children into an unknown world than into the one she knew? What might have been the possibilities she imagined lay on the other side of that journey? What had Gorée already been emptied of for her to make her desire to leave behind the possibility of being safe and secure in that place? And what might have happened to that desire as she traveled as a free black female subject aboard a slave ship? And finally, what was the cost of her survival, her freedom, in this new, bewildering place? How is that calculated?

NOTES

1. While the facts of the woman's appearance in the archive and her journey aboard *La Galathée* are not in dispute, Hall's and Spear's books indicate different years. Hall's appendix of slave ship voyages indicates that *La Galathée* departed Gorée in October 1728 and arrived in New Orleans on February 23, 1729 (*Africans*, 390). Spear states, "The ship's log for *Le [sic] Galathée*, which arrived in Louisiana in 1727 from Senegal ... included among its passengers a Senegalese mulâtresse who was joining her husband, Jean Pinet" (*Race*, 80). The archival document I cite here states that the woman, "Pinet's wife," departed in 1728. See Délibérations priser en l'assemblée des directeurs, June 3, 1729, Sous Series C 13, fol. 11, Archives nationales d'outre mer, Aix-en-Provence, France.

2. The archival record indicates that the gunsmith's name was Pinet. Spear informs us, "The 1732 census of New Orleans identifies a Pinet, occupation gunsmith, living on Rue St. Pierre with an unnamed and unraced woman" (*Race*, 256n6). Because the woman is unnamed in both records, we cannot know whether the woman living with Pinet in 1732 is the same woman who followed him in 1728.

3. As VèVè Clark and Sara E. Johnson note in their introduction to *Kaiso!*, the varied orthography of Francophone Creoles in general and Haitian vodou terms in particular "has been the subject of sustained debate and is often indicative of political and class divisions in each nation" (xv). I follow Clark and Johnson's lead in "follow[ing] the current trend in scholarship in Creole orthography that is essentially phonetic" (xv). Thus, while some of my sources and direct quotes employ "vodou," "vodu," or "vodun," among other spellings, I have opted for "vodou" to name the religious practice. The name signifying Haitian deities as a group is as often spelled "loa" as "lwa"; here I've used the latter. And while Erzulie has been the historically appropriate spelling, current scholarship more often uses Ezili, as I have here. Following Dayan's example in *Haiti* and in an effort to underscore the fact that vodou is something more than a religious practice, I have opted not to capitalize the term. In addition, except for direct quotations, in order to mark their coequivalent production of knowledge within an African diasporic framework, I do not italicize vodou terms.

4. The fancy slave trade was the informal, albeit heavily documented, name given to the sale and purchase of enslaved black women and girls for the specific purpose of their sexual desirability to white men. Textual and visual representations of the fancy trade emphasized the light or near-white skin color of the enslaved women and girls. See Baptist, "'Cuffy.'"

5. Emily Clark's recent monograph, *The Strange History of the American Quadroon*, offers a richly documented and generative genealogy of discursive and historical manifestations of the mulatta concubine across the eighteenth- and nineteenth-century Americas.

6. See also Hartman, *Scenes*; Garraway, *Libertine Colony*, chap. 4; and Sharpe, Ghosts, chap. 2.

7. See especially Jacobs, *Incidents*; Harper, *Iola Leroy*; Hopkins, *Contending Forces*. Key contemporary scholarship includes White, *Ar'n't I a Woman?*; Davis, "Reflections"; Spillers, "'Mama's Baby'"; Hartman, *Scenes*; and Carby, *Reconstructing*.

8. Screen caps of Touré's tweets, which he subsequently deleted and denied posting, ascribing blame to an unnamed cousin, are posted on the blog *Gawker* in a post by O'Connor, "Mysterious Case."

9. For an informative overview of nineteenth-century incarnations of the literary trope of the tragic mulatta and twentieth-century interrogations of and interventions in reading the figure, see Sollors, *Neither Black nor White*, esp. chap. 8. For provocative rereadings of the figure's social and political work in nineteenth-century literature, see Foreman, "Who's Your Mama?"; Sánchez-Eppler, *Touching Liberty*; and Zackodnik, *Mulatta*.

10. "Ces femmes sont des maîtresses fort impérieuses & très-redoutées, quoiqu'il soit très-commun de voir des Mulâtresses libres, vivant dans la plus grande familiarité avec des femmes esclaves: mais ce ne sont pas les leurs» (Moreau, *Description*, 96). Unless otherwise noted, all translations are mine.

11. "Et j'observe à cet égard que cette familiarité, quelquefois fondée sur la parenté, a très-souvent pour cause, les présens que des Affranchies reçoivent des esclaves qui ont des amans [*sic*] dans leurs maîtres ou dans d'autres Blancs, qui leur donnent les moyens d'être genereuses. En general, les Mulâtres tirent meme de grands secours des esclaves avec lesquels ils ont des rapports de différens genres, sans s'en croire humiliés» (Moreau, *Description*, 96).

12. On the roles these groups would play in nineteenth-century and twentieth-century Senegal, see Jones, *Métis*; and Diouf, "French Colonial Policy."

13. For a detailed discussion of official French policies governing sexual relations on Gorée and Saint-Louis, see Brooks, *Eurafricans*, 210–12.

14. That the term eventually came to denote all mulattas living on the island, with women who owned property further "distinguished by the name 'de dame' or 'd'habitante,'" suggests a discursive and knowing negotiation on the part of the island's women in order to achieve legitimacy and recognition within the islands' racial and sexual economies (Knight-Baylac, "La vie," 401).

15. I am not suggesting that work is unimportant or that all work on the figure does this. See note 9 above for some of the most productive interventions in theorizing the mulatta.

16. The full quote asserts that these characteristics describe a "colonial femininity" specifically performed by the intrepid "nineteenth-century Jamaican freeborn mulatta Mary Grant Seacole" (MacDonald-Smythe, "Trading Places," 89).

17. Here, I wish neither to obscure nor to exaggerate the "difference place makes" in reading and theorizing the figure's signification. Certainly, both the term and the figure of the mulatta vary in their valence across Atlantic spaces, with African-descended subjects positioning themselves variously regarding the term's appropriateness and value.

And within each space, the term and its meanings were always negotiated and contested. As Zackodnik's work makes clear, black writers often invoked the stereotype of the tragic mulatta in order to critique it and "interrogate constructed identities and notions of identity that defy categories serving the interests of a racialized imbalance of power" (*Mulatta*, xxxii). However, it remains true that across time and space, the invocation of the term signals a racial hierarchy that values whiteness and devalues blackness.

18. For an illuminating examination of the complex negotiations of kinship in a slave society, see Johnson, "Death Rites."

19. My use of "controlling archives" also draws on and invokes Patricia Hill Collins's theorization of stereotypes of black women as "controlling images" in order to make visible how these stereotypes "are designed to make racism, sexism, poverty, and other forms of social injustice appear to be natural, normal, and inevitable parts of everyday life" (*Black Feminist Thought*, 69).

20. The field has given birth to a rich tradition in monographs that directly engage the problem of the archive in producing and theorizing African diasporic histories. See Trouillot, *Silencing*; Dayan, *Haiti*; Hartman, *Lose*; Palmié, *Wizards*; Scott, *Conscripts*; Matory, *Black Atlantic Religion*; Edwards, *Practice*; and Smallwood, *Saltwater*. In addition, a recent proliferation of special journal issues and articles devoted to the problem of the archive in African diaspora studies signals that the field is at a watershed moment in theorizing and articulating experiences and histories made otherwise unimaginable and unrecognizable by traditional framings and readings of the archive.

21. Dayan's meditation of Ezili as an embodiment of Haitian women's history is generative and indispensable. I both draw from her analysis and build upon it, extending and complicating it in order to read a history of diasporic black womanhood.

CHAPTER I. ECHO AND THE MYTH OF ORIGINS

1. "Les métives, métifs, mulâtres, mulâtresses, quartrons, quatronnes, & les négresses libres avec tous leur captifs" (Pruneau, *Description*, 3). Unless otherwise noted, all translations are mine.

2. "Les femmes de cette isle en général, sont fort attachées aux blancs, & les soignent on ne peut mieux, lors-qu'ils sont malades" (Pruneau, *Description*, 3).

3. "Avec cet or, ces femmes font fabriquer une partie en bijoux, & l'autre partie est employée à acheter des vêtemens, car elles aiment, comme par-tout ailleurs, la parure" (Pruneau, *Description*, 4).

4. "Elles portent sur la tête un mouchoir blanc fort artistement arrangé, par-dessus lequel elles placent un petit ruban noir étroit, ou de couleur, autour de la tête. Une chemise à la françoise, garnie, un corset de taffetas ou de mousseline, une jupe de même, & pareille au corset, des boucles d'oreilles d'or, des chaînes de pieds d'or ou d'argent, lorsqu'elles n'en ont point d'autres, avec des bembouches de maroquin rouge, aux pieds; par-dessus leur corset, elles portent un morceau de deux aulnes de mousseline, dont les bouts se jettent par-dessus l'épaule gauche.... Les femmes escortées ainsi lorsqu'elles sortent, rencontrent souvent un *quiriot* (espece d'hommes qui chantent les louanges de chacun, pour de l'argent); alors il ne manque pas de marcher devant elles, en débitant à leurs louanges toutes les hyperboles qui lui viennent dans l'idée, & quelques grossières, qu'elles soient, ces femmes en sont si flattées, que dans te transport qu'excitent ces adulations, elles

jettent souvent partie de leurs nippes au chanteur, lorsqu'elles n'ont rien, dans leurs poches, qu'elles puissant lui donner" (Pruneau, *Description*, 4–6, translated and quoted in Brooks, "*Signares* of Saint-Louis," 24).

5. The most detailed history of the emergence and rise of the signares is in Brooks, *Eurafricans*, esp. 206–21.

6. In Deren's portrayal, Ezili's arrival in the peristyle signals that Deren is describing ritual possession, as the peristyle is the public space of the temple where rituals are performed. According to Leslie Desmangles, the peristyle "is a microcosmic representation of the universe. The four poles sustaining the structure symbolize mythologically the four cardinal points of the universe, covered by an overarching roof that represents the cosmic vault above the earth.... [T]he floor of the peristil symbolizes the profane world, while the vertical pole (potomitan) in the center of the peristil represents the axis mundi, the avenue of communication between the two worlds" (*Faces*, 105).

7. "La plupart vivent avec beaucoup d'aisance, & plusieurs de ces négresses ont à elles trente à quarante esclaves" (Pruneau, *Description*, 3).

8. By public archive, I mean the numerous published sources on Ezili available to those outside vodou, whether those sources are scholarly imprints or popular representations across a variety of print and digital media.

9. I am grateful to Sara Johnson for asking me whether Deren actually names Ezili a mulatta.

10. Due to limited natural resources on both islands, Saint-Louis and Gorée were uninhabited by local African communities (Searing, *West African Slavery*, 94).

11. Emily Clark's archaeology of the discourse of the quadroon in the United States in her monograph *The Strange History of the American Quadroon* is instructive. Her first chapter's examination of the "quadroon press war" in 1807 Philadelphia decidedly challenges prevailing genealogies and geographies of the quadroon and thus demonstrates the stakes of reading and mapping the figure of the free(d) mulatta concubine, whether marked as mulatta, mulâtresse, or quadroon, as a transnational Atlantic figure.

12. I do not want to trivialize or otherwise reduce the imaginative and material significance of these other African diasporic deities. What I do want to suggest is that the historicity of the signares makes legible another dimension of these goddesses' signatures across a black Atlantic.

13. For descriptions of these communities, see, for example, Rodney, *History*, chap. 8; Jobson, *Golden Trade*; Brooks, *Eurafricans*; and Thorton, *Cultural History*.

14. As Gerdès Fleurant explains, vodou "consists of many rites or styles of worship such as Rada, Kongo, Nago, Petwo, Ibo, and Makanda, or Bizango. But in actual practice, Haitian Vodun is divided into two major rites: the Rada, whose music and structure are retained quite faithfully from the Fon/Ewe and Yoruba of Dahomey and Nigeria, and the Petwo, which might be called Kongo-Petwo, for it retains syncretic elements from the Kongo/Angola region that were redefined in the crucible of the colonial plantation system of Saint Domingue" ("Vodun," 47). Each rite has distinctive characteristics; Robert Farris Thompson explains: "*Rada* ... is the 'cool' side of *vodun*, being associated with the achievement of peace and reconciliation. *Petro* ... is the hot side, being associated with the spiritual fire of charms for healing and for attacking evil forces" (*Flash*, 164). At the same time, Fleurant contends, "contrary to what was believed in the past, the division between Rada and Kongo-Petwo is not so rigid," and finally, "many Lwa, known as '*an*

de zo,' or 'in two substances,' are worshipped in both the Rada and Kongo-Petwo cults" ("Vodun," 47).

15. *Bousen* is a Haitian Creole term for "prostitute." The interview between René and Houlberg is published in English; the published transcript of the taped interview does not indicate whether Houlberg conducted the interview in French and Kreyòl and then translated to English for publication or if she and René conversed in English. In either case, René often offers a Kreyòl term preceded and followed by a translation of that term. His use of language underscores the simultaneous translatability and untranslatability of place-specific worldviews in diaspora.

16. On Ezili Dantò as lesbian, see Bellegarde-Smith, "Broken Mirrors"; and Michel, Bellegarde-Smith, and Racine-Toussaint, "From the Horses' Mouths," 70.

17. Karen McCarthy Brown states unequivocally, "Ezili Freda is a white woman" (*Mama Lola*, 246). Leslie Desmangles informs us, "In Haitian mythology and folklore, Ezili is depicted as an astonishingly wealthy upper-class mulatto woman of luxury" (*Faces*, 132). And in his interview with Marilyn Houlberg, vodouist Georges René explains that his connection to Ezili Freda is due, in part, to his being "very charmed by the white women," linking Ezili Freda's racial identity to that of his "first girlfriend . . . a French girl, her father was Haitian." Houlberg asks, "She was light-skinned?" René responds, "No, she was white" ("My Double," 290).

18. While George Brooks asserts that the 1763 memoir is the earliest written account of the signares, Sylvain Sankalé cites a 1720 document reporting salaries of the company employees that mentions a "Signare Paula, de Rufisk" ("Une société métisse"). Jessica Marie Johnson first drew my attention to the document; she informs me that the original document reads "Sig." and that the likelihood that "Sig." refers to the honorific "Signare" is overwhelming (personal communication, August 24, 2014). See also Knight-Baylac, "La vie à Gorée," 399, 402–3.

19. Of course, eighteenth-century Europeans did not elide their roles in the slave trade the same way; the elision of European accountability in travelers' narratives came rather by framing the colonial enterprise as a benevolent, civilizing mission and displacing the barbarity of the slave trade onto Africans, captive and free. Thus, one might certainly say that origins stories of "Africa" were always already revisions of what actually happened. What I want to emphasize here is how the travelers' narratives characterized the autonomy and authority of the signares in a way that made such portrayals ripe for subsequent revisions that worked to elide the accountability (however uneven and distorted) of both black African merchants and chiefs and European commercial agents and militaries.

20. For examples of family photos of signare families that subvert the dominant representation of the women and oral history accounts from descendants, see Jones, *Métis*.

21. For examples of this iconography, see Cosentino, *Sacred Arts*, 148–49, 240–41, and 200–201.

22. On Lasirèn's relationship to Ezili Freda and Ezili Dantò and her position within Rada and Petwo, and for examples of Lasirèn's iconography, see Houlberg, "Sirens," 32.

23. For a trenchant analysis of the relationship between vodou and Haitian history, see Bellegarde-Smith, "Broken Mirrors."

24. On Mami Wata's roots in transnational trade routes, see Drewal, "Introduction."

25. See especially Hartman, "Seduction"; and Spillers, "'Mama's Baby.'"

26. And of course, underscoring the tensions in representing vodou are the persistent

debates around retention and syncretism in African-diasporic cultures and traditions. For a cogent overview and analysis of the debates, see Matory, *Black Atlantic Religion*, 10–16.

27. On women as traders in West Africa, see White, "Creole Women Traders"; Morgan, *Laboring Women*, 62–63; and Brooks, *Eurafricans*, 124–29.

28. "L'être entier d'une Mulâtresse est livré à la Volupté, & le feu de cette Déesse brûle dans son Coeur pour ne s'y éteindre qu'avec la vie. Ce culte, voilà tous son code, tous ses voeux, tout son bonheur. Il n'est rien que l'imagination la plus enflammée puisse concevoir, qu'elle n'ait pressenti, deviné, accompli. Charmer tous les sens, les livrer aux plus délicieuses extases, les suspendre par les plus séduisans ravissements: voilà son unique étude" (Moreau, *Description*, 92).

29. Equally important, of course, is the passage's invocation of a legal lexicon and how such juridical vocabulary underscores the supposed threat of the free(d) mulatta concubine to social and legal order in the colony. On this question especially instructive are Garraway, *Libertine Colony*; Dayan, "Codes."

30. "Au surplus comme on a fait violence à ces jeunes filles, elles ne se croyent point déflorées: elles prétendent qu'il faut pour qu'elles le soyent, qu'elles ayent donné leur consentement à la chose. Elles disent en plaisantant, & cette opinion est assez généralement reçue, qu'elles ont trois pucelages; celui que les Maures prennent de force, celui qu'elles donnent d'amitié à leur ami & celui qu'achète leur mari" (Lamiral, *L'Affrique*, 245).

31. On tactics as tools of the weak or oppressed, see Certeau, *Practice*.

32. Of course, Vincent Carretta's argument that Equiano was in fact born in colonial South Carolina disrupts any reading of Equiano's eyewitness account of his experiences as a captive African. While the question of Equiano's nativity is beyond the limits of my discussion here, I suggest that the ensuing conversations regarding the authority and legitimacy of official documents versus Equiano's own testimony underscore two points central to my own argument: (1) the fact that African diasporic subjects produced memories and artifacts that contradict official records should not necessarily render such evidence false or inaccurate; (2) whether or not the testimony is "true," what is important is that it demands that we attend to the process and problem of witnessing and testifying to experiences that are otherwise beyond or outside the history told by the official record. See Carretta, *Equiano*.

33. See Geggus, "French Slave Trade." Of course, it is almost impossible to account for the contraband trade—pirates and privateers—that brought captives to Saint-Domingue. Nonetheless, scholarly consensus locates the Bight of Benin and west-central Africa as the main source of captives for Saint-Domingue.

34. "Admirez la peau veloutée de la jeune métisse: elle va de la teinte crème jusqu'au café au lait foncé" (Seck, *Gorée*, 26).

35. "Avec sa carnation d'Andalouse, ses lèvres délicatement bleuies, ses cheveux noirs de jais qu'encadrent deux volutes harmonieuses d'or filigrané, sa coiffure pointe en l'air de quelques centimètres, qu'elle nomme Dioumbeul. Faits de mouchoirs flamboyants de madras ou de simples mouchoirs sénégalais à carreaux bleus et blancs ou de satin blanc brodé de roses rouge et feu, ces étranges couvre-chefs en forme de pain de sucre, sont fixés sur le pourtour de la tête par un étroit bandeau noir ou de couleur. Ce 'dioumbeul' monumental présente l'allure de la tiare papale à triple couronne, car une guirlande de broderie d'or à petite frange le 'spirale' trois fois. Une longue chemise blanche de toile fine,

serre la taille au moyen de pagnes d'étoffe de coton formés par une réunion de bandes tissées à trente centimètres de largeur et brodées de fils de laine où dominent le bleu, le rouge le jaune [*sic*], le vert et l'aurore. Les pagnes de fabrication européenne sont peints de divers motifs ou rayés. Tous ces pagnes pendent jusqu'à terre et balayent les babouches marocaines rouge et jaune. Un autre pagne, souvent très fin, jeté négligemment sur les épaules, confère à certaines silhouettes l'aspect vaguement romain. Les mains de ces mulâtresses, leur bras, leurs oreilles et leur poitrine scintillent de bijoux d'or artistement travaillés" (Seck, *Gorée*, 26).

36. Drawing from the same colonial archive as Searing, Brooks is also forced to speculate and does so explicitly. Explaining that "the identities and social standing of the [signares] are matters of speculation, since few sources recorded the name or status of a woman," Brook asserts that "many of the women" who cohabited with Europeans were of slave descent, while some were the daughters of "grumetes" (free African seamen) (*Eurafricans*, 213).

37. "La maison romantique qui abrite le Musée goréen de l'I.F.A.N. a contenu des captifs pendant trente ans, de 1777 à 1807, et appartenait à la riche signare Victoria Albir" (Seck, *Gorée*, 20).

38. "En 1936, il ne restait plus sur l'île que des maisons tombant en ruines, où vivaient environ cinq cents Goréens. Ceux-là descendent des 'signares,' métisses d'origine plus ou moins Gasconne, Bretonne ou Normande" (Seck, *Gorée*, 28).

39. "La maison où habita la Mère Javouhey sur la rue de Boufflers angle rue des Dongeons. . . . La rue Boufflers, principale artère de l'île, rappelle le souvenir de l'illustre chevalier Stanislas de Boufflers. Que de 'Signares' ont pleuré son départ de Gorée et particulièrement Anne Pépin. On raconte même que le sable de ses derniers pas sur la plage a été ramassé et gardé dans de petits sacs, souhaitant ainsi son retour" (Seck, *Gorée*, 31).

40. In an H-Africa discussion addressing how UNESCO's presentation of Gorée persists in its inaccurate presentation of the "Door of No Return," scholars' interventions in the mythos of Gorée, Ana Lucia Araujo notes, "The description provided on the website is actually almost a transcription of Mr. Ndiaye's speech when touring the house" (Badassy, "Gorée").

41. "L'un des spectacles qui nous impressionna le plus étrangement"; "antérieurement à l'abolition de la traite des noirs"; "bienheureux temps" (Frey, *Côte Occidentale*, 10).

42. "A cette époque, l'orgue de Barbarie et sa prétentieuse contre-façon, le piano mécanique, qui depuis lors ont fait les délices des bals de plus d'un fonctionnaire colonial, était peu ou n'étaient point encore connus à Saint-Louis. On se contentait donc d'y danser au son du tam-tam, que des griots, l'œil lubrique, faisaient vibrer avec rage, et qu'accompagnaient les frénétiques claquements de mains des jeunes négresses. Au son de cette musique infernale, et malgré une température torride, souvent le bal était encore dans tout son entrain que, depuis longtemps, les premières lueurs de l'aube avaient blanchi l'horizon!" (Frey, *Côte Occidentale*, 14).

43. "C'est des *griottes* que les jeunes filles apprennent ces postures lascives qu'elles savent si bien figure dans leurs danses" (Boilat, *Esquisses*, 314).

44. "A la damalice foubine! A la damalice foubine!" is the phrase Frey says the griottes use to call dancers to this particular dance. His textual description of the Wolof dance echoes his explanation of the music played at the signare ball. He describes how the

women "vigorously clap their hands . . . and, rolling their eyes in which pleasure shines, opening their mouths to show two rows of splendid teeth, arouse the dancers" by calling "A la damalice foubine! A la damalice foubine!" ("Les femmes . . . batten vigoureusement des mains . . . roulant des yeux où brille le plaisir, ouvrant la bouche et montrant deux rangées de dents magnifiques, elles excitent les danseurs . . . *A la damalice foubine! A la damalice foubine!*") (Frey, *Côte Occidentale d'Afrique*, 7).

45. Deborah Heath's ethnology of Wolof dance in contemporary Senegal is suggestive of how the signares' ball performance may have enacted multiple and conflicting relationships of belonging and service and offers the possibility of reading the signare ball as a site of resistance and/or subversion ("Politics").

CHAPTER 2. INTIMATE ACTS

1. Darcy Grigsby describes the "iconography of the mulatta" as portraying her as a "desirable sexual object, emphasizing her demure but entreating gaze, her revealing shoulders, and her full round breasts, a nipple protruding from the caressing folds of a white blouse" (*Extremities*, 260).

2. As I discuss in this book's introduction, the free(d) mulatta concubine signifies women from a range of skin tones and racial categories who are represented in the archive as hypersexual, mixed-race, and often near-white seductresses of white men. In antebellum New Orleans and contemporary histories of that city, the free(d) women of color known for their sexual liaisons with white men are most often and persistently named "quadroons." "Quadroon balls," for example, refer to a spectacular public site wherein such liaisons were supposedly commenced and negotiated. Therefore, when discussing New Orleans specifically, unless otherwise noted, I employ "quadroon" to refer to this particular class of women.

3. The term "voodoo" in a U.S. context has historically misrepresented, at best, and continues to reflect both a misunderstanding and often a demonization of "any form of spiritual beliefs and practices remotely associated with the Black continent" and specifically associated with black subjects in Louisiana (Fandrich, "Yorùbá Influences," 777). And as Stephan Palmié demonstrates ("Conventionalization"), the historiography of voodoo practices in New Orleans is imbued with "distortion" in its repeated, unacknowledged verbatim reiterations of Moreau de Saint-Méry's eighteenth-century descriptions of vodou in colonial Saint-Domingue, which themselves represent the religion as an orgiastic, animalistic cult carried directly from a savage Africa. Despite (or perhaps because of) its vexed etymology and problematic archive, the term "voodoo" is paradoxically precise in locating its racialized and geographic subjects in the city of New Orleans. I therefore use it when speaking specifically of the African-diasporic religious practices in New Orleans and popular (mis)representations of such.

4. In addition to the biographies by Long and Ward is one more full-length published scholarly biography of Laveau: Fandrich, *The Mysterious Voodoo Queen*. While each work reflects careful and extensive archival research, to varying degrees each also articulates the impossibility of knowing the "real" Marie Laveau.

5. Many thanks to Sara Johnson for drawing my attention to this specific aspect of the portrait's work and for providing this phrase.

6. The free people of color of Louisiana have attracted the interest of historians

throughout the twentieth century. Due to prodigious research and the vast repository of civil and church records in Louisiana, the overwhelming majority of these accounts are rich and detailed in their attention to this class's relationship to Louisiana's civic, political, military, and religious institutions. In addition to the numerous dissertations and articles produced on this aspect of Louisiana's history, some of the most useful book-length works include the following: H. E. Sterkx, *The Free Negro in Ante-bellum Louisiana* (1972); John Blassingame, *Black New Orleans: 1860–1880* (1973); Caryn Cossé Bell, *Revolution, Romanticism and the Afro-Creole Protest Tradition in Louisiana, 1718–1868* (1997); Kimberly S. Hanger, *Bounded Lives, Bounded Places: Free Black Society in Colonial New Orleans, 1769–1803* (1997); Jennifer Spear, *Race, Sex, and Social Order in Early New Orleans* (2009); Shirley Elizabeth Thomson, *Exiles at Home: The Struggle to Become American in Creole New Orleans* (2009); and Emily Clark, *The Strange History of the American Quadroon: Free Women of Color in the Atlantic World* (2013).

7. Congo Square was a parade ground just outside the city walls of New Orleans. Here, slaves were permitted to attend Sunday afternoon activities, including dancing. See Gary A. Donaldson, "A Window on Slave Culture: Dances at Congo Square in New Orleans, 1800–1862," *Journal of Negro History* 69, no. 2 (Spring 1984): 63–72.

8. Long (*New Orleans*, 43) and Bryan (*Myth*) also note the origin of these descriptions.

9. Marcus B. Christian, "Voodooism and Mumbo Jumbo," unpublished manuscript, Marcus Christian Collection. See also Fandrich, *Mysterious*; Long, *New Orleans*; and Touchstone, "Voodoo."

10. Of course, it was not only African-descended women who had sexual relations and relationships with European settlers. Spear, for example, traces the scope and dynamics of French relationships with indigenous women in Louisiana. For a thoughtful critique of assumptions about desire and racial demographics in studies of métissage, see Spear, "Colonial Intimacies."

11. Madame Laurette Aimée Mozard Nicodami Ravient (1788–1864), *Mémoires d'une créole du Port-au-Prince* (1844; Paris, 1973), 24, quoted in Dayan, "Codes of Law," 297; Long, *New Orleans*, 21; Liliane Crété, *Daily Life in Louisiana, 1815–1830*, trans. Patrick Gregory (Baton Rouge: Louisiana State University Press, 1981), 81, quoted in Gould, "'Chaos,'" 238.

12. I borrow the term "public transcripts" from James C. Scott, whose analysis of public and private transcripts of the oppressed informs my reading here.

13. Here, of course, I draw from Spillers's generative and influential meditation on the "ungendering" of black female subjects via the transatlantic slave trade and American slavery ("Mama's Baby").

14. On the sacred aspects of hair braiding and hairdressing in West African religious practices, see Abiodun, "Hidden Power"; Seiber and Herreman, "Hair."

15. Thanks to Sara Johnson for suggesting this line of questioning.

16. Mrs. Marie Dede, folder 203, Federal Writers' Project Papers.

17. On the headwrap's "coded messages," see Buckridge, *Language*, 86–93.

18. See Thompson, *Exiles*, for a nuanced examination that unravels traditional binary framings of "Creole" and "American" in antebellum New Orleans.

19. A notable exception is Thompson's treatment of free women of color, the institution of plaçage, and these women's negotiation of the color line in antebellum New Orleans in *Exiles at Home*.

20. For accounts of this robbery, see Ward, *Voodoo Queen*; Fandrich, *Mysterious*; and Long, *New Orleans*.

21. In parsing the accuracy of the reporting of Toledano's words here I draw on Nell Irvin Painter's excavation of the various and divergent representations of Sojourner Truth's iconic speech, "Ar'n't I a Woman?" ("Representing Truth").

22. "The Voudous vs. Municipality No. Three," *Daily Delta*, July 14, 1850, quoted in Fandrich, *Mysterious*, 139.

23. In her careful biography of Laveau, Long writes against the popular "belief that Glapion was a person of mixed race from Saint Domingue" and insists that the documentary trail, including Christophe's "baptismal entry, military service documents, his death certificate and property succession, plus a wealth of civil and ecclesiastical records relating to his grandparents, parents, and siblings, indicate that he was born in Louisiana" and demonstrate unequivocally Glapion's legal white racial status (*New Orleans*, 51).

24. 3C3, March 14, 1940, folder 203, Federal Writers' Project Papers.

25. "Toutes les Négresses libres et riches, et toutes les Mulâtresses, se faisaient appeler Signares, et l'usage de prendre ce titre est assez general dans toute la partie de l'Afrique occidentale ... il date de l'arrivée des Portugais en Afrique" (Golberry, *Fragmens*, 1:156–57, cited in Brooks, *Eurafricans*, 215).

26. Reading against the grain of the official archive in order to discern some truth of the signares' experiences as subjects is a challenging endeavor in that it assigns a certain validity to a white European heterosexual patriarchal colonizing desiring gaze even as it works to undermine the authority of this gaze. That is, we have to presume a certain honesty from travelers' narratives that, according to Mary Louise Pratt, simultaneously operated as "innocent" observer and "imperial" conqueror (*Imperial Eyes*, 33).

27. In his reference to Lindsay's description of the saw knife, Brooks cites another example of violence amongst the women of Gorée, noting, "A French resident living on Gorée later in the century mentioned an instance of an African woman using solanum ... to poison her former lover and the Eurafrican for whom he abandoned her" (*Eurafricans*, 219).

28. As Brooks explains, over the course of the seventeenth and eighteenth centuries, "French trading companies underwent a series of transmutations." For example, the 1664 incorporation of the Compagnie des Indes Occidentales "lasted until 1674 when a second company of the same name was formed. Following the latter's bankruptcy, in 1681 the Compagnie du Sénégal was restricted to trade between Cape Blanco and the Gambia River" (Brooks, *Eurafricans*, 123). Both Searing and Brooks detail the various and numerous dissolutions and reconstitutions of chartered and monopolistic French concessionary companies in the region. For ease of reading, I will use "Senegal Company" throughout.

29. On colonial rule and the uses of concubinage in policing morality, race, and gender in order to maintain domination, see Stoler, *Carnal Knowledge*.

30. Whether Lindsay excluded evidence of other possible causes or was not as privy to the women's intimate lives as he suggests, the absence of such acknowledgment underscores the problem of the archive in reading the black women's lives. For example, if the women refused to discuss or mention or otherwise make public the sexual violence they endured, what does it mean to speculate on the possibilities of that sexual violence?

CHAPTER 3. AUTHORITY, KINSHIP, AND POSSESSION

1. By narrative accounts by free women of color, I mean documents such as letters and journals written by women in these relationships that would reveal how the women experienced the events of their lives. I am not suggesting that there do not exist such narratives in the archives. Rather, there are two issues at stake: first, if and where they do exist, they are hidden or otherwise submerged by inadvertent or deliberate choices in how archivists (both amateur and professional) select, assemble, catalog, and index collections; second, scholars' own biases may prevent them from seeing or acknowledging texts produced by women that are there. When it comes to the signares, such silences are particularly striking. John Hargreaves's essay "Assimilation in Eighteenth-Century Senegal" is thus remarkable for not only acknowledging the signares as political agents but also directly quoting the words of one signare. Furthermore, beyond narrative accounts, a textual archive documenting the existence and lives of these women does exist, including court documents, manumission records, wills and probate documents, baptismal records, and so forth; these documents offer invaluable evidence for piecing together free(d) women's private and public experiences. However, even with this rich archive, historians interested in tracing how the women experienced their slavery, manumission, and freedom must imagine the women's interiority. For an extraordinary and generative example, see Rebecca Scott and Jean Hébrard's revelatory work on the life and fortunes of the descendants of Rosalie, a young girl captured in Senegambia and brought to Saint-Domingue who eventually gave birth to mixed-race children and who struggled repeatedly and continuously to achieve freedom for herself and her children. Striking in Scott and Hébrard's account is the juxtaposition between the meticulous excavation, mining, and reading of an extraordinarily rich and diverse archive and the speculative lexicon necessary to recount the events of Rosalie's life: Rosalie's name "can reasonably be assumed to refer to a single individual," "it seems quite possible that Michel Vincent [a white Frenchman] was the father of all of Rosalie's children," "Rosalie seems to have hoped," and so forth ("Rosalie," 118, 123, 125).

2. An important and recent exception to the invisibility of free men of color in works that otherwise focus on free women of color is Emily Clark's *Strange History*, wherein she explores the antebellum literary critiques of *plaçage* by New Orleans free men of color, many of them of Haitian descent (see especially 155–61). The twentieth century also offers notable and troubling examples of African, black, and mulatto men within colonial spaces writing about the mulatta and her significance within diaspora. The most pressing of these is Frantz Fanon's chapter in *Black Skin, White Masks*, "The Woman of Color and the White Man," wherein he develops psychoanalytic critiques of two colonial literary works depicting relationships between mulatta women and white men: Martiniquan writer Mayotte Capécia's *Je suis martiniquaise* (1948) and Abdoulaye Sadji's *Nini: Mulâtresse de Sénégal* (1954); Sadji's novel is especially relevant here, as it centers on descendants of the habitant society produced by the signares.

3. Aside from a handful of notable exceptions, scholarly and popular examinations of free(d) women of color across the Atlantic depend almost exclusively upon representations of these subjects produced by white European and American men and fail to attend

to the archival silence of these women. In the case of the signares, the absence of their voices—those free(d) women of color in diaspora who acquired wealth and status from their relationships with white men—from the published record is striking. Indeed, across academic and popular histories that focus on eighteenth-century life in Gorée and Saint-Louis, what receives little discernible remark is that our understandings of these African and Euro-African women's subjectivities rely almost entirely upon the writings of colonizing European and colonized African men.

4. "peindre avec vérité & sans fard leurs meurs" (Lamiral, *L'Affrique*, "Advertissement" n.p.).

5. A—— Gusban to the Compagnie des Indes, July 6, 1737, Sous Series C 6, box 11, Archives nationales d'outre mer, Aix-en-Provence, France. The letter writer's first name is illegible. All subsequent quotes from this letter come from this source.

6. In thinking about intimacy, understanding the public and private spheres to be mutually constitutive rather than mutually discrete, especially in colonial and slave societies, is a point of departure. And certainly the writers of both the petition and Gusban's letter desired a public response to their entreaties. But what I am interested in here is something that moves beyond a focus on sexual relationships in explorations of intimacy in colonial and slave societies and seeks to explore how free(d) women of color defined and negotiated notions of intimacy, the private, and interiority. My understanding of intimacy and the intimate draws from and builds upon Ann Laura Stoler's work. Especially helpful is her examination of the work of memory in understanding colonial intimacies: "By treating memory as interpretive labor, the focus is on not only *what* is remembered, but *how*" (*Carnal Knowledge*, 170, emphasis in original). Within my own project, I am less interested in marking what intimacy is or looks like as an analytical frame to ask other questions; instead, I am more concerned with how free(d) black and mulatta women may have negotiated both the lexicon and the laws of racial, sexual, and familial intimacy as they experienced their freedom.

7. For some of the more provocative meditations on this tension, see Phillips, *Atlantic Sound*; Hartman, *Lose*; Brand, *Map*; and Edwards, "Evidence."

8. "afin d'assurrer à jamais la liberté et le bonheur de ses Sujets"; "Daignez, Messieurs, lui faire entendre la voix timide et plaintive des malheureux Habitans du Sénégal, *courbés sous le joug insupportable du despotisme affreux d'une Compagnie Priviligiée*"; "Nègres ou Mulâtres nous sommes tous Français puisque c'est le sang de Français qui coule dans nos veines ou dans celles de nos neveux" (Lamiral, *L'Affrique*, 1–2, emphasis in original).

9. It is important to note that Gorée and Saint-Louis are two distinct places in terms of how the habitants organized and exercised their political authority; they are also distinct in their shared imaginative and discursive space in black Atlantic history and memory.

10. Boubacar Barry describes two petitions, one sent in 1775 and the second in 1776 (during British control of Saint-Louis), both of which "deplor[ed] the personal business activities of [British governor O'Hara], arguing that he was ruining trade" (*Senegambia*, 68). Curtin also outlines tensions between the habitants and the French: "The Afro-French community of Gorée or of Saint Louis could usually have its way when it felt strongly about an issue, so long as the issue was not fundamental to the French position" (*Economic Change*, 116). Curtin's caveat here is important: while they exercised a great deal

of authority, at a certain point the habitants were subject to French authority. Hargreaves also notes that in "January 1776 a whole series of complaints, from both men and women, was presented before his (British Governor O'Hara) successor in Council, and in a formal petition written in very adequate English" ("Assimilation," 182). Hargreaves's essay is notable for mentioning that women, too, appealed to European authorities.

11. For a detailed overview of government and company policies against "private trade or traffic with African women" and on-the-ground proliferation of these relationships, see Brooks, *Eurafricans*, 210–15.

12. Regarding an earlier petition, Searing reads the habitants' assertion of their French blood as a "profession of loyalty to France" (*West African Slavery*, 112). My analysis concurs with and complicates this assessment.

13. Here again, Spear's intervention in such framings is exceptional ("Colonial Intimacies").

14. Foundational to my understanding of black geographies and the possibilities for resistance is McKittrick, *Demonic Grounds*.

15. "Elle voudroit nous réduire à un tel état de misere que nous fussions obliges de les lui vendre, faute d'avoir de quoi les alimenter. Elle a grand tort de former un tel projet; car il est beaucoup de ces esclaves qui ne le sont que de nom, que nous regardons comme nos frères & nos enfans" (Lamiral, *L'Affrique*, 24, translated and quoted in Searing, *West African Slavery*, 118).

16. My textual analysis here echoes and finds support in Mamadou Diouf's examination of the contours of the habitants' political strategies over the course of the nineteenth century.

17. For examinations of references to *plaçage* and quadroon balls in literary production by free men of color, see Clark, *Strange History*, 155–59; and Thompson, *Exiles*, 180–90.

18. Regarding the household captives on Saint-Louis, John Hargreaves explains: "The majority of these were Bambaras; . . . since their homeland was several hundred miles away they were unlikely to abscond" ("Assimilation," 179–80). While, as Martin Klein argues, "with time, a new language and new ways, the slave became part of both household and community," scholars (including Klein) concur that, against the romanticized notions of benign West African slavery, slaves were in fact socially "alien" vis-à-vis the master class (*Slavery*, 10). Thus, Claude Meillassoux argues, "If, *by the purely ideological extension of kinship*, the slave is sometimes assimilated to a sort of perpetual cadet, with the obligations of a dependant in terms of customary notions of morality, he never acquires the essential prerogatives—those bound up with paternity" (*Anthropology*, 14, emphasis in original). Orlando Patterson is perhaps most emphatic when he states, "It would be a great mistake, however, to confuse these fictive kin ties with the claims and obligations of real kinship or with those involving genuine adoption" (*Slavery*, 63).

19. Here, of course, I am drawing on Edouard Glissant's insistence that African diasporic subjects must return to the "point of entanglement, from which we were forcefully turned away" (*Caribbean Discourse*, 26).

20. "Elles sont au reste pleines de graces & de gentillesse"; "les femmes vont nues jusques à la ceinture"; "laborieuses, infatigables"; "les gens de couleur & quelques Nègres, professent la religion Catholique; mais avec un mélange singulier de Mahométisme &

d'Idolâtrie"; "ils parlent bien plus de bonne heure que les nôtres le langage de la raison" (Lamiral, *L'Affrique*, 43, 44, 45, 49).

21. "Presque tous les Blancs qui ont habité le Sénégal se sont associés avec des Négresses, en ont eu des enfans, qui ensuite mariés sans distinction de couleurs, ont mêlé les races, & ont formé une espece particulière qui constitue la population de l'Isle St-Louis"; "Ils sont inviolablement attachés aux Français, mais je crois que cet attachement tient plutôt aux préjugés de la naissance, aux habitudes de l'enfance, qu'à acun sentiment rasionné & à aucune vue politique" (Lamiral, *L'Affrique*, 74–75, 76).

22. "par environ trois cents habitans libres, Nègres ou Mulâtres, & environ cinq à six mille esclaves, ou étrangers des diverse nations qui avoisinent le pays" (Lamiral, *L'Affrique*, 42).

23. "En voyant les femmes de ce pays-là on ne peut que regretter infiniment qu'elles ne soient pas blanches. Elles sont au reste pleines de graces & de gentillesse, l'accent de leur voix est d'une douceur séduisante, leurs chansons ne respirent que volupté"; "elles sont capricieuses et aussi changeantes que nos élégantes" (Lamiral, *L'Affrique*, 44, 47).

24. "Elles les aiment tendrement, rien ne leur est refusé, & quoiqu'esclaves, la plupart, ces enfans vivent dans la liberté la plus indéfinie, jusqu'à l'âge de porter les armes, ou de travailler aux champs. C'est pourquoi ils deviennent si fiers, si robustes & auqu'ils acquièrent cette demarche hardie & aisée. Ils parlent bien plus de bonne heure que les nôtres le langage de la rasion, parce qu'ils sont, presqu'en naissant, regardés comme des homes, & qu'ils n'ont pas été humiliés par les corrections ni intimidés par la ferule d'un Pédagogue. Ils ne connoissent ni les arts ni les sciences, mais à douze ans ils connoissent très-bien & par tradition l'histoire de leur pays, ainsi que les intérêts civils & politiques de la societé où ils vivent" (Lamiral, *L'Affrique*, 49–50).

25. "Au Sénégal les femmes sont comme par-tout" (Lamiral, *L'Affrique*, 48).

26. "Dan leurs pillages les Maures prennent beaucoup plus d'enfans que de femmes & d'hommes, parce qu'il leur est plus facile de s'en saisir" (Lamiral, *L'Affrique*, 243–44).

27. "Les Blancs choisissent les plus jolis & les plus alertes pour en faire de petits domestiques. Il est peu de Blancs qui n'ait une de ces petites filles dont ils se propose de faire sa ménagère, & qui par la suite deviennent de grandes signares. Mais il faut qu'ils les prennent bien jeunes s'ils veulent obtenir cette fleur à laquelle nos préjugés attachent un si grand prix; il est bien rare que ces jeunes filles, quand elles ont passées par les mains des Maures, nous parviennent avec leur virginité. Le soin le plus empressé de leurs infâmes ravisseurs lorsqu'ils n'ont plus à craindre de poursuites, est de cueillir cette rose précisuese. Ils souillent l'innocence par leurs baisers impurs, les pleurs, les gémissemens que le chagrin & la douleur arrachent à ces tremblantes victimes ne sauroient mouvoir l'ame [*sic*] de ces doubles monstres de la nature" (Lamiral, *L'Affrique*, 244–45).

28. "Celles de ces femmes que les Blancs ont adoptées se sentent bientôt énorgueillies de cette distinction"; "J'ai cependant vu des Blancs qui ont eu la bassesse & l'abomination de vendre & d'envoyer à l'Amérique des esclaves qui avoient partagés leur couche. Cette atrocité m'a toujours revolté, jamais je n'ai pu supporter l'idée qu'il y eut des hommes assez inhumains pour laisser dans les fers une femme don't ils avoient desiré & obtenue les faveurs" (Lamiral, *L'Affrique*, 245, 246).

29. On the male heterosexual gaze, see Berger, *Ways*.

30. Searing also notes that the "composition of the slave population showed a clear

preference for women: 979 female slaves compared to 478 men in 1779" (*West African Slavery*, 116).

31. One nineteenth-century illustration that makes unambiguous the children's relationships to their signare mothers portrays the children as visibly closer to whiteness and wearing European-style clothing. See Frey, *Côte*, 16, fig. 9.

32. Curtin (279), Brooks (*Eurafricans*, 204), and Searing (213n113) all cite *Voyages to the Coast of Africa by Mess. Saugnier and Brisson* (London, 1792), but none offers a first name or much biographical detail for the French traveler, besides the fact that he "engaged in the slave trade as well" (Searing 127).

33. Curtin's footnote states that another source insisted that "a bloody insurrection actually did take place, but the evidence of Le Brasseur, who was commandant at Gorée in 1774–77, is preferred" (*Economic Change*, 116n10).

34. On the panopticon, see Foucault, *Discipline and Punish*. See also Scott, "Evidence."

35. "Je prens la liberté de vous representer les droits de ma fille Anne Gusban»; "Votre tres humble et tres obeisant servante, A—— Gusban, Negresse."

36. Hilary Jones is remarkable here in persistently attending to gender in her political history, *The Métis of Senegal*.

37. Citing Delcourt and Searing, Brooks explains that while company practice was initially not to allow "children to inherit property acquired by an employee," by the time of Gusban's letter, this policy "seems to have been abandoned. . . . A communication concerning circumstances at Gorée in June 1736 indicated that the official practice was to allow children to inherit the property of their mothers" (*Eurafricans*, 211).

38. "il y a trois captifes, dont un vielle femme, un jeune Rapace, et une Negresse d'environs 17 ans."

39. "Lorsqu'il n'y a point de navire européen sur la côte, souvent un maître indulgent admet au nombre de ses domestiques des esclaves qu'il avoit achetés pour les revendre. Ce sont le plus souvent des enfans de l'un ou de l'autre sexe que l'on emploie pour les petits détails de la maison; on nomme les garcons *rapaces*, les filles *rapacilles*; ces enfans jouissent des memes privileges que les esclaves nés dans la case du maître" (Villeneuve, *L'Afrique*, 55).

40. "qu'en osant les captifes de ma fille (qui a que 10 ans) on lui osent sa nouriture"; "Je supplie la Compagnie d'avoir egard a mes représentations en faisant cette acte de justice, et on ne pourra dire dans le païs que la Compagnie fait faire des pillages comme le Roy Damel."

41. On the Damel and relationships with the French, see also Barry, *Senegambia*, 81–87; and Curtin, *Economic Change*, 300.

CHAPTER 4. MAPPING FREEDOM AND BELONGING

1. On the impact of the abolition of slavery in Senegal, see Klein, *Slavery*.

2. See Trouillot, *Silencing*, esp. chap. 1.

3. For a productive and relevant critique of contemporary assertions of transnationalism as "radically or qualitatively new," especially in terms of the history of an African diaspora, see Matory, *Black Atlantic Religion*, esp. chap. 2.

4. I use "country" here advisedly; as Murphy points out, during Boilat's stay, Senegal was neither yet colony nor nation ("Birth," 57).

5. "indispensables pour la parfaite intelligence de l'histoire que j'ai tracée dans mes *Esquisses sénégalaises*" (Boilat, *Atlas*, n.p.).

6. Of course, without any familiarity with the text's written language, one's understanding of who these people were would be constrained. However, while the incompleteness of such comprehension may disrupt or shift how one reads the visual *Atlas*, it does not absolutely negate one's ability to make some sort of sensible meaning of the plates.

7. As Thomas Bassett explains, late nineteenth-century "map readers interpreted blank spaces as areas open for exploration and ultimately colonization. . . . In the apparent absence of human habitation and signs of indigenous territorial control, the public might be more willing to support imperialist ventures overseas" ("Cartography," 324).

8. As Abdoulaye-Bara Diop explains in his introduction to the 1984 republication of *Esquisses*, the work "aligns itself less with those works by explorers charged with discovering Africa's interior" and more with those works that assert a "familiarity with the country and the people whose conquest these works prepare and justify" (10). Boilat's project was "evangelism, instruction, 'civilization' of the population, all aided by colonization" (10). Most importantly, *Esquisses* "glorifies conquest of Senegal, even a military one, for which [Governor] Faidherbe is the best instructor and architect" (10). Thus, as "one of the first books on Africa written by an African," *Esquisses sénégalaises* demonstrates the complex and often contradictory interactions between place, race, ethnicity, and nation in parsing the subject formation of "Africans" subjected to European incursion and the process of being "systematically and violently colonized by the French" (Murphy, "Birth," 59). The fact of Boilat's personal history compounds the complexity of this negotiation. As Bernard Mouralis notes, Boilat, the "author of two foundational works on Senegal, spent only twenty-three years in his native country and sixty-four in France" ("Les 'Esquisses sénégalaises,'" 821). Furthermore, Mouralis insists that given Boilat's apparent silence on the conditions surrounding his permanent return to France, "one is reduced to speculation and must therefore ignore in particular whether the period he spent in France until his death was in effect an exile, more or less imposed by colonial or church authorities and from which the writer would have wished to be freed" (821). More specifically, Mouralis offers his literary analysis of *Esquisses* as evidence that the work reflects Boilat's engagement with Senegal as someone who was "never an outsider to Senegal" nor a mere "traveler" but rather "someone who is a national of that country" (821). As David Murphy points out, "In 1853 when the book was published, the colony of Senegal was largely a fiction; the colonization of the country now known as Senegal had not yet taken place" ("Birth," 57). Furthermore, "even the map of 'Senegal' produced by Boilat to accompany his text includes vast areas of land that do not belong to the current Senegalese state" (57). At the same time, while Boilat's geographical origin and racial and ethnic identities appear transparent in the archive, and his work is indeed central to examinations of a Senegalese national literary tradition, how he and his work fit into the definition and formation of this tradition engenders a bit of debate. For example, Murphy insists that *Esquisses* is one of a "small number of texts from the 1850s to 1920s" that "occupy a deeply ambiguous position within the [Senegalese] national literary canon because of their open support for French colonialism" (49). For a concise and productive overview of the idea of a Senegalese national literature and Boilat's fit, see Murphy, "Birth."

9. I am again influenced by Matory's work in *Black Atlantic Religion*, where he examines "how Afro-Brazilian talk and action helped to generate a so-called Yòrùbá culture in West Africa that is in fact *younger than its Brazilian diaspora*" (50, emphasis in original). While Matory focuses on an "Afro-Atlantic" dialogue between subjects in Africa and subjects in its American diaspora, I am interested in thinking about how Boilat's encounters with differently located black subjects in his "homeland" of Senegal help him produce or invent "authentic" representations of his nation's peoples and cultures.

10. "Je n'ai point donné de costume ni de type d'hommes de couleur, appelés *habitants* du Sénégal; leur type tient de la race caucasique, et leur costume est tout à fait français" (Boilat, *Atlas*, 5).

11. "[Elles] ont encore conservé leur costume particulier"; "leur intérieur"; "Les dames signares sont logées à peu près comme en France; leurs maisons sont bâties de brique ou de pierre" (Boilat, *Atlas*, 5).

12. "Les signares sont divisées par sociétiés ou compagnies connues sous le nom de *Mbotaye*"; "la première sortie de l'enfant"; "elles s'y rendent avec les parents et les amis, suivies chacune de plusieurs domestiques"; "vêtues richement de *mboubes* brodés avec finesse et avec art; le cou, les oreilles, les bras et les pieds ornés de bijoux d'or" (Boilat, *Atlas*, 5, 6).

13. Hinchman contends that because Boilat's subjects consented to him sketching them, they therefore consented to how he represented them in his work. While I disagree with this conclusion, I find the question underlying Hinchman's argument, that of how Boilat's subjects understood and theorized his portraits of them, to be compelling and provocative.

14. "Elle est en tenue de fête; son costume est très riche; les mouchoirs de la tête sont de beaux madras, et son mboube est de soie. Le collier se termine en petits anneaux de paille travaillés avec soin" (Boilat, *Atlas*, 31).

15. "Le plus grand défaut chez eux, après celui de n'avoir aucune religion, est de n'avoir aucune espèce d'affection de famille. Pour eux, la femme n'est qu'une esclave que l'on emploie quand elle peut être utile et dont on se débarrasse quand on n'en veut plus. Il arrive fréquemment qu'un Bambara, après trois ou quatre ans de mariage, vend sa femme et ses enfants en esclavage, et se remarie avec une autre femme plus jeune"; "Elle a beaucoup d'intelligence; son caractère est très jovial" (Boilat, *Atlas*, 31).

16. On the various Senegalese ethnic groups' encounters with and relationship to slavery in the eighteenth and nineteenth centuries, see Searing, "'No Kings'"; and Klein, "Slave Trade."

17. Bernard Moitt cites a 1905 report that takes "note that young girls were generally sold to Wolof traders who sometimes obtained a *certificat de liberté* (certificate of freedom) for them before putting them to work in Wolof households under conditions similar to slavery" ("Slavery," 34). Noting that the author of the report states that this was a "special trade," Moitt concludes, "Some of these girls were obviously used as concubines." Those girls sent to "urban centers," including Saint-Louis and Gorée, were "classified as minors and placed in the care of legal guardians . . . a subterfuge for slavery" (35).

18. Here I am drawing on Alejo Carpentier's and Jacques Stéphan Alexis's meditations on the "marvelous real" in the Americas.

19. In her survey of nineteenth-century travelers' narratives, Florence Roos Brink

notes, "With one or two exceptions all those who have recorded their visits to Louisiana have arrived and left Louisiana by boat" ("Literary Travellers," 403).

20. On the impact of Saint-Domingue refugees on the city's population, see Lachance, "The 1809 Immigration." See also Scott, "Paper Thin"; Clark, *Strange History*, esp. chap. 2; Thompson, *Exiles*, 73–81.

21. While New Orleans's free women of color occupied a range of skin colors, travelers' narratives most often employed the term *quadroon*, sometimes substituting it with *octoroon* or *mulatta*.

22. According to Clark, Pierre-Louis Berquin-Duvallon, a white refugee of Saint-Domingue, was the writer who explicitly "transported the trope of the *mulâtresse* to New Orleans" (*Strange History*, 52).

23. While Clark rightly characterizes Olmsted's description of New Orleans's quadroons as more tempered and "credible" than most in that he "offered a glimpse of the much more mundane arrangement [than plaçage] that may actually have existed" (*Strange History*, 171), I contend that he nonetheless ascribes to them a fantastic power propelled by their charm and beauty, as evidenced by the quote provided here.

24. For the myriad threats against free blacks' liberty in New Orleans, see Schafer, *Becoming Free*. For a historical analysis of the "Negro Seaman Acts" enacted throughout southern ports, see Bolster, *Black Jacks*.

25. For a particularly trenchant critique of the romance of benevolent black slaveholders in antebellum Louisiana specifically and the Americas more broadly, and the concomitant romance of shared interests between black slaveholders and those held as slaves, see Johnson, *Fear*, 104–14.

26. Until recently, Sharon Dean's research had produced nearly all of the biographical information on Potter, including details from the 1860 census for Cincinnati (introduction). Xiomara Santamarina's recent annotated edition of and introduction to Potter's narrative offer new biographical details, as well as generative framings for the underexamined work. However, as Santamarina states, Potter "remains elusive in historical records. It has not been possible to corroborate many of her biographical claims" ("Introduction [Appendix A]," 179). Potter's narrative emerges as subversive in its relationship to the archive in its claim to authority and offering into evidence accounts of events otherwise not in the historical record. See also Santamarina, *Belabored Professions*, 107, 123–32.

27. For an examination of how the works of Potter and other underexamined nineteenth-century African American women writers invite us to revise the critical lens through which we read African American literature as a whole, see Santamarina, *Belabored Professions*.

28. As Santamarina details, the circumstances of the marriage Potter mentions here are elusive, but other evidence of Potter's life suggests that she would have been very young when she married the first time (she married a second time). Santamarina thus reminds us that we cannot make assumptions about why Potter considered marriage a "weakness."

29. Mexico and the western territories offered similar possibilities; however, in terms of the landscape of abolitionist literature, heading north toward freedom was the predominant narrative. On Mexico and the western territories as sites of freedom, see Carrigan, *Making*. Special thanks to Kidada Williams for directing me to this source.

30. As Zafar speculates, Potter "may here be punning on 'previous condition,' the nineteenth-century American legal term for former enslavement" (*We Wear*, 160).

31. Particularly remarkable here is Potter's ability to resist making herself fully visible to her reader even as the entire description centers on her hypervisibility to the ship's other passengers. This resistance is particularly compelling given the possibilities of Potter's own racial status. Marked "mulatto" in the 1860 census, Potter describes explicitly neither her appearance nor her racial status. We do not know whether Potter identified herself to the census taker as "mulatto" or whether the official made an assumption based on her skin color.

32. Potter's sojourn in Canada and description of how she "was welcomed by her own relatives and their numerous friends and acquaintances" are remarkable and deserve further investigation (*Hairdresser's Experience*, 14).

33. For an analysis of the spatial proximity of quadroon balls to the fancy trade in New Orleans, see Guillory, "Under One Roof."

34. Baptist's essay provides an excellent and detailed analysis of the fetishism and disavowal at work in planters' descriptions of the fancy trade. See also the discussion in Johnson, *Soul*, 113–15. Overwhelmingly, the historiography of the fancy trade has focused on white male desire and power. Baptist's essay, for example, mines traders' letters about fancy girls in order to provide a psychoanalytical analysis of white male desire. A recent essay by Sharony Green offers a productive and revelatory counternarrative to Baptist's essay by examining the same archival repository he examines, the papers of Rice C. Ballard, "a former Virginia slave trader." Analyzing the letters written to Ballard by women previously and still owned by Ballard, Green speculates on how these women may have enjoyed some agency because of their status as "fancy girls." While I do not agree with all of Green's conclusions, I find her intervention extraordinary, especially as it presses upon the limits of the archive and reminds us that evidence was indeed produced by the very subjects we so often presume to have been silenced. See Green, "'Mr. Ballard.'"

35. For an especially productive analysis, see Brody, *Impossible Purities*.

36. I am extremely grateful to Lara Langer Cohen for pressing me to consider the implications of the log of wood here.

37. Potter's clear description of the logistics of writing and circulating the petition is remarkable, in that she alludes to her own standing outside citizenship even as she makes a claim upon the rights of citizenship.

WORKS CITED

ARCHIVAL SOURCES

Marcus Christian Collection, Series 13, Literary and Historical Manuscripts, Special Collections, Earl K. Long Library, University of New Orleans.
Federal Writers' Project Papers, Cammie G. Henry Research Center, Watson Memorial Library, Northwestern State University of Louisiana.
Sous Series C 6, C 13, Archives nationales d'outre mer, Aix-en-Provence, France.

NEWSPAPERS

Daily Picayune
New Orleans Daily Crescent

EIGHTEENTH- AND NINETEENTH-CENTURY PRIMARY SOURCES

Bibb, Henry. *Narrative of the Life and Adventures of Henry Bibb, an American Slave.* 1849. Mineola, N.Y.: Dover Publications, 2005.
Boilat, L'Abbé P.-D. *Esquisses sénégalaises: Physionomie du pays, peuplades, commerce, religions, passé et avenir, récits et légendes.* Paris: P. Bertrand, 1853.
————. *Esquisses sénégalaises: Physionomie du pays, peuplades, commerce, religions, passé et avenir, récits et légendes. Atlas.* Paris: P. Bertrand, 1853. HathiTrust Digital Library.
Buckingham, James. *The Slave States of America.* Vol. 1. London: Fisher, Son and Co., 1842.
Craft, William. *Running a Thousand Miles for Freedom: The Escape of William and Ellen Craft from Slavery.* 1860. Baton Rouge: Louisiana State University Press, 1999.
Durand, Jean Baptiste Léonard. *A Voyage to Senegal; or, Historical, philosophical, and political memoirs relative to the discoveries, establishments and commerce of Europeans in the Atlantic Ocean, from Cape Blanco to the river of Sierra Leone.* London: Richard Phillips, 1806.
Equiano, Olaudah. *The Interesting Narrative of the Life of Olaudah Equiano, or Gustavus Vassa, the African. Written by Himself.* 1814. In *The Classic Slave Narratives*, edited by Henry Louis Gates, Jr., 1–182. New York: Penguin Books, 1987.
Frey, Colonel Henri. *Côte Occidentale d'Afrique: Vues, scènes, croquis.* Paris, 1890.
Golberry, Silv. Mienrad Xavier. *Fragmens d'un voyage en Afrique.* Paris, 1802.
Jacobs, Harriet. *Incidents in the Life of a Slave Girl.* 1861. Edited by Nellie Y. McKay and Frances Smith Foster. New York: W. W. Norton, 2001.
Jobson, Richard. *The Golden Trade or a Discovery of the River Gambia, and the Golden Age of the Aethiopians.* 1623. Teignmouth and Devonshire: E. E. Spieght & R. H. Walpole, 1904.

Lamiral, Dominique Harcourt. *L'Affrique et le peuple affriquain considérés sous tous leurs rapports avec notre commerce & nos colonies.* Paris: Dessenne, 1789.

Lindsay, Rev. John. *A Voyage to the Coast of Africa, in 1758. Containing a Succinct Account of the Expedition to, and the taking of the Island of Gorée, by a squadron commanded by the Honourable Augustus Keppel.* London, 1759. Microfilm. Newspapers and Microforms Library, University of California, Berkeley.

Moreau de Saint-Méry, Médéric-Louis-Elie. *Description topographique, physique, civile, politique et historique de la partie française de l'isle Saint-Domingue, tome premier.* Philadelphia, 1797. Gallica bibliothèque numérique, Bibliothèque nationale de France. http://gallica.bnf.fr/ark:/12148/bpt6k111179t.

Olmsted, Frederick Law. *A Journey in the Seaboard Slave States, with Remarks on Their Economy.* New York: Dix & Edwards, 1856.

Potter, Eliza. *A Hairdresser's Experience in High Life.* 1859. New York: Oxford University Press, 1991.

Prince, Nancy. *A Narrative of the Life and Travels of Mrs. Nancy Prince. Written by Herself.* 2nd ed., 1853. In *Collected Black Women's Narratives.* Introduction by Anthony G. Barthelemy. New York: Oxford University Press, 1988.

Pruneau de Pommegorge, Antoine. *Description de la Nigritie.* Amsterdam, 1789. HathiTrust Digital Library.

Robin, Charles César. *Voyage to Louisiana, 1803–1805.* Translated by Stuart O. Landry, Jr. New Orleans: Pelican Publishing Company, 1966.

Trollope, Frances. *Domestic Manners of the Americans.* 1832. Edited by Donald Smalley. New York: Alfred A. Knopf, 1949.

Villeneuve, René Geoffroy de. *L'Afrique, ou histoire, moeurs, usages et coutumes des Africains.* Vol. 4, *Le Sénégal.* Paris, 1814. Gallica bibliothèque numérique, Bibliothèque nationale de France. http://gallica.bnf.fr/ark:/12148/bpt6k85224c.

CONTEMPORARY LITERARY WORKS AND SECONDARY SOURCES

Abiodun, Rowland. "Hidden Power: Ọṣun, the Seventeenth Odù." In *Ọṣun across the Waters: A Yoruba Goddess in Africa and the Americas,* edited by Joseph M. Murphy and Mei-Mei Sanford, 10–31. Bloomington: Indiana University Press, 2001.

Alexis, Jacques Stéphan. "Of the Marvellous Realism of the Haitians." *Présence Africaine* 8–10 (June–November 1956): 249–75.

Badassy, Prinisha. "Gorée and Its House of Slaves: Almost 20 Years Later." 2012. *H-Africa.* Michigan State University. http://h-net.msu.edu/cgi-bin/logbrowse.pl?trx=vx&list=H-Africa&month=1203&week=e&msg=gi8YboOJ41%2bKTMLbzSzPnQ&user=&pw=.

Baker, Houston A. *Blues, Ideology, and Afro-American Literature: A Vernacular Theory.* Chicago: University of Chicago Press, 1987.

Baptist, Edward E. "'Cuffy,' 'Fancy Maids,' and 'One-Eyed Men': Rape, Commodification, and the Domestic Slave Trade in the United States." *American Historical Review* 106 (2001): 1619–50. http://www.jstor.org/stable/2692741.

Barrett, Lindon. "Hand-Writing: Legibility and the White Body in *Running a Thousand Miles for Freedom.*" *American Literature* 69, no. 2 (1997): 315–36. http://www.jstor.org/stable/2928273.

Barry, Boubacar. *Senegambia and the Atlantic Slave Trade*. Cambridge: Cambridge University Press, 1998.

Bassett, Thomas J. "Cartography and Empire Building in Nineteenth-Century West Africa." *Geographical Review* 84, no. 3 (1994): 316–35. http://www.jstor.org/stable/215456.

Baucoum, Ian. *Specters of the Atlantic: Finance Capital, Slavery, and the Philosophy of History*. Durham, N.C.: Duke University Press, 2005.

Bellegarde-Smith, Patrick. "Broken Mirrors: Mythos, Memories, and National History." In *Haitian Vodou: Spirit, Myth, and Reality*, edited by Patrick Bellegarde-Smith and Claudine Michel, 19–31. Bloomington: Indiana University Press, 2006.

Berger, John. *Ways of Seeing*. New York: Penguin, 1990.

Berlin, Ira. *Slaves without Masters: The Free Negro in the Antebellum South*. New York: Oxford University Press, 1975.

Bolster, W. Jeffrey. *Black Jacks: African American Seamen in the Age of Sail*. Cambridge, Mass.: Harvard University Press, 1997.

Bost, Suzanne. *Mulattas and Mestizas: Representing Mixed Identities in the Americas, 1850–2000*. Athens: University of Georgia Press, 2003.

Brand, Dionne. *A Map to the Door of No Return: Notes to Belonging*. Toronto: Doubleday, 2001.

Brink, Florence Roos. "Literary Travellers in Louisiana between 1803 and 1860." *Louisiana Historical Quarterly* 31 (1948): 394–424.

Brody, Jennifer DeVere. *Impossible Purities: Blackness, Femininity, and Victorian Culture*. Durham, N.C.: Duke University Press, 1998.

Brooks, George E. "Artists' Depictions of Senegalese Signares: Insights Concerning French Racist and Sexist Attitudes in the Nineteenth Century." *Genève—Afrique/Geneva—Africa* 18, no. 1 (1980): 75–90.

———. *Eurafricans in Western Africa: Commerce, Social Status, Gender, and Religious Observance from the Sixteenth to the Eighteenth Century*. Athens: Ohio University Press, 2003.

———. *Landlords and Strangers: Ecology, Society, and Trade in Western Africa*. Boulder, Colo.: Westview Press, 1993.

———. "The *Signares* of Saint-Louis and Gorée: Women Entrepreneurs in Eighteenth-Century Senegal." In *Women in Africa: Studies in Social and Economic Change*, edited by Nancy J. Hafkin and Edna G. Bay, 19–44. Stanford, Calif.: Stanford University Press, 1976.

Brown, Karen McCarthy. *Mama Lola: A Vodou Priestess in Brooklyn*. Berkeley: University of California Press, 1991.

———. "Olina and Erzulie: A Woman and a Goddess in Haitian Vodou." *Amina* 5 (Spring 1979): 110–16.

Brown, Stacia L. "Is Olivia Pope the New Sally Hemings?" *Clutch*, May 11, 2012. http://www.clutchmagonline.com/2012/05/is-olivia-pope-is-the-new-sally-heming/.

Brown, William Wells. *Clotel; or, the President's Daughter*. 1853. New York: First Carol Publishing Group, 1969.

Bryan, Violet. *The Myth of New Orleans in Literature: Dialogues of Race and Gender*. Knoxville: University of Tennessee Press, 1993.

Buckridge, Steeve O. *The Language of Dress: Resistance and Accommodation in Jamaica, 1760–1890.* Kingston, Jamaica: University of West Indies Press, 2004.

Camp, Stephanie M. H. "The Pleasures of Resistance: Enslaved Women and the Body Politics in the Plantation South, 1830–1861." *Journal of Southern History* 68, no. 3 (2002): 533–72. JSTOR. http://www.jstor.org/stable/3070158.

Carby, Hazel. *Reconstructing Womanhood: The Emergence of the Afro-American Woman Novelist.* New York: Oxford University Press, 1989.

Caron, Peter. "'Of a Nation which the Others Do Not Understand': Bambara Slaves and African Ethnicity in Colonial Louisiana, 1718–60." *Slavery and Abolition: A Journal of Slave and Post-slave Studies* 18, no. 1 (1997): 98–121. DOI: 10.1080/01440399708575205.

Carpentier, Alejo. "On the Marvelous Real in America." 1949. Translated by Tanya Huntington and Lois Parkinson Zamora. In *Magical Realism: Theory, History, Community,* edited by Lois Parkinson Zamora and Wendy B. Faris, 75–88. Durham, N.C.: Duke University Press, 1995.

Carretta, Vincent. *Equiano, the African: Biography of a Self-Made Man.* Athens: University of Georgia Press, 2005.

Carrigan, William D. *Making of a Lynching Culture: Violence and Vigilantism in Central Texas, 1836–1916.* Urbana: University of Illinois Press, 2004.

Certeau, Michel de. *The Practice of Everyday Life.* Translated by Steven Rendall. Berkeley: University of California Press, 1984.

Christian, Barbara. "Fixing Methodologies: *Beloved.*" In *Female Subjects in Black and White: Race, Psychoanalysis, Feminism,* edited by Elizabeth Abel, Barbara Christian, and Helene Moglen, 363–70. Berkeley: University of California Press, 1997.

Clark, Emily. *The Strange History of the American Quadroon: Free Women of Color in the Revolutionary Atlantic World.* Chapel Hill: University of North Carolina Press, 2013.

Clark, Emily, and Virginia Meacham Gould. "The Feminine Face of Afro-Catholicism in New Orleans, 1727–1852." *William and Mary Quarterly* 59, no. 2 (2002): 409–48.

Clark, VèVè A. "Developing Diaspora Literacy and Marasa Consciousness." In *Comparative American Identities: Race, Sex, and Nationality in the Modern Text,* edited by Hortense Spillers, 40–61. New York: Routledge, 1991.

Clark, VèVè A., and Sara E. Johnson, eds. *Kaiso! Writings by and about Katherine Dunham.* Madison: University of Wisconsin Press, 2005.

Collins, Patricia Hill. *Black Feminist Thought: Knowledge, Consciousness and the Politics of Empowerment.* 2nd ed. New York: Routledge, 2000.

Cosentino, Donald J., ed. *Sacred Arts of Haitian Vodou.* Los Angeles: Regents of the University of California, 1995.

Curtin, Philip D. *Economic Change in Precolonial Africa: Senegambia in the Era of the Slave Trade.* Madison: University of Wisconsin Press, 1975.

Dakar et le Sénégal: Les guides bleus illustrés Librairie Hachette. Paris: Librairie Hachette, 1972.

Davis, Angela. "Reflections on the Black Woman's Role in a Community of Slaves." In *Words of Fire: An Anthology of African American Feminist Thought,* edited by Beverly Guy Sheftal, 200–218. New York: New Press, 1998.

Dayan, Colin (Joan). "Codes of Law and Bodies of Color." *New Literary History* 26, no. 2 (1995): 283–308. http://www.jstor.org/stable/20057283.

———. "Erzulie: A Women's History of Haiti." *Research in African Literatures* 25, no. 2 (1994): 5–31.

———. *Haiti, History and the Gods.* Berkeley: University of California Press, 1995.

———. "Paul Gilroy's Slaves, Ships, and Routes: The Middle Passage as Metaphor." *Research in African Literatures* 27, no. 4 (1996): 7–14. http://www.jstor.org/stable/3819981.

Dean, Sharon. Introduction to *A Hairdresser's Experience in High Life,* by Eliza Potter, xxxiii–lix. New York: Oxford University Press, 1991.

Deren, Maya. *Divine Horsemen: The Living Gods of Haiti.* 1953. Kingston, N.Y.: McPherson, 2004.

Desmangles, Leslie. *The Faces of the Gods: Vodou and Roman Catholicism in Haiti.* Chapel Hill: University of North Carolina Press, 1992.

Diop, Abdoulaye-Bara. Introduction to *Esquisses sénégalaises: Physionomie du pays, peuplades, commerce, religions, passé et avenir, récits et légendes,* by David Boilat, 5–26. Paris: Karthala, 1984.

Diouf, Mamadou. "The French Colonial Policy of Assimilation and the Civility of the Originaires of the Four Communes (Senegal): A Nineteenth Century Globalization Project." *Development and Change* 29 (1998): 671–96. DOI: 10.1111/1467-7660.00095.

Drewal, Henry John. "Introduction: Sources and Currents." In *Mami Wata: Arts for Water Spirits in Africa and Its Diasporas,* edited by Henry John Drewal, 23–69. Los Angeles: Fowler Museum at UCLA, 2008.

Ebron, Paulla A. *Performing Africa.* Princeton, N.J.: Princeton University Press, 2002.

Edwards, Brent Hayes. "Evidence." *Transition* 90 (2001): 42–67.

———. "Langston Hughes and the Futures of Diaspora." *American Literary History* 19, no. 3 (2007): 689–711. http://www.jstor.org/stable/4497007.

———. *The Practice of Diaspora: Literature, Translation, and the Rise of Black Internationalism.* Cambridge, Mass.: Harvard University Press, 2003.

Fandrich, Ina Johanna. "Defiant African Sisterhoods: The Voodoo Arrests of the 1850s and 1860s in New Orleans." In *Fragments of the Bone: Neo-African Religions in a New World,* edited by Patrick Bellegarde-Smith, 187–207. Urbana: University of Illinois Press, 2005.

———. *The Mysterious Voodoo Queen: Marie Laveaux: A Study of Powerful Female Leadership in Nineteenth-Century New Orleans.* New York: Routledge, 2005.

———. "Yorùbá Influences on Haitian Vodou and New Orleans Voodoo." *Journal of Black Studies* 37, no. 5 (2007): 775–91.

Fanon, Frantz. *Black Skin, White Masks.* Translated by Richard Philcox. New York: Grove Press, 2008.

Fleurant, Gerdès. "Vodun, Music, and Society in Haiti: Affirmation and Identity." In *Haitian Vodou: Spirit, Myth, and Reality,* edited by Patrick Bellegarde-Smith and Claudine Michel, 46–57. Bloomington: Indiana University Press, 2006.

Foreman, P. Gabrielle. "'Who's Your Mama?' 'White' Mulatta Genealogies, Early Photography, and Anti-passing Narratives of Slavery and Freedom." *American Literary History* 14, no. 3 (Fall 2002): 506–39.

Foster, Helen Bradley. *"New Raiments of Self": African American Clothing in the Antebellum South.* New York: Berg, 1997.

Foucault, Michel. *Discipline and Punish: The Birth of the Prison.* Translated by Alan Sheridan. New York: Vintage Books, 1995.

Fouchard, Jean. *The Haitian Maroons: Liberty or Death.* Translated by A. Faulkner Watts. New York: Edward W. Blyden Press, 1981.

Garraway, Doris. *The Libertine Colony: Creolization in the Early French Caribbean.* Durham, N.C.: Duke University Press, 2005.

Gates, Henry Louis, Jr. *The Signifying Monkey: A Theory of African-American Literary Criticism.* New York: Oxford University Press, 1988.

Geggus, David. "The French Slave Trade: An Overview." "New Perspectives on the Transatlantic Slave Trade." Special issue, *William and Mary Quarterly* 58, no. 1 (2001): 119–38. http://www.jstor.org/stable/2674421.

Gehman, Mary. *Women and New Orleans: A History.* New Orleans: Margaret Media, 2000.

Gilroy, Paul. *The Black Atlantic: Modernity and Double-Consciousness.* Cambridge, Mass.: Harvard University Press, 1993.

Glissant, Edouard. *Caribbean Discourse.* Translated by Michael Dash. Charlottesville: University Press of Virginia, 1989.

Glover, Kaiama L. *Haiti Unbound: A Spiralist Challenge to the Postcolonial Canon.* Liverpool: Liverpool University Press, 2010.

Gordon, Avery. *Ghostly Matters: Haunting and the Sociological Imagination.* Minneapolis: University of Minnesota Press, 1997.

Gordon-Reed, Annette. *Thomas Jefferson and Sally Hemings: An American Controversy.* Charlottesville: University of Virginia Press, 1997.

Gorée: Island of Memories. Paris: UNESCO, 1985.

Gould, Virginia Meacham. "'A Chaos of Iniquity and Discord': Slave and Free Women of Color in the Spanish Ports of New Orleans, Mobile, and Pensacola." In *The Devil's Lane: Sex and Race in the Early South,* edited by Catherine Clinton and Michele Gillespie, 232–46. New York: Oxford University Press, 1997.

Gourdine, Angeletta KM. *The Difference Place Makes: Gender, Sexuality, and Diaspora Identity.* Columbus: Ohio University Press, 2003.

Green, Sharony. "'Mr. Ballard, I Am Compelled to Write Again': Beyond Bedrooms and Brothels, a Fancy Girl Speaks." *Black Women, Gender + Families* 5, no. 1 (2011): 17–40. http://www.jstor.org/stable/10.5406/blacwomegendfami.5.1.0017.

Grigsby, Darcy Grimaldo. *Extremities: Painting Empire in Post-revolutionary France.* New Haven, Conn.: Yale University Press, 2004.

Guillory, Monique. "Some Enchanted Evening on the Auction Block: The Cultural Legacy of the New Orleans Quadroon Balls." PhD diss., New York University, 1999. Ann Arbor, Mich.: University Microfilms, 1999.

———. "Under One Roof: The Sins and Sanctity of New Orleans Quadroon Balls." In *Race Consciousness: African-American Studies for the New Century,* edited by Judith Jackson Fossett and Jeffery A. Tucker, 67–92. New York: New York University Press, 1997.

Hall, Gwendolyn Midlo. *Africans in Colonial Louisiana: The Development of Afro-Creole Culture in the Eighteenth Century.* Baton Rouge: Louisiana State University Press, 1992.

Hall, Stuart. "Cultural Identity and Diaspora." In *Identity: Community, Culture, Difference*, edited by Jonathan Rutherford, 222–37. London: Lawrence & Wishart, 1990.

Hanchard, Michael. "Identity, Meaning, and the African-American." *Social Text* 24 (1990): 31–42.

Hanger, Kimberly S. "Coping in a Complex World: Free Black Women in Colonial New Orleans." In *The Devil's Lane: Sex and Race in the Early South*, edited by Catherine Clinton and Michele Gillespie, 218–29. New York: Oxford University Press, 1997.

Hargreaves, John D. "Assimilation in Eighteenth-Century Senegal." *Journal of African History* 6, no. 2 (1965): 177–84.

Harper, Frances. *Iola Leroy or, Shadows Uplifted*. 1892. Introduction by Frances Smith Foster. New York: Oxford University Press, 1988.

Hartman, Saidiya. *Lose Your Mother: A Journey along the Atlantic Slave Route*. New York: Farrar, Straus and Giroux, 2007.

———. *Scenes of Subjection: Terror, Slavery, and Self-Making in Nineteenth-Century America*. New York: Oxford University Press, 1997.

———. "Seduction and the Ruses of Power." *Callaloo* 19, no. 2 (1996): 537–60. http:// www.jstor.org/stable/3299219.

———. "Venus in Two Acts." *Small Axe* 12, no. 2 (2008): 1–14. http://muse.jhu.edu /journals/smx/summary/v012/12.2.hartman.html.

Heath, Deborah. "The Politics of Appropriateness and Appropriation: Recontextualizing Women's Dance in Urban Senegal." *American Ethnologist* 21, no. 1 (1994): 88–103. http://www.jstor.org/stable/646523.

Hinchman, Mark. "African Rococo: House and Portrait in Eighteenth-Century Senegal." PhD diss., University of Chicago, 2000. Ann Arbor, Mich.: University Microfilms, 2000.

———. "House and Household on Gorée, Senegal, 1758–1837." *Journal of the Society of Architectural Historians* 65, no. 2 (2006): 166–87. http://www.jstor.org/stable/25068263.

———. "When Stereotypes Go Left: An African Priest in 19th-Century Senegal." *Mots Pluriels*, no. 10 (May 1999). http://www.arts.uwa.edu.au/MotsPluriels/MP1099mh .html.

Hine, Darlene Clark. "Rape and the Inner Lives of Black Women in the Middle West." *Signs* 14, no. 4 (Summer 1989): 912–20. http://www.jstor.org/stable/3174692.

hooks, bell. "Whiteness in the Black Imagination." In *Displacing Whiteness: Essays in Social and Cultural Criticism*, edited by Ruth Frankenberg, 165–78. Durham, N.C.: Duke University Press, 1997.

Hopkins, Pauline. *Contending Forces: A Romance Illustrative of Negro Life North and South*. 1899. Introduction by Richard Yarborough. New York: Oxford University Press, 1988.

Hopkinson, Natalie. "The Truth about White Masters, Black Mistresses and Touré." *Root*, March 23, 2010. http://www.theroot.com/views/ truth-about-white-masters-black-mistresses-and-tour.

Houlberg, Marilyn. "Sirens and Snakes: Water Spirits in the Arts of Haitian Vodou." *African Arts* 29, no. 2 (1996): 30–35 + 10. http://www.jstor.org/stable/3337364.

Hunt, Lynn. *The French Revolution and Human Rights: A Brief Documentary History*. Boston: St. Martin's Press, 1996.

Hurston, Zora Neale. *Folklore, Memoirs, & Other Writings.* Edited by Cheryl A. Wall. New York: Library of America, 1995.

Johnson, Jessica Marie. "Death Rites as Birthrights in Atlantic New Orleans: Kinship and Race in the Case of María Teresa v. Perine Dauphine." *Slavery & Abolition: A Journal of Slave and Post-slave Studies,* September 25, 2014. DOI: 10.1080/0144039X.2014.943931.

Johnson, Sara E. *The Fear of French Negroes: Transcolonial Collaboration in the Revolutionary Americas.* Berkeley: University of California Press, 2012. http://wayne .eblib.com.proxy.lib.wayne.edu/patron/FullRecord.aspx?p=977265.

Johnson, Walter. *Soul by Soul: Life inside the Antebellum Slave Market.* Cambridge, Mass.: Harvard University Press, 1999.

Jones, D. H. "The Catholic Mission and Some Aspects of Assimilation in Senegal, 1817– 1852." *Journal of African History* 21 (1980): 323–40. http://www.jstor.org/stable/181187.

Jones, Hilary. *The Métis of Senegal: Urban Life and Politics in French West Africa.* Bloomington: Indiana University Press, 2013.

King, Wilma. "Out of Bounds: Emancipated and Enslaved Women in Antebellum America." In *Beyond Bondage: Free Women of Color in the Americas,* edited by David Barry Gaspar and Darlene Clark Hine, 127–44. Urbana: University of Illinois Press, 2004.

Klein, Martin. "Review of *Esquisses Sénégalaises.*" *Canadian Journal of African Studies / Revue Canadienne des Études Africaines* 20, no. 3 (1986): 449–50. http://www.jstor.org /stable/484455.

———. *Slavery and Colonial Rule in French West Africa.* Cambridge: Cambridge University Press, 1998.

———. "The Slave Trade and Decentralized Societies." *Journal of African History* 42, no. 1 (2001): 49–65. http://www.jstor.org/stable/3647215.

Knight-Baylac, Marie-Hélène. "La vie à Gorée de 1677 à 1789." *Revue française d'histoire d'outre-mer* 57, no. 209 (1970): 377–420. Persee. DOI: 10.3406/outre.1970.1519

Kriz, Kay Dian. *Slavery, Sugar, and the Culture of Refinement: Picturing the British West Indies 1700–1840.* New Haven, Conn.: Yale University Press, 2008.

Lachance, Paul. "The 1809 Immigration of Saint-Domingue Refugees to New Orleans: Reception, Integration and Impact." *Louisiana History* 29, no. 2 (1988): 109–41.

Leymarie-Ortiz, Isabelle. "The Griots of Senegal and Change." *Africa: Rivista Trimestrale di Studi e Documetazione dell'Istituto Italiano per l'Africa e l'Oriente* 34, no. 3 (1979): 183–97. http://www.jstor.org/stable/40759177.

Long, Carolyn Morrow. *A New Orleans Voudou Priestess: The Legend and Reality of Marie Laveau.* Gainesville: University Press of Florida, 2006.

Lunel, Armand. *Senegal.* Lausanne: Éditions Rencontre, 1966.

MacDonald-Smythe, Antonia. "Trading Places: Market Negotiations in *Wonderful Adventures of Mrs. Seacole in Many Lands.*" In *Gendering the African Diaspora: Women, Culture, and Historical Change in the Caribbean and Nigerian Hinterland,* edited by Judith A. Byfield, LaRay Denzer, and Anthea Morrison, 88–113. Bloomington: Indiana University Press, 2010.

Matory, J. Lorand. *Black Atlantic Religion: Tradition, Transnationalism, and Matriarchy in the Afro-Brazilian Candomblé.* Princeton, N.J.: Princeton University Press, 2005.

McKittrick, Katherine. *Demonic Grounds: Black Women and the Cartographies of Struggle*. Minneapolis: University of Minnesota Press, 2006.

Meillassoux, Claude. *The Anthropology of Slavery: The Womb of Iron and Gold*. Translated by Alide Dasnois. Chicago: University of Chicago Press, 1991.

Michel, Claudine, Patrick Bellegarde-Smith, and Marlène Racine-Toussaint. "From the Horses' Mouths: Women's Words / Women's Worlds." In *Haitian Vodou: Spirit, Myth, and Reality*, edited by Patrick Bellegarde-Smith and Claudine Michel, 70–83. Bloomington: Indiana University Press, 2006.

Mintz, Sidney, and Michel-Rolph Trouillot. "The Social History of Haitian Vodou." In *Sacred Arts of Haitian Vodou*, edited by Donald J. Cosentino, 123–47. Los Angeles: UCLA Fowler Museum of Cultural History, 1995.

Moitt, Bernard. "Slavery and Emancipation in Senegal's Peanut Basin: The Nineteenth and Twentieth Centuries." *International Journal of African Historical Studies* 22, no. 1 (1989): 27–50. http://www.jstor.org/stable/219223.

Montilus, Guérin. "Africa in Diaspora: Myth of Dahomey in Haiti." *Journal of Caribbean Studies* 2, no. 4 (1981): 73–84.

Moreau de Saint-Méry, Médéric-Louis-Elie. *A Civilization That Perished: The Last Years of White Colonial Rule in Haiti*. 1797–98. Translated and edited by Ivor D. Spencer. Lanham, Md.: University Press of America, 1985.

Morgan, Jennifer L. *Laboring Women: Reproduction and Gender in New World Slavery*. Philadelphia: University of Pennsylvania Press, 2004.

———. "'Some Could Suckle over Their Shoulder': Male Travelers, Female Bodies, and the Gendering of Racial Ideology, 1500–1770." *William and Mary Quarterly* 54, no. 1 (1997): 167–92.

Mouralis, Bernard. "Les 'Esquisses sénégalaises' de l'abbé Boilat, ou le nationalism sans la négritude" (Abbot Boilat's 'Esquisses sénégalaises': On nationalism without Negritude). *Cahiers d'Études Africaines* 34 (1995): 819–37. http://www.jstor.org/stable/4392644.

Murphy, David. "Birth of a Nation? The Origins of Senegalese Literature in French." *Research in African Literatures* 70, no. 1 (2008): 48–69. http://www.jstor.org.stable/20109559.

Murphy, Joseph M., and Mei-Mei Sanford, eds. *Ọṣun across the Waters: A Yoruba Goddess in Africa and the Americas*. Bloomington: Indiana University Press, 2001.

Myerhoff, Barbara. "Rites of Passage: Process and Paradox." In *Celebration: Studies in Festivity and Ritual*, edited by Victor Turner, 109–35. Washington, D.C.: Smithsonian Institution Press, 1982.

Myers, Amrita Chackrabarti. *Forging Freedom: Black Women and the Pursuit of Liberty in Antebellum Charleston*. Chapel Hill: University of North Carolina Press, 2011.

O'Connor, Maureen. "The Mysterious Case of Touré Praising Raped Slaves for Seducing 'Massa.'" *Gawker*, March 1, 2010. http://gawker.com/5482474/the-mysterious-case-of-toure-praising-raped-slaves-for-seducing-massa.

Painter, Nell Irvin. "Representing Truth: Sojourner Truth's Knowing and Becoming Known." *Journal of American History* 81, no. 2 (1994): 461–92. http://links.jstor.org/sici?sici=0021-8723%28199409%2981%3A2%3C461%3ARTSTKA%3E2.0.CO%3B2-N.

Palmié, Stephan. "Conventionalization, Distortion, and Plagiarism in the Historiography of Afro-Caribbean Religion in New Orleans." In *Creoles and Cajuns: French Louisiana—La Louisiane française*, edited by Wolfgang Binder, 315–44. Frankfurt am Main: Peter Lang, 1998.

———. *Wizards and Scientists: Explorations in Afro-Cuban Modernity and Tradition.* Durham, N.C.: Duke University Press, 2002.

Paskin, Willa. "Network TV Is Broken. So How Does Shonda Rhimes Keep Making Hits?" *New York Times*, May 9, 2013. http://www.nytimes.com/2013/05/12/magazine/shonda-rhimes.html?pagewanted=1&_r=1&emc=eta1&.

Patterson, Orlando. *Slavery and Social Death: A Comparative Study.* Cambridge, Mass.: Harvard University Press, 1982.

Patterson, Tiffany, and Robin D. G. Kelley. "Unfinished Migrations: Reflections on the African Diaspora and the Making of the Modern World." *African Studies Review* 43, no. 1 (2000): 11–45.

Phillips, Caryl. *The Atlantic Sound.* New York: Knopf, 2000.

Pietz, William. "The Problem of the Fetish, IIIa: Bosman's Guinea and the Enlightenment Theory of Fetishism." *RES: Anthropology and Aesthetics* 16 (1988): 105–24.

Pollock, Griselda. *Differencing the Canon: Feminist Desire and the Writing of Art's Histories.* London: Routledge, 1999.

Pratt, Mary Louise. *Imperial Eyes: Travel Writing and Transculturation.* New York: Routledge, 1992.

René, Georges, and Marilyn Houlberg. "My Double Mystic Marriages to Two Goddesses of Love. An Interview." In *Sacred Arts of Haitian Vodou*, edited by Donald J. Cosentino, 287–99. Los Angeles: Regents of the University of California, 1995.

Roach, Joseph. *Cities of the Dead: Circum-Atlantic Performance.* New York: Columbia University Press, 1996.

Rodney, Walter. *A History of the Upper Guinea Coast 1545–1800.* New York: Monthly Review Press, 1970.

Sánchez-Eppler, Karen. *Touching Liberty: Abolition, Feminism, and the Politics of the Body.* Berkeley: University of California Press, 1993.

Sankalé, Sylvain. "Une société métisse originale Saint-Louis du Sénégal aux 18ᵉ et 19ᵉ siècles." *Éthiopiques: Revue Negro-Africaine de Littérature et de Philosophie* 64–65 (2000). http://ethiopiques.refer.sn/spip.php?article1193.

Santamarina, Xiomara. *Belabored Professions: Narratives of African American Working Womanhood.* Chapel Hill: University of North Carolina Press, 2005.

———. Introduction to *A Hairdresser's Experience in High Life*, by Eliza Potter, xi–xxxv. Edited by Xiomara Santamarina. Chapel Hill: University of North Carolina Press, 2009.

———. "Introduction (Appendix A)." In *A Hairdresser's Experience in High Life*, by Eliza Potter. Edited by Xiomara Santamarina. Chapel Hill: University of North Carolina Press, 2009.

———. "'... So You Can See, Color Makes No Difference': Race, Slavery and Abolition in *A Hairdresser's Experience in High Life*." *Legacy* 24, no. 2 (2007): 171–86. http://muse.jhu.edu.proxy.lib.wayne.edu/journals/legacy/v024/24.2santamarina.html.

Schafer, Judith Kelleher. *Becoming Free, Remaining Free: Manumission and Enslavement in New Orleans, 1846–1862.* Baton Rouge: Louisiana State University Press, 2003.

Scott, David. *Conscripts of Modernity: The Tragedy of Colonial Enlightenment.* Durham,
    N.C.: Duke University Press, 2004.
————. "That Event, This Memory: Notes on the Anthropology of African Diasporas
    in the New World." *Diaspora* 1, no. 3 (1991): 261–84.
Scott, James C. *Domination and the Arts of Resistance: Hidden Transcripts.* New Haven,
    Conn.: Yale University Press, 1990.
Scott, Joan. "The Evidence of Experience." *Critical Inquiry* 17, no. 4 (Summer 1991):
    773–97.
————. "Fantasy Echo: History and the Construction of Identity." *Critical Inquiry* 27,
    no. 2 (2001): 284–304. http://www.jstor.org/stable/1344251.
Scott, Rebecca J. "Paper Thin: Freedom and Re-enslavement in the Diaspora of the
    Haitian Revolution." *Law and History Review* 29, no. 4 (2011): 1061–87. DOI: http://
    dx.doi.org/10.1017/S0738248011000538.
Scott, Rebecca J., and Jean M. Hébrard. *Freedom Papers: An Atlantic Odyssey in the Age of
    Emancipation.* Cambridge, Mass.: Harvard University Press, 2012.
————. "Rosalie of the Poulard Nation: Freedom, Law, and Dignity in the Era of the
    Haitian Revolution." In *Assumed Identities: The Meanings of Race in the Atlantic World,*
    edited by John D. Garrigus and Christopher Morris, 116–43. Arlington: Texas A & M
    University Press, 2010.
Searing, James F. "'No Kings, No Lords, No Slaves': Ethnicity and Religion among the
    Sereer-Safèn of Western Bawol, 1700–1914." *Journal of African History* 43, no. 3 (2002):
    407–29. http://www.jstor.org/stable/3647215.
————. *West African Slavery and the Atlantic Commerce: The Senegal River Valley, 1700–
    1860.* Cambridge: Cambridge University Press, 1993.
Seck, Babacar. *Gorée: Guide touristique.* Dakar, Senegal: SAFER, 1966.
Seiber, Roy, and Frank Herreman. "Hair in African Art and Culture." *African Arts* 33, no.
    3 (2000): 54–69 + 96. http://www.jstor.org/stable/3337689.
Sharpe, Jenny. *Ghosts of Slavery: A Literary Archaeology of Black Women's Lives.*
    Minneapolis: University of Minnesota Press, 2002.
"Slavery and Indentured Servants." Library of Congress, American Memory. http://
    memory.loc.gov/ammem/awhhtml/awlaw3/slavery.html.
Smalls, James. "Slavery Is a Woman: 'Race,' Gender, and Visuality in Marie Benoist's
    Portrait d'une négresse (1800)." *Nineteenth-Century Art Worldwide* 3, no. 1 (2004).
    http://www.19thc-artworldwide.org/index.php/spring04/286-slavery-is-a-woman
    -race-gender-and-visuality-in-marie-benoists-portrait-dune-negresse-1800.
Smallwood, Stephanie E. *Saltwater Slavery: A Middle Passage from Africa to American
    Diaspora.* Cambridge, Mass.: Harvard University Press, 2007.
Sollors, Werner. *Neither Black nor White yet Both: Thematic Explorations of Interracial
    Literature.* New York: Oxford University Press, 1997.
Spear, Jennifer M. "Colonial Intimacies: Legislating Sex in French Louisiana." *William
    and Mary Quarterly* 16, no. 1 (2003): 75–98.
————. *Race, Sex, and Social Order in Early New Orleans.* Baltimore, Md.: Johns
    Hopkins University Press, 2009.
Spillers, Hortense. "'Mama's Baby, Papa's Maybe': An American Grammar Book."
    Diacritics 17 (1987): 65–81. http://www.jstor.org/stable/464747.
————. "Notes on an Alternative Model—neither/nor." In *Black, White, and in Color:*

Essays on American Literature by Hortense Spillers, 301–18. Chicago: University of Chicago Press, 2003.

Stoler, Ann Laura. *Carnal Knowledge and Imperial Power: Race and the Intimate in Colonial Rule.* Berkeley: University of California Press, 2002.

Sturtz, Linda L. "Mary Rose: 'White' African Jamaican Woman? Race and Gender in Eighteenth-Century Jamaica." In *Gendering the African Diaspora: Women, Culture, and Historical Change in the Caribbean and Nigerian Hinterland,* edited by Judith A. Byfield, LaRay Denzer, and Anthea Morrison, 59–87. Bloomington: Indiana University Press, 2010.

Tallant, Robert. *Voodoo in New Orleans.* 1946. Gretna: Pelican Publishing Company, 1998.

Thompson, Robert Farris. *Flash of the Spirit: African and Afro-American Art and Philosophy.* New York: Vintage Books, 1984.

Thompson, Shirley Elizabeth. *Exiles at Home: The Struggle to Become American in Creole New Orleans.* Cambridge, Mass.: Harvard University Press, 2009.

Thorton, John K. *A Cultural History of the Atlantic World, 1250–1820.* Cambridge: Cambridge University Press, 2012.

Touchstone, Blake. "Voodoo in New Orleans." *Louisiana History* 13, no. 4 (1972): 371–86. http://www.jstor.org/stable/4231284.

Trouillot, Michel-Rolph. *Silencing the Past: Power and the Production of History.* Boston: Beacon Press, 1995.

Turner, Victor W. "Betwixt and Between: The Liminal Period in *Rites of Passage.*" In *Magic, Witchcraft, and Religion: An Anthropological Study of the Supernatural,* 6th ed., edited by Arthur C. Lehmann, James E. Myers, and Pamela A. Moro, 96–105. Boston: McGraw Hill, 2005.

Virtual Visit of Gorée Island, Dakar, Senegal. UNESCO. http://webworld.unesco.org/goree/en/index.shtml.

Ward, Martha. *Voodoo Queen: The Spirited Lives of Marie Laveau.* Jackson: University of Mississippi Press, 2004.

Washington, Kerry. "Emmys 2013: Kerry Washington's Favorite 'Scandal' Season 2 Moments." *Daily Beast.* August 22, 2013. http://www.thedailybeast.com/articles/2013/08/22/emmys-2013-kerry-washington-s-favorite-scandal-season-2-moments.html.

White, Deborah Gray. *Ar'n't I a Woman? Female Slaves in the Plantation South.* Rev. ed. New York: W. W. Norton, 1999.

White, E. Frances. "Creole Women Traders in the Nineteenth Century." *International Journal of African Historical Studies* 14, no. 4 (1981): 626–42. http://www.jstor.org/stable/218229.

Wood, Marcus. *Slavery, Empathy and Pornography.* Oxford: Oxford University Press, 2002.

Young, Hershini Bhana. *Haunting Capital: Memory, Text, and the Black Diasporic Body.* Hanover: University Press of New England, 2006.

Zackodnik, Teresa C. *The Mulatta and the Politics of Race.* Jackson: University of Mississippi Press, 2004.

Zafar, Rafia. *We Wear the Mask: African Americans Write American Literature, 1760–1870.* New York: Columbia University Press, 1997.

INDEX

Page numbers in italics refer to illustrations.

Adanson, Michel, 33–34

African diaspora. *See* diaspora

agency: of free mulatta women, 7, 75; as illusory, 11, 161, 166, 169, 178; and skin color, 91; and stereotypes of hypersexuality, 5; and tignon (headwrap), 78

Albiri, Victoria, 54

Americas, free mulatta women in, 31–32

appearance and dress: in *Atlas* (Boilat), 151–53; in *Un bal de signares (mulatresses) a Saint-Louis (Senegal)* (Nousveaux), 60–62; of Bambara woman, in *Atlas* (Boilat), 155–57; of Ezili Freda, 26–28, 30; fluidity of, 50; function of, 43; in *Gorée: Guide touristique* (Seck), 50–55; hair care, 80; of mulatta women, 5, 7, 8, 14, 30–31, 151–52, 161, 192n11; as resistance, 69–70, 79; as ritual and performance, 40, 43, 79; of signares, 25–26, 28, 30–31, 50–55, 121–22, 129, 151–53. *See also* tignon (headwrap)

Araujo, Ana Lucia, 191n40

archives, 73–74; and African diaspora studies, 15; emphasis of, on sexuality, 70; of Ezili, 35; and free black men, 107–8, 171; inadequacy of, 48, 180; Lasirèn as, 104–5; on Laveau, 71, 72–73, 89–90; linearity of dominant versions, 17; and privacy, 73–74; and signares' viewpoints, 34, 52–53, 107–8, 109, 135; on slave trade, 46–47; Toledano's trial and testimony, 85–87; and vodou, 74; as voyeuristic, 71–72. *See also* counterarchives

Atlas (Boilat): appearance and dress in, 151–53; Bambara woman in, 155–58; and diaspora, 150; habitants' exclusion from, 147; overview of, 146–47; sequence of plates in, 154–55; signares in, 148–49, 151–53; subjects' understanding of, 201n13. See also *Esquisses sénégalaises* (Boilat)

Un bal de signares (mulatresses) a Saint-Louis (Senegal) (Nousveaux), 60–62

Ballard, Rice C., 203n34

Bambara woman, 155–58

Baptist, Edward, 168–69, 203n34

Barrett, Lindon, 176

Barry, Boubacar, 68, 196n10

Bartolozzi, Francesco, *Joanna*, 92

Bassett, Thomas J., 149, 200n7

Baucoum, Ian, 14

beauty. *See* appearance and dress

Belasario, Isaac Mendes, *French Set Girls*, 62

Bellegarde-Smith, Patrick, 102

Berger, John, 125, 131

Berlin, Ira, 161

Bibb, Henry, 161, 162

binaries, 38; Ezili and, 19–21; marasa consciousness and, 19

black men, enslaved: *laptots*, 128–29; and white male desire, 172–73. *See also* slaves

black men, free: archival invisibility of, 107–8, 109, 171, 195n2; New Orleans as dangerous for, 161–62, 164. *See also* habitants

black people. *See* black women; mulatta women; mulatta women, free; slaves

black women: New Orleans as dangerous for, 161–62, 164; savagery of, 194n27; as sexual commodities, 115, 159, 162, 168–70, 201n17; sexual violence in lives of, 5; as slaveholders, 162, 175; surveillance of, by whites, 70, 78; "ungendering" of, 36, 37, 79, 98, 193n13. *See also* mulatta women, free

black women, enslaved, 58, 88, 132–33; in *A Hairdresser's Experience* (Potter) 168–70. *See also* slaves

Boilat, David, 64, 200n8; *Atlas*, 146–59; background, 149; and diaspora, 149–50; *Esquisses sénégalaises*, 145–49, 153–56, 158–59;

217

RACE IN THE ATLANTIC WORLD, 1700–1900

CPSIA information can be obtained
at www.ICGtesting.com
Printed in the USA
LVOW03s2059150218
566747LV00003B/429/P